# Harriman's
# Stock Market Almanac
# 2018

Stephen Eckett

HARRIMAN HOUSE LTD
18 College Street
Petersfield
Hampshire
GU31 4AD
GREAT BRITAIN
Tel: +44 (0)1730 233870
Email: enquiries@harriman-house.com
Website: www.harriman-house.com

First edition published in Great Britain in 2004
This 11th edition published in 2017


Print ISBN: 978-0-85719-605-7
eBook ISBN: 978-0-85719-606-4

British Library Cataloguing in Publication Data
A CIP catalogue record for this book can be obtained from the British Library.



Page number cross references are for the print edition.

# CONTENTS

# INTRODUCTION

Welcome to the 2018 edition of *Harriman's Stock Market Almanac,* where we celebrate the Efficient Market Theory – that is, the failure of the theory. This book could alternatively be titled, *The Inefficient Almanac*, as it revels in the trends and anomalies of the market that the Efficient Market Theory says shouldn't exist.

## New format

The *Almanac* has a new format! Previously, a large part of the book was comprised of a weekly diary. We have discontinued this format for two reasons.

Firstly, most people today have digital diaries and it was becoming something of an anachronism to think readers would actually use the *Almanac* as a diary. For those readers who liked the weekly diary format, the good news is that we have moved much of the diary online, which is a more suitable platform for the content. To find this online diary, go to the *Almanac's* website (stockmarketalmanac.co.uk > Reference > Market Calendar). If you like, you can now add the continuously updated online *Almanac* calendar to your own digital calendar.

The second reason for the change is that the previous format was quite limiting in the length of articles that accompanied each week. In the new version, strategies and analysis can be fully explained without any length constraint.

Like, or hate, the new format? We'd like to hear your views. Do contact us via Twitter or the Harriman House website with your thoughts.

The structure of the new *Almanac* is explained in the Preface.

## Updated strategies and analysis

This edition of the *Almanac* comprises updates on strategies and analysis, including:

- **Bounceback Portfolio** – a strategy that buys the worst performing shares in a year, and then sells them after three months into the new year; the strategy has outperformed the index in 13 of the last 15 years [page 38].
- **Construction Sector 4M Strategy** – exploits a seasonality anomaly of the construction sector that greatly outperforms the FTSE 100 index [page 41].
- **Sell in May** – this extraordinary effect remains as strong as ever: since 1982 the market in the winter months has outperformed the market in the summer months by an average 8.2 percentage points annually [page 43].
- **Sell in May Sector Strategy** – how to exploit the Sell in May effect with sectors [page 46].
- **Summer Share Portfolio** – a portfolio of seven stocks that has outperformed the market in nine of the last ten summers [page 48].

- **Sell Rosh Hashanah, Buy Yom Kippur** – the US equity market tends to be weak between these two Jewish holidays; is there a similar effect in the UK market [page 50]?
- **Santa Rally** – does a Santa Rally exist for shares and, if so, when does it start [page 52]?
- **Day of the Week Strategy** – a strategy exploiting the day of the week anomaly that outperforms the FTSE 100 index [page 53].
- **Tuesday Reverse Monday** – do market returns on Tuesdays reverse those on Monday [page 55]?
- **Turn of the Month Strategy** – all the market's gains occur in the six days around the turn of the month [page 58].
- **FTSE 100/250 Monthly Switching Strategy** – on the back of research into the comparative monthly performance of the two indices, a strategy of switching between the two markets is found that greatly outperforms either index individually [page 60].
- **FTSE 100/S&P 500 Switching Strategy** – the strong/weak months for the FTSE 100 index relative to the S&P 500 index are identified; and a strategy of switching between the two markets is found that produces twice the returns of either market individually [page 62].
- **Monthly Share Momentum Strategy** – a monthly rebalanced momentum portfolio of FTSE 100 stocks beats the market [page 67].
- **Quarterly Sector Strategy** – The strongest/weakest sectors for each quarter are identified; and the Quarterly Sector Strategy continues to beat the market. Is this strategy even easier than the World's Simplest Trading System mentioned below [page 69]?
- **Quarterly Sector Momentum Strategy** – a portfolio comprising the best FTSE 350 sector from the previous quarter, and rebalanced quarterly, outperforms the FTSE All-Share index by an average of 2.0 percentage points per month. A variant – buying the worst sector of the previous quarter – has performed even better [page 72]?
- **Low/High Share Price Strategy** – a portfolio of the 20 lowest priced shares in the market has outperformed a portfolio of the 20 highest priced shares by an average 39 percentage points each year since 2002 [page 74]?
- **World's Simplest Trading System** – a simple trading system based on moving averages with an impressive performance [page 78].

## Outlook for 2018

What can we look forward to in 2018?

The big sporting event in 2018 will be the football World Cup held in Russia, so expect that to go without a hitch. Previous editions of the *Almanac* have poked fun at the United Nations and their International Year observances (who can forget the intoxicating 2016 UN International Year of Pulses?), but the UN has nothing at all planned for 2018! Do they not care any more? Or have they come to their senses? Or perhaps we're truly looking at the end of times?

Away from the apocalyptic nihilism of the UN, NASA, as ever, can be relied on to keep the space probes going to justify their budget; in 2018 they'll be off to search out exoplanets. More interestingly, courtesy of the private sector, there is a plan in 2018 for humans (i.e. space tourists) to go beyond low-earth orbit for the first time since 1972.

*Onto the serious stuff – whither the stock market in 2018?*

Since 1800 the market has generally been relatively strong in the eighth year of the decade. It has been especially strong since 1958, with an average annual return of 11.0% and up every decade until... yep, 2008. In that year the market fell 33% – which has rather hit the performance of the eigth years. Remove 2008 from the calculation and the average annual return in eigth years since 1958 has been 19.3%.

The guidance from the centennial cycle is also encouraging; in 1718, 1818 and 1918 the respective annual returns for the UK market were +0.6%, +5.5%, and +11.0% – a steady progression of increasing returns suggesting a return of around 16% in 2018!

In the Chinese calendar it will be the year of the dog, which is excellent news. Since 1950, dog years (despite the name) have the best record of returns of the 12 zodiac signs. Since 1950, the average annual return for the S&P 500 index has been 16.8% in dog years.

How about that for congruence? The above gives us 19%, 16% and 17% as forecasts for equity market returns in 2018 – spooky!

Turning to the Long-Term Formula (more information on this on page 195), it is a little less bullish but still positive: the trend line from 1920 suggests the long-term trend value of the market will be 7% above the current level by the end of 2018.

The US presidential cycle has a significant effect on equity markets worldwide, including in the UK. 2018 will be the second year in the cycle and on average the UK market has seen returns of 2.0% in the second year.

Finally, the 1975 film *Rollerball* was set in the corporate-controlled future world of... 2018. In the film, Rollerball is a violent, globally popular sport – which today probably better describes Twitter than anything else. The *Almanac* predicts that Rollerball will have a revival in 2018, and perhaps Rollertwitter will become a thing? In the film, one of the characters says:

> What do you want books for? Look Johnny, if you wanna learn somethin', just get a Corporate Teacher to come and teach it to ya'.

Wise words. But for those of you who don't happen to have a Corporate Teacher, I hope you find this book useful.

Stephen Eckett

# PREFACE

*Definition*

*almanac (noun): an annual calendar containing dates and statistical information*

## What the book covers

The *Almanac* provides an in-depth study of the anomalies and seasonality effects in the UK and international markets. As such, it subjects the markets to quantitative analysis, rather than fundamental or technical analysis. By studying price and other data the *Almanac* looks for patterns of behaviour that can help give traders and investors an edge.

So, the *Almanac* highlights daily, weekly and monthly seasonality effects in shares, sectors and market indices. It also looks at momentum effects, size effects, and other market anomalies. Old market sayings, such as the famous "Sell in May", are analysed to discover if they have any relevance to the market today. In short, the markets are put under a statistical microscope to determine the underlying real nature of prices.

It should be noted that the type of quantitative analysis contained in the *Almanac* in some cases is best exploited by an arbitraged or hedged strategy, not a simple long position.

In summary, the *Almanac* is a unique work providing everything from essential reference information to informative and profitable trading and investing ideas for the UK and international markets.

## How the book is structured

The *Almanac* has four major parts:

1. **Calendar**: A two-page summary of the main features of each month. This includes the historic average performance, the sectors and shares that tend to be strong or weak in the month, the month's major anomalies and seasonality patterns, the significant dates coming up, and a chart of the average daily performance throughout the month (for more information on the construction of the average month charts see page 118).

2. **Strategies**: This section describes the major anomalies and seasonality effects in the UK market and how they can be exploited.

3. **Analysis**: In depth analysis of the characteristics of the UK and international markets, to help give traders and investors an edge in the markets they are active in.

4. **Reference**: Information on UK and international markets useful to all traders and investors.

## Supporting website

The website supporting this book can be found at: stockmarketalmanac.co.uk.

## Follow the Almanac on Twitter

@UKAlmanac

## Free eBook

Every owner of a physical copy of *The Harriman Stock Market Almanac 2018* can download the eBook edition for free direct from us at Harriman House, in a format that can be read on any eReader, tablet or smartphone.

Simply head to ebooks.harriman-house.com/almanac2018 to get your copy now.

# 1.
# CALENDAR

# CONTENTS

## Market performance this month

The performance of the stock market in January has changed dramatically over time. From 1984 to 1999 the average FTSE All-Share return in the month was 3.3% and, as can be seen in the accompanying chart, in those 16 years the market only fell twice in January. But then things changed completely. Since year 2000 the average market return in January has been -1.6%, with the market seeing positive returns in only six years. This makes January the worst of all months for shares since 2000.

In an average January, the euphoria of December (the second strongest month of the year) carries over into the first few days of the month as the market continues to climb for the first couple of days. But by around the fourth trading day the exhilaration is wearing off and the market then falls for the next two weeks – the second week of January is the weakest week for the market in the whole year. Then, around the middle of the third week, the market has tended to rebound sharply.

## January Effect

In the world of economics the month is famous for the January Effect. This describes the tendency of small-cap stocks to outperform large-caps in the month. This anomaly was first observed in the US, but it certainly seems to apply to the UK market as well. For example, since 1999 the FTSE Fledgling has outperformed the FTSE 100 in January in every year except two. The interesting thing is those two weak years for small-caps were seen in January in the last two years – 2015 and 2016. Is this effect on the wane?

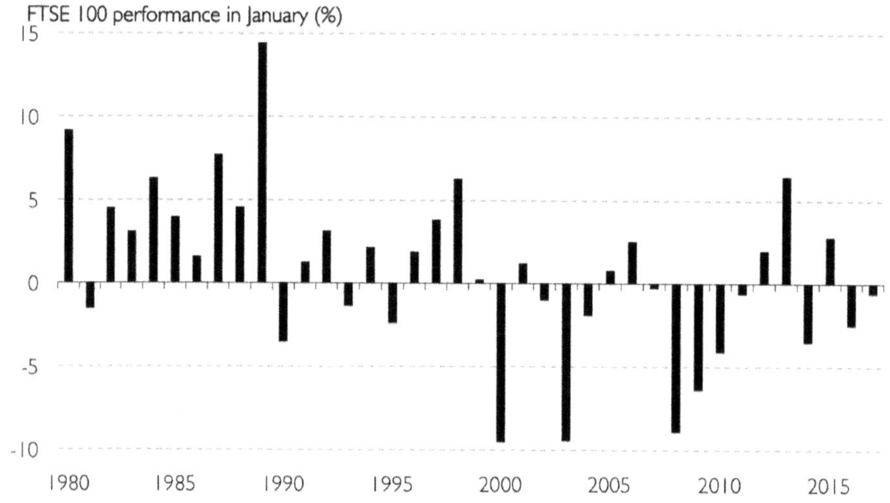

## January dashboard

| | | | |
|---|---|---|---|
| Market performance | Avg change (%): 0.8% | Positive (%): 58% | Ranking: 7th |
| Sector performance | *Strong*<br>Health Care Equipment & Services, Software & Computer Services, General Industrials | *Weak*<br>Electricity, Food Producers, Oil & Gas Producers | |
| Share performance | *Strong*<br>JD Sports Fashion [JD.], Paysafe Group [PAYS], Domino's Pizza Group [DOM], Mitchells & Butlers [MAB], St James's Place [STJ] | *Weak*<br>FirstGroup [FGP], Berkeley Group Holdings (The) [BKG], Paragon Banking Group [PAG], Royal Dutch Shell [RDSB], Dairy Crest Group [DCG] | |
| Main features | Small-cap stocks often outperform large-cap stocks in January (January Effect)<br>The FTSE 250 is particularly strong relative to the FTSE 100 in this month<br>FTSE 100 often underperforms the S&P 500 in January<br>Busy month for FTSE 100 interim dividend payments<br>First trading day average return: 0.30%; positive: 58%<br>Last trading day average return: 0.20%; positive: 58% (year's 2nd strongest)<br>Strong month for silver<br>GBPUSD historically weak this month | | |
| Significant dates | 01 Jan: LSE, NYSE, TSE, HKEX closed [New Year's Day]<br>05 Jan: US nonfarm payroll report<br>15 Jan: NYSE closed [Martin Luther King Day]<br>25 Jan: ECB Governing Council Meeting (monetary policy)<br>30 Jan: Two-day FOMC meeting starts<br>Don't forget: the last date to file your 2016/17 tax return online is 31 January | | |
| Average chart of the month | 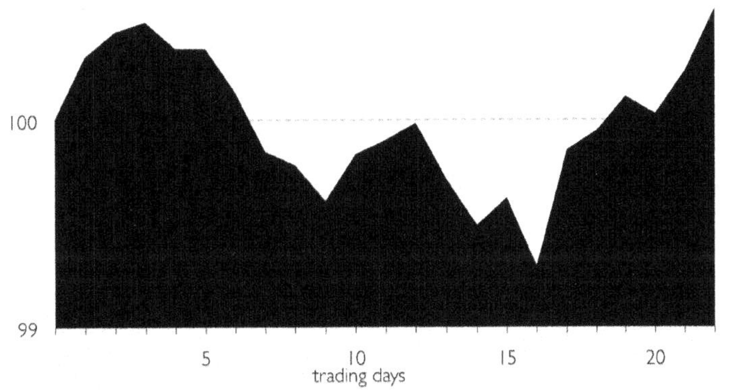<br> | | |

## Market performance this month

Since 1970 the average month return of the FTSE All-Share index in February has been 1.6%, with the month seeing positive returns in 64% of years. But a glance at the accompanying chart will show quite how strong the market has been in February in recent years.

Since 2009 the market has been up every February, and since 1994 the market has only seen significant negative returns in three years. There's no obvious reason why the market has been so strong in recent years in this month; one possible explication might be that, also in recent years, shares have been weak in January and so they experience a bounce back rally in February.

In an average February shares tend to rise strongly on the first trading day, then trade flat for a couple of weeks, before gaining strongly in the middle of the month and finally drifting off slightly to month end.

## Mid-caps outperform large-cap stocks

A feature of February is that, with January, it is the best month for mid-cap stocks relative to the large-caps. Since 2000 on average the FTSE 250 has outperformed the FTSE 100 by 1.6 percentage points in this month, and in that time the large-cap index has underperformed mid-caps in February in only four years.

## FTSE 100 outperforms S&P 500

On the international front, February is one of the four months in the year that the FTSE 100 has historically outperformed the S&P 500. Since 1999 the UK index has underperformed the US index in February in only three years. Although the outperformance is somewhat attenuated once currency is taken into account as GBPUSD is historically weak in February.

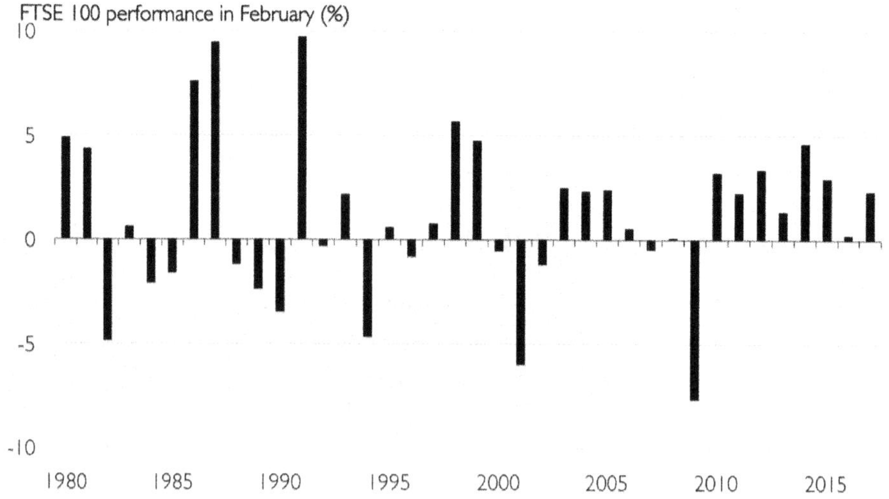

## February dashboard

<table>
<tr><td>Market performance</td><td colspan="2">Avg change (%): 1.1% | Positive (%): 63% | Ranking: 4th</td></tr>
<tr><td>Sector performance</td><td>Strong<br>Industrial Engineering, Mining, Household Goods</td><td>Weak<br>Mobile Telecommunications, Pharmaceuticals & Biotechnology, Banks</td></tr>
<tr><td>Share performance</td><td>Strong<br>Fidessa Group [FDSA], Galliford Try [GFRD], Bodycote [BOY], Croda International [CRDA], Bunzl [BNZL]</td><td>Weak<br>Vodafone Group [VOD], AstraZeneca [AZN], Vectura Group [VEC], Redefine International [RDI], JPMorgan Indian Investment Trust [JII]</td></tr>
<tr><td>Main features</td><td colspan="2">The FTSE 250 is particularly strong relative to the FTSE 100 in this month<br>GBPUSD historically weak this month<br>Busiest month for FTSE 250 preliminary results announcements<br>Strong month for gold, silver<br>First trading day average return: 0.52%; positive: 58% (year's 2nd strongest)<br>Last trading day average return: -0.05%; positive: 46% (year's 2nd weakest)<br>Close out Construction Sector 4M Strategy</td></tr>
<tr><td>Significant dates</td><td colspan="2">02 Feb: US Nonfarm payroll report<br>08 Feb: MPC interest rate announcement at 12 noon<br>08 Feb: MPC inflation report<br>12 Feb: MSCI Quarterly Index Review [announcement date]<br>16 Feb: Chinese New Year (Year of the dog)<br>19 Feb: NYSE closed [Washington's Birthday]<br>28 Feb: FTSE index reviews announced</td></tr>
<tr><td>Average chart of the month</td><td colspan="2">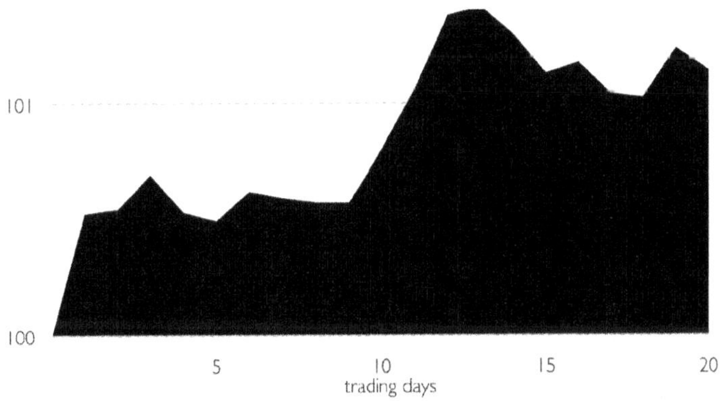
</td></tr>
</table>

# MARCH MARKET

## Market performance this month

What can we expect from shares as we move into spring? Since 1984 the market has had an average return of 0.5% in March, with returns positive in 55% of all years. This ranks March seventh among months of the year for market performance. Although, as can be seen in the accompanying chart, negative returns have been seen in March with increasing frequency in recent years.

The general trend for the market in March is to rise for the first three weeks and then fall back in the final week – the last week of March has historically been one of the weakest weeks for the market in the whole year.

## Large-cap v small-cap stocks

Generally, small-cap stocks outperform large-cap stocks at the beginning of the year, and March marks the final month of the three-month period when the FTSE 250 strongly outperforms the FTSE 100. In March on average the FTSE 250 has outperformed the FTSE 100 by 0.9 percentage points.

## Dividends and results

March is the busiest month of the year for FTSE 100 companies paying dividends. And it's also a busy month for company announcements: the busiest for FTSE 250 companies in the year with 71 companies announcing their prelims this month (along with 24 FTSE 100 companies).

Aside from stocks, March has often been a weak month for gold and a strong month for oil.

## Holiday Effect

It's Good Friday at the end of the month. A famous anomaly in stock markets is that prices tend to be strong on the day preceding and the day following a holiday. This effect is strongest in the year around the Easter holiday.

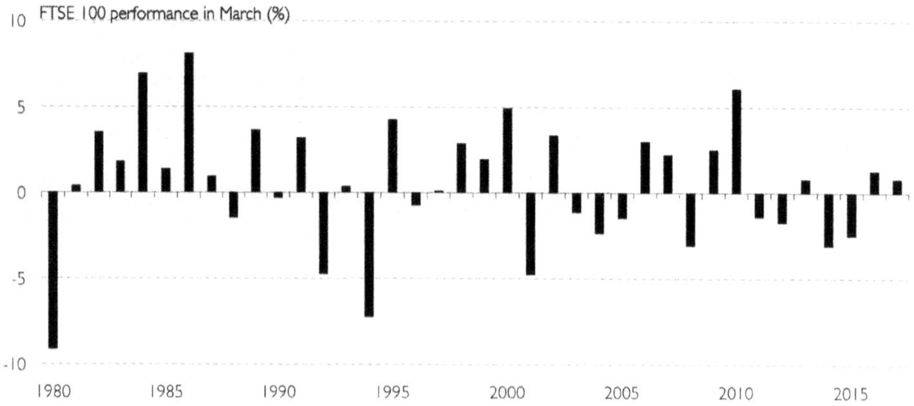

## March dashboard

| | | |
|---|---|---|
| Market performance | Avg change (%): 0.5% \| Positive (%): 61% | Ranking: 9th |
| Sector performance | *Strong*<br>Oil Equipment, Services & Distribution, Chemicals, Support Services | *Weak*<br>Banks, Fixed Line Telecommunications, Nonlife Insurance |
| Share performance | *Strong*<br>IWG [IWG], Clarkson [CKN], Senior [SNR], Intertek Group [ITRK], Petrofac Ltd [PFC] | *Weak*<br>Vectura Group [VEC], Lancashire Holdings Ltd [LRE], Kier Group [KIE], Renishaw [RSW], HSBC Holdings [HSBA] |
| Main features | The FTSE 250 is particularly strong relative to the FTSE 100 in this month<br>Market abnormally strong on day before and day after Easter holiday<br>Busiest month for FTSE 250 preliminary results announcements<br>Busiest month for FTSE 100 dividend payments<br>Weak month for gold, strong month for oil<br>First trading day average return: 0.03%; positive: 58% (2nd weakest in year)<br>Last trading day average return: 0.02%; positive: 46%<br>Liquidate Bounceback Portfolio (if not done so already) | |
| Significant dates | 01 Mar: MSCI Quarterly Index Review [effective date]<br>08 Mar: ECB Governing Council Meeting (monetary policy)<br>09 Mar: US Nonfarm payroll report<br>16 Mar: Triple Witching<br>16 Mar: FTSE index series quarterly changes effective today<br>20 Mar: Two-day FOMC meeting starts<br>22 Mar: MPC interest rate announcement at 12 noon (anticipated)<br>25 Mar: Daylight Saving Time starts<br>30 Mar: LSE, NYSE, HKEX closed [Good Friday] | |
| Average chart of the month | 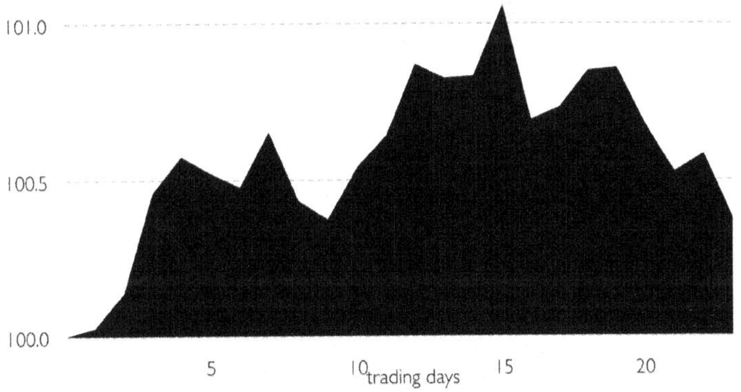 | |

### Market performance this month

Historically, April has been one of the best months for equities. Since 1970 the average return for the FTSE All-Share index in the month has been 2.6%, with positive returns seen in 83% of Aprils in the last 47 years. This is the best record, by quite a margin, for any month in the year. And the strong performance has continued in recent years. Since 2000 the average month return for the index has been 2.0% and, as can be seen in the accompanying chart, the market has only fallen in April in five years since 2000.

### The average April

The market often gets off to a strong start in the month – the first trading day of April is the second strongest first trading day of all months in the year. The market then tends to be fairly flat for the middle two weeks and then rises strongly in the final week.

Investors need to make the most of April. After this month the market enters a six-month period when equities have tended to tread water (the Sell in May Effect).

### FTSE 100 v S&P 500

This is the strongest month for the FTSE 100 relative to the S&P 500 (in sterling terms), the former outperforms the latter by an average of 1.3 percentage points in April – the UK index has outperformed the US index (in sterling terms) in April in 13 of the past 15 years.

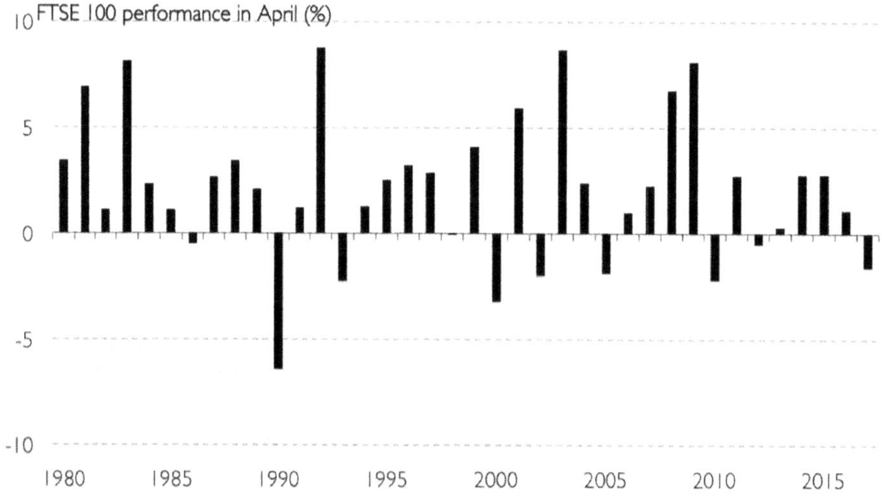

## April dashboard

| | | | |
|---|---|---|---|
| Market performance | Avg change (%): 2.1% | Positive (%): 74% | Ranking: 2nd |
| Sector performance | *Strong*<br>Industrial Engineering, General Retailers, Oil & Gas Producers | *Weak*<br>Construction & Materials, Household Goods, Media | |
| Share performance | *Strong*<br>JD Sports Fashion [JD.], Ashmore Group [ASHM], Renishaw [RSW], UDG Healthcare [UDG], Weir Group [WEIR] | *Weak*<br>Balfour Beatty [BBY], BAE Systems [BA.], RELX [REL], Booker Group [BOK], Pearson [PSON] | |
| Main features | Second strongest month of the year for shares<br>FTSE 100 strong relative to S&P 500 this month<br>GBPUSD historically strong this month<br>Strong month for oil<br>First trading day average return: 0.38%; positive: 67% (3rd strongest in year)<br>Last trading day average return: 0.11%; positive: 53% | | |
| Significant dates | 02 Apr: LSE, HKEX closed [Easter Monday]<br>06 Apr: US Nonfarm payroll report<br>26 Apr: ECB Governing Council Meeting | | |
| Average chart of the month | 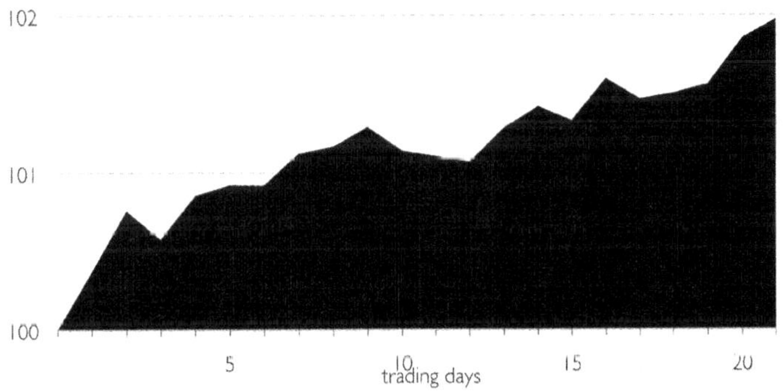 | | |

## Market performance this month

*Sell in May?*

One of the most famous adages in the stock market is "Sell in May". And often this can be good advice. But not always. Since 1984 the market in May has seen roughly an equal proportion of positive and negative returns (the proportion of years with positive returns in May is 51%).

*So, why does May have a bad reputation for shares, and why is the saying "Sell in May" so popular?*

One reason can be seen in the chart. Although the proportion of positive and negative returns in May are roughly equal, it can be seen that the positive returns in May are relatively small, whereas when the market falls in May it can suffer quite a large sell-off. Since 1970 the average market return in May has been -0.5%, which is the third worst record of all months.

The other reason why investors should take note of "Sell in May" is that, longer term, May marks the start of the underperforming half of the year (May through to October); a period over which share performance can tend to be lacklustre.

## The average May

In an average May the market trades fairly flat for the first two weeks of the month, and then prices drift lower in the second half.

## FTSE 100 v S&P 500

There are some months that the UK market fairly consistently outperforms the US market. May isn't one of them. In fact, May is the weakest month of the year for the FTSE 100 relative to the S&P 500; on average the UK index underperforms the US by 1.3 percentage points in May.

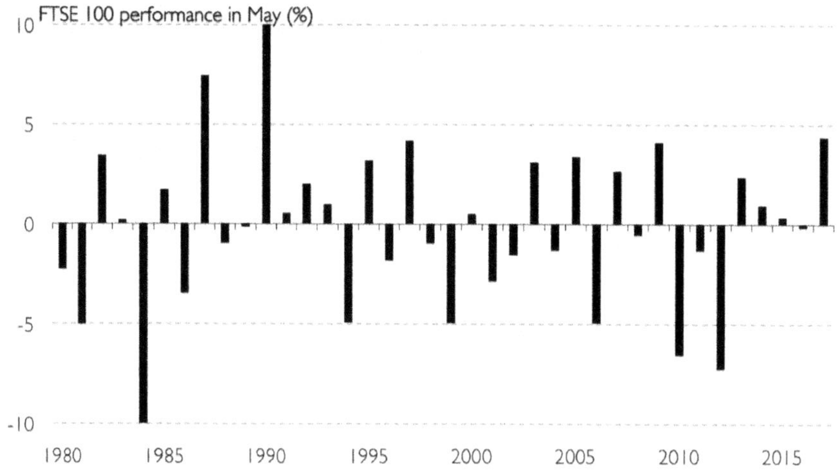

## May dashboard

<table>
<tr><td>Market performance</td><td>Avg change (%): -0.1%</td><td>Positive (%): 50%</td><td>Ranking: 10th</td></tr>
<tr><td>Sector performance</td><td>Strong<br>Gas, Water & Multiutilities, Electricity, Tobacco</td><td colspan="2">Weak<br>Oil & Gas Producers, Real Estate Investment Trusts, Construction & Materials</td></tr>
<tr><td>Share performance</td><td>Strong<br>Aveva Group [AVV], 3i Group [III], Babcock International Group [BAB], Cranswick [CWK], Severn Trent [SVT]</td><td colspan="2">Weak<br>Petra Diamonds Ltd [PDL], Ferrexpo [FXPO], Thomas Cook Group [TCG], Acacia Mining [ACA], Carillion [CLLN]</td></tr>
<tr><td>Main features</td><td colspan="3">Sell in May effect: start of the weak six months of the year<br>FTSE 100 often underperforms the S&P 500 in this month<br>Busy month for FTSE 100 final dividend payments<br>First trading day average return: 0.9%; positive: 56%<br>Last trading day average return: -0.02%; positive: 44% (3rd weakest in year)</td></tr>
<tr><td>Significant dates</td><td colspan="3">01 May: Two-day FOMC meetings starts<br>04 May: US Nonfarm payroll report<br>07 May: May Day bank holiday, LSE closed<br>10 May: MPC interest rate announcement at 12 noon (anticipated)<br>10 May: MPC inflation report<br>14 May: MSCI semi-annual index review [announcement date]<br>28 May: LSE closed [Spring bank holiday]<br>28 May: NYSE closed [Memorial Day]<br>30 May: FTSE quarterly reviews announced</td></tr>
<tr><td>Average chart of the month</td><td colspan="3">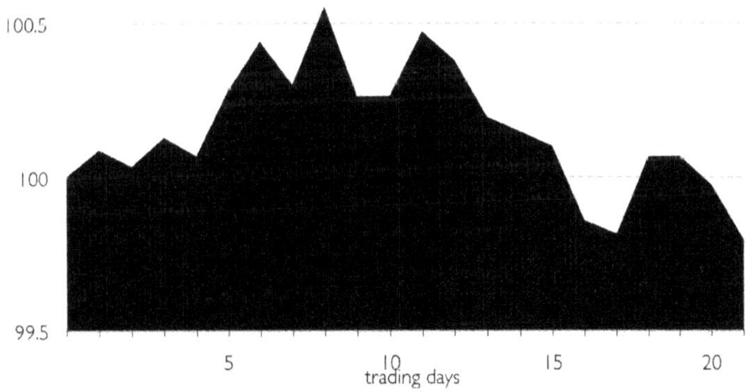
</td></tr>
</table>

# JUNE MARKET

## Market performance this month

June is not usually a good month for investors. One can see from the accompanying chart that the market falls more often than it rises in June, and when the market does decline the falls can be quite large, whereas the positive returns are usually only modest.

Putting some numbers to this, in the 47 years since 1970 the FTSE All-Share index has seen positive returns in June 21 times (45%), with an average month return of -1.0%. In recent years the record is even worse. In the 17 years since 2000 the market has seen positive returns in June just seven times (41%), with an average month return of -1.6%. Last year saw an unusually positive return in June when the market rose 2.5% (over the turbulent time of the EU referendum).

Not surprisingly, June has the second worst record for equity returns of all months. And the May–June period has been the weakest two-month period in the year for the market.

## The average June

In an average June the market starts strong, hitting its month high on the second or third trading day, but prices then drift down steadily for the rest of the month, although the market ends the month on a positive note – the last trading day is the second strongest in the year.

## Company results

Not much action on the results front this month, June is the quietest month for results from FTSE 100 companies – just two companies make announcements this month.

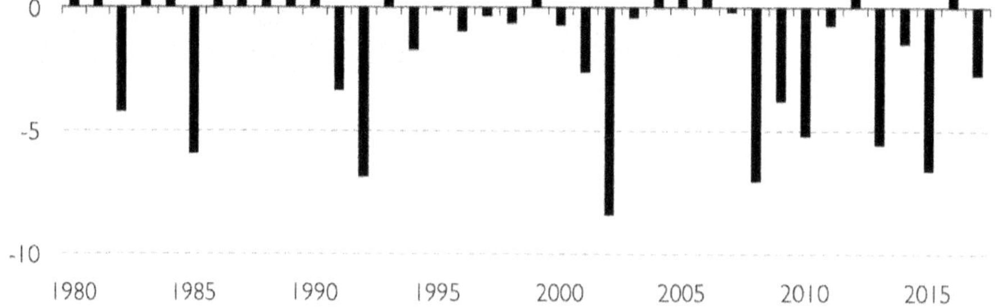

## June dashboard

<table>
<tr><td>Market performance</td><td>Avg change (%): -0.5%</td><td>Positive (%): 42%</td><td>Ranking: 11th</td></tr>
<tr><td>Sector performance</td><td>Strong<br>Pharmaceuticals & Biotechnology, Health Care Equipment & Services, Fixed Line Telecommunications</td><td colspan="2">Weak<br>General Retailers, Real Estate Investment Trusts, Food & Drug Retailers</td></tr>
<tr><td>Share performance</td><td>Strong<br>BTG [BTG], RPC Group [RPC], Halma [HLMA], Telecom plus [TEP], Ted Baker [TED]</td><td colspan="2">Weak<br>Barclays [BARC], Thomas Cook Group [TCG], Grafton Group [GFTU], Travis Perkins [TPK], Marston's [MARS]</td></tr>
<tr><td>Main features</td><td colspan="3">Second weakest month of the year for shares.<br>Weak month for silver<br>Summer starts 21 June, consider the Summer Share Portfolio stocks<br>First trading day average return: 0.17%; positive: 53%<br>Last trading day average return: 0.16%; positive: 62% (3rd strongest in year)</td></tr>
<tr><td>Significant dates</td><td colspan="3">01 Jun: MSCI semi-annual index review [effective date]<br>01 Jun: US Nonfarm payroll report<br>12 Jun: Two-day FOMC meeting starts<br>14 Jun: ECB Governing Council Meeting (monetary policy)<br>15 Jun: Triple Witching<br>15 Jun: FTSE Index series quarterly changes effective today<br>21 Jun: MPC interest rate announcement at 12 noon (anticipated)</td></tr>
<tr><td>Average chart of the month</td><td colspan="3">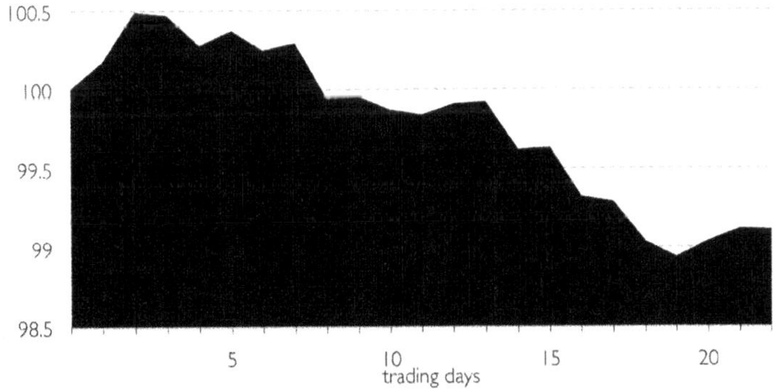</td></tr>
</table>

# JULY MARKET

## Market performance this month

After traditional weakness in June, share prices often bounce back in July – making this month a short period of strength in an otherwise weak six-month period (May to October).

Since 1970 the FTSE All-Share index has seen an average return of 0.8% in July, with 53% of years seeing positive returns in this month. This makes July the fifth strongest month of the year for shares. As can be seen in the accompanying chart, in recent years the market has been stronger than its longer-term performance. In the last eight years the market has only seen falls in July twice, and the average return in July has been 3.3%. So currently July is on a roll.

## The average July

In an average July the start of the month tends to be strong – the first week of the month is among the top ten strongest weeks in the year. After that, the market has a tendency to drift lower for a couple of weeks until finishing strongly in the final week of the month.

## Large-caps v mid-caps

July is one of only three months (the others being September and October) where the FTSE 100 tends to outperform the mid-cap FTSE 250, although the outperformance in July is not significantly large (an average of 0.2 percentage points since 1986). Better is the performance of the FTSE 100 relative to the S&P 500; in sterling terms July is the second-best month for the FTSE 100 (the UK index has outperformed the US index by an average of 1.0 percentage points since 1984).

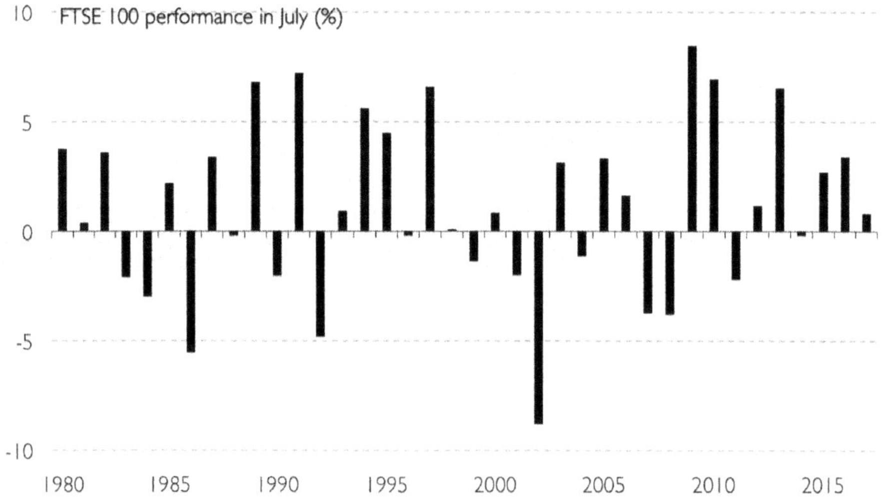

## July dashboard

| | | | |
|---|---|---|---|
| Market performance | Avg change (%): 1.1% | Positive (%): 61% | Ranking: 5th |
| Sector performance | *Strong*<br>Banks, Real Estate Investment Trusts, Software & Computer Services | *Weak*<br>Electricity, Industrial Transportation, Health Care Equipment & Services | |
| Share performance | *Strong*<br>Travis Perkins [TPK], Renishaw [RSW], Morgan Advanced Materials [MGAM], Bodycote [BOY], Elementis [ELM] | *Weak*<br>TalkTalk Telecom Group [TALK], SSE [SSE], CRH [CRH], Redefine International [RDI], Babcock International Group [BAB] | |
| Main features | FTSE 100 strong relative to S&P 500 this month<br>2nd busiest month for FTSE 100 interim results<br>Busy month for FTSE 100 final dividend payments<br>First trading day average return: 0.55%; positive: 74% (strongest of the year)<br>Last trading day average return: 0.14%; positive: 50%<br>GBPUSD historically strong this month<br>Strong month for silver | | |
| Significant dates | 04 Jul: NYSE closed [Independence Day]<br>06 Jul: US Nonfarm payroll report (anticipated)<br>26 Jul: ECB Governing Council Meeting (monetary policy)<br>31 Jul: Two-day FOMC meeting starts | | |
| Average chart of the month | 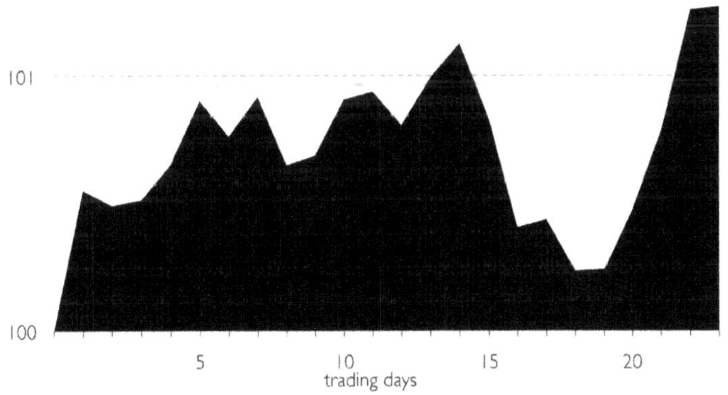 | | |

# AUGUST MARKET

## Market performance this month

August used to be a good month for the stock market, but this has changed in recent years. Indeed, as can be seen in the accompanying chart, the market has fallen by over 6% in this month in two of the last six years. As it's a month for holidays, trading volumes tend to be low for stocks, which in some years can lead to some increased volatility. The average return for the market in the month is 0.6%, while the probability of a positive return in August is 63%. Internationally, August is not a good month for equities; August has the second lowest average monthly returns for 70 world equity markets.

## The average August

In an average month for August the market tends to drift lower for the first couple of weeks and then increase for the final two weeks of the month. The final trading day of the month has historically been strong.

Finally, August is the busiest month for interim results announcements for both FTSE 100 (30 companies reporting) and FTSE 250 (80 companies).

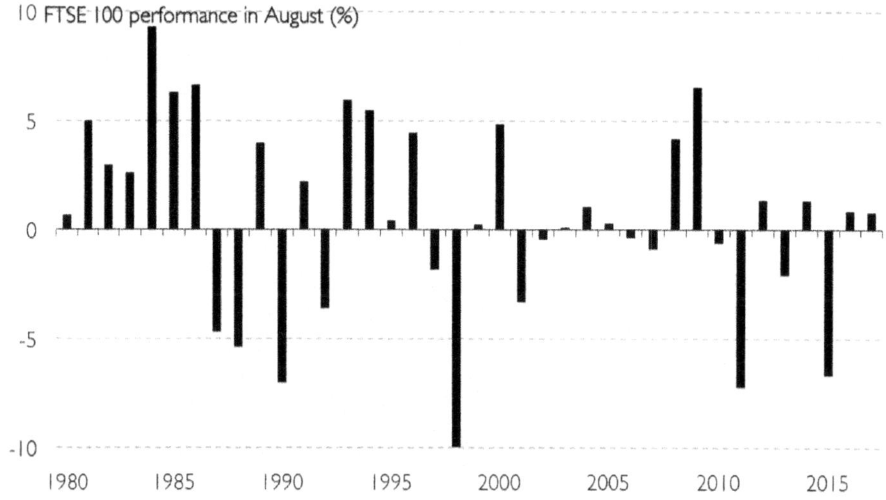

## August dashboard

| | | | |
|---|---|---|---|
| Market performance | Avg change (%): 0.6% | Positive (%): 63% | Ranking: 8th |
| Sector performance | *Strong*<br>Oil Equipment, Services & Distribution, Gas, Water & Multiutilities, Software & Computer Services | *Weak*<br>Fixed Line Telecommunications, Mining, Oil & Gas Producers | |
| Share performance | *Strong*<br>Redrow [RDW], Taylor Wimpey [TW.], Paysafe Group [PAYS], Synthomer [SYNT], Fisher (James) & Sons [FSJ] | *Weak*<br>Standard Chartered [STAN], BT Group [BT.A], Man Group [EMG], Rio Tinto [RIO], William Hill [WMH] | |
| Main features | Busiest month for FTSE 100 and FTSE 250 interim results announcements<br>First trading day average return: 0.04%; positive: 59% (3rd weakest of the year)<br>Last trading day average return: 0.13%; positive: 62%<br>GBPUSD historically weak this month<br>Weak month for silver | | |
| Significant dates | 02 Aug: MPC interest rate announcement at 12 noon<br>03 Aug: US Nonfarm payroll report (anticipated)<br>13 Aug: MSCI quarterly index review [announcement date]<br>27 Aug: Summer bank holiday, LSE closed | | |
| Average chart of the month | 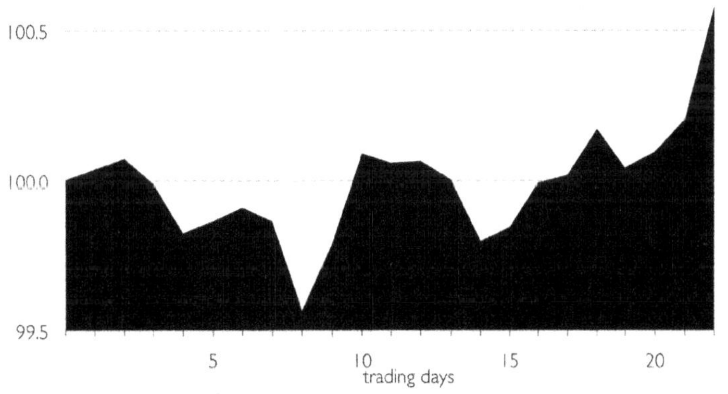 | | |

## Market performance this month

After summer the stock market tends to burst back into life in September. Unfortunately, the renewed activity in shares tends to be on the downside. Since 1984, the FTSE 100 index has an average return of -1.2% in this month; this gives September the worst record for shares for any month in the year. And things haven't improved recently, since year 2000 the average month return in the month has been -1.7%.

However, although the average return is bad in the month, about half of all Septembers actually have positive returns. The problem is that when the market does fall in this month, the falls can be very large. For example, as can be seen in the accompanying chart, the market has fallen over 8% in three years since 2000.

## The average September

In an average month for September the market tends to gently drift lower for the first three weeks before rebounding slightly in the final week – although the final trading day (FTD) of the month has historically been one of the weakest FTDs of all months in the year.

## Strategies

This is the month to consider the Sell Rosh Hashanah, Buy Yom Kippur trade, and also at the end of the month the Construction Sector 4M Strategy.

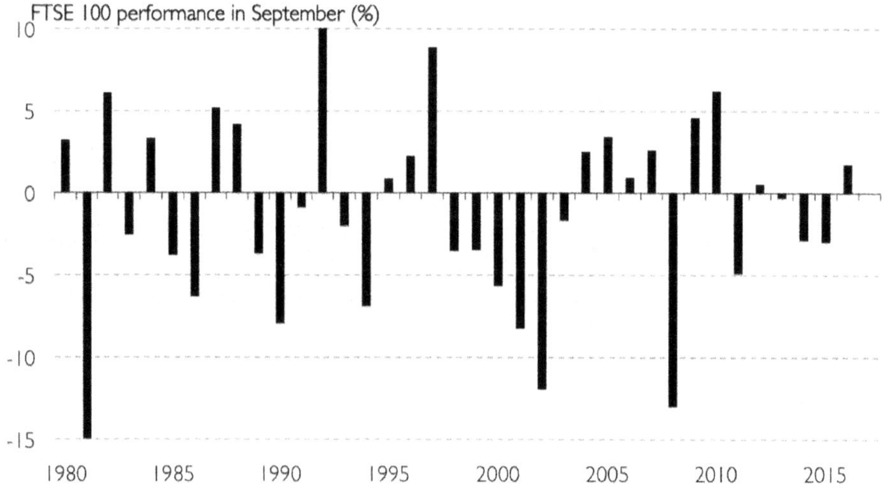

## September dashboard

| | | |
|---|---|---|
| Market performance | Avg change (%): -1.2% · Positive (%): 46% · Ranking: 12th | |
| Sector performance | *Strong*<br>Tobacco, Nonlife Insurance, Beverages | *Weak*<br>Industrial Transportation, Real Estate Investment Trusts, Electronic & Electrical Equipment |
| Share performance | *Strong*<br>JD Sports Fashion [JD.], SuperGroup [SGP], Genus [GNS], Jupiter Fund Management [JUP], Dechra Pharmaceuticals [DPH] | *Weak*<br>Standard Chartered [STAN], BT Group [BT.A], Man Group [EMG], Rio Tinto [RIO], William Hill [WMH] |
| Main features | Weakest month of the year for shares<br>The FTSE 250 is particularly weak relative to the FTSE 100 in this month<br>Strong month for gold<br>Strong month for silver<br>Busy month for FTSE 100 interim dividend payments<br>First trading day average return: 0.16%; positive: 64%<br>Last trading day average return: -0.01%; positive: 42%<br>Consider implementing Construction Sector 4M Strategy<br>Sell Rosh Hashanah, Buy Yom Kippur strategy<br>Summer ends Sep, consider liquidating the Summer Share Portfolio | |
| Significant dates | 03 Sep: NYSE closed [Labor Day]<br>03 Sep: MSCI quarterly index review [effective date]<br>05 Sep: FTSE quarterly reviews announced<br>07 Sep: US Nonfarm payroll report<br>13 Sep: MPC interest rate announcement at 12 noon<br>13 Sep: ECB Governing Council Meeting (monetary policy)<br>21 Sep: Triple Witching<br>21 Sep: FTSE Index series quarterly changes effective today<br>25 Sep: Two-day FOMC meeting starts | |
| Average chart of the month | 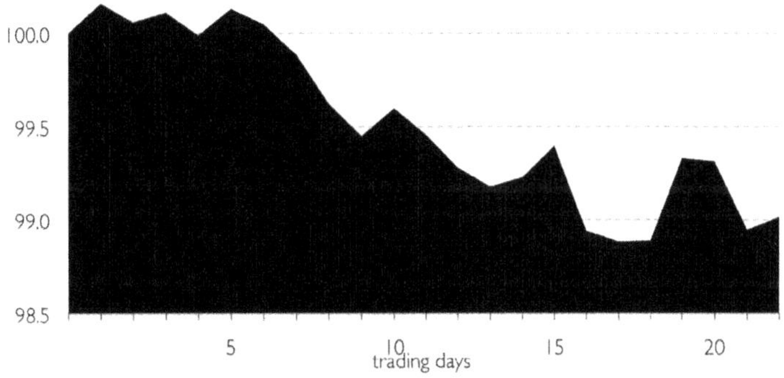 | |

# OCTOBER MARKET

## Market performance this month

October can be a volatile month for equities. Since 1984, seven of the ten largest one-day falls in the market have occurred in October. The largest fall happening on 20 October 1987 when the FTSE 100 index fell 12.2%. So, this would appear to bode ill for investors in October. However, if you look at the accompanying chart you will see why averages don't tell the whole story and how things have changed in recent years. For example, since 1992 the market has only fallen in five years (and two of those years were the exceptional years of 2008 and 2009). And since 2000 the average stock market return for October has been 1.8%, making it the second best month for equities after April.

The strength of equities in October may not be unconnected with the fact that the strong six-month period of the year starts at the end of October (part of the Sell in May Effect) and investors may be anticipating this by increasing their weighting in equities during October. But while October, therefore, should be regarded as a good month for shares, any occasional weakness in the month can be severe.

## The average October

In an average month for October the market tends to rise in the first two weeks, then to fall back, before a surge in prices in the last few days of the month (Sell in May Effect – aka Halloween Effect – again!).

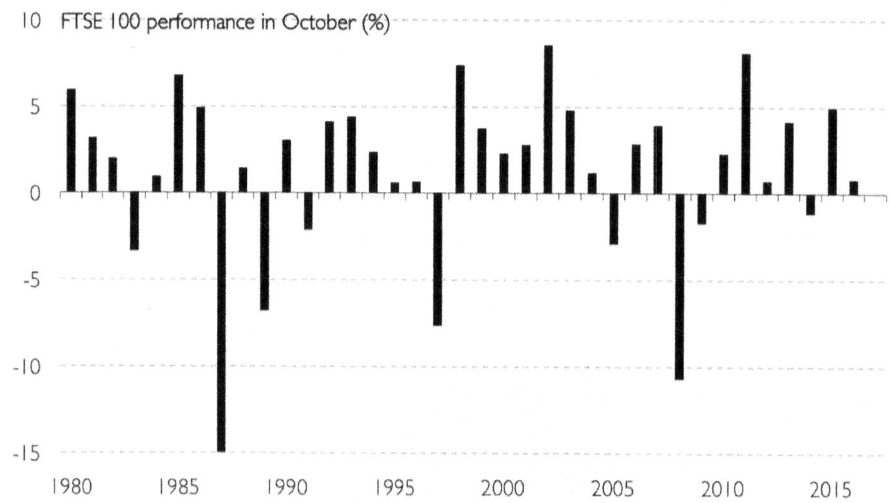

## October summary

<table>
<tr><td>Market performance</td><td>Avg change (%): 1.0%</td><td>Positive (%): 76%</td><td>Ranking: 3rd</td></tr>
<tr><td>Sector performance</td><td>Strong<br>Oil & Gas Producers, Beverages, Real Estate Investment & Services</td><td colspan="2">Weak<br>Software & Computer Services, Health Care Equipment & Services, General Industrials</td></tr>
<tr><td>Share performance</td><td>Strong<br>BP [BP.], Hargreaves Lansdown [HL.], Booker Group [BOK], Elementis [ELM], Tate & Lyle [TATE]</td><td colspan="2">Weak<br>Marshalls [MSLH], William Hill [WMH], UDG Healthcare [UDG], Morgan Advanced Materials [MGAM], Smiths Group [SMIN]</td></tr>
<tr><td>Main features</td><td colspan="3">Sell in May effect: end of the weak 6 months of the year<br>The FTSE 100 is particularly strong relative to the FTSE 250 in this month<br>Weak month for gold, silver and oil<br>GBPUSD historically strong this month<br>First trading day average return: 0.18%; positive: 61%<br>Last trading day average return: 0.43%; positive: 67% (year's strongest)</td></tr>
<tr><td>Significant dates</td><td colspan="3">05 Oct: US Nonfarm payroll report (anticipated)<br>25 Oct: ECB Governing Council Meeting<br>28 Oct: Daylight Saving Time ends</td></tr>
<tr><td>Average chart of the month</td><td colspan="3">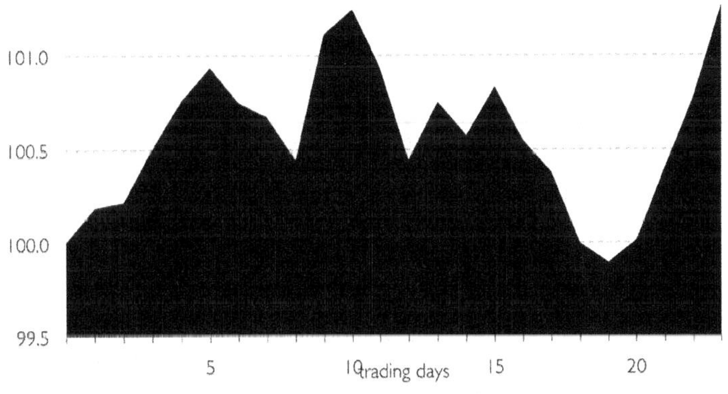</td></tr>
</table>

# NOVEMBER MARKET

## Market performance this month

Since 1984 the FTSE 100 index has risen in 59% of years in November, with an average return over the period of 1.0%. This gives it a rank of 6th place for monthly performance. From 1980 its relative performance had been steadily improving, but that trend has reversed since 2006 – the market has risen only three times in November in the last nine years.

Although the longer-term performance of November is only average, the significant feature of November is that it marks the start of the strong six-month period of the year (November to April). In other words, investors should be increasing exposure to the market this month (if they haven't already done so in October).

## The average November

On average the market tends to rise for the first three days of the month, then give up those gains over the following few days, before rising again and then falling back, until finally increasing quite strongly over the final seven trading days of the month.

Elsewhere, November is a strong month for gold and weak for GBPUSD.

This is a busy month for interim results: 64 companies from the FTSE 350 make their announcements this month.

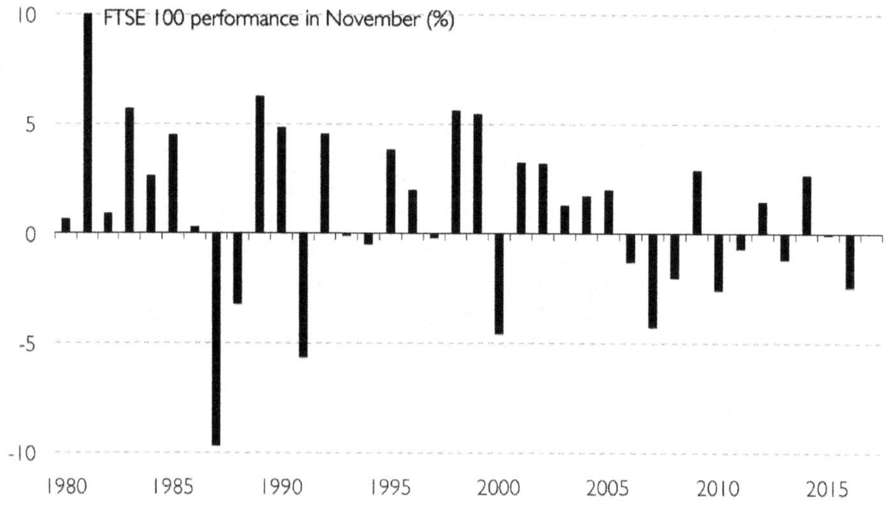

## November summary

| | | | |
|---|---|---|---|
| Market performance | Avg change (%): 1.0% | Positive (%): 59% | Ranking: 6th |
| Sector performance | *Strong*<br>Food Producers, Aerospace & Defense, Media | *Weak*<br>Oil Equipment, Services & Distribution, Real Estate Investment Trusts, Industrial Transportation | |
| Share performance | *Strong*<br>CRH [CRH], Shire [SHP], Britvic [BVIC], Babcock International Group [BAB], Compass Group [CPG] | *Weak*<br>Galliford Try [GFRD], Royal Bank of Scotland Group [RBS], Ashmore Group [ASHM], Hochschild Mining [HOC], Petrofac Ltd [PFC] | |
| Main features | Start of the strong six-month period for shares<br>Busy month for FTSE 350 interim results<br>First trading day average return: 0.11%; positive: 64%<br>Last trading day average return: -0.11%; positive: 42% (year's weakest)<br>Strong month for gold<br>Weak month for oil<br>GBPUSD historically weak this month | | |
| Significant dates | 02 Nov: US Nonfarm payroll report (anticipated)<br>07 Nov: Two-day FOMC meeting starts<br>08 Nov: MPC interest rate announcement at 12 noon<br>08 Nov: MPC inflation report<br>13 Nov: MSCI semi-annual index review [announcement date]<br>23 Nov: NYSE closed [Thanksgiving Day] | | |
| Average chart of the month | 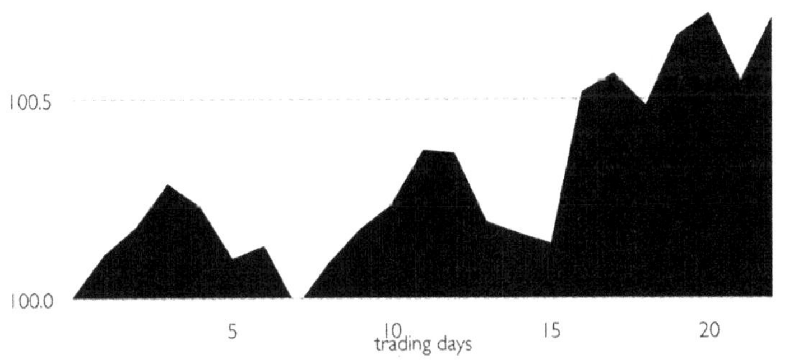 | | |

# DECEMBER MARKET

## Market performance this month

Towards the end of the year shares tend to rise strongly – a characteristic sometimes called the end of the year rally, or the Christmas rally. It makes December the best month of the year for investors. Since 1984 the FTSE 100 index has risen in 78% of all years with an average monthly return of 2.0%. Incredibly, the index has only fallen three times in December since 1995, although two of those times were in 2014 and 2015 – so things may be changing.

## The average December

As can be seen in the accompanying chart, the market tends to increase gently in the first two weeks of the month, but then goes into overdrive and rises strongly in the final two weeks. Indeed, this is the strongest two-week period in the whole year, with the three strongest days of the year all occurring in this two-week period.

## Strategies

In this month investors may like to look at the Santa Rally Portfolio, and also to consider implementing the Bounceback Portfolio at the end of the month.

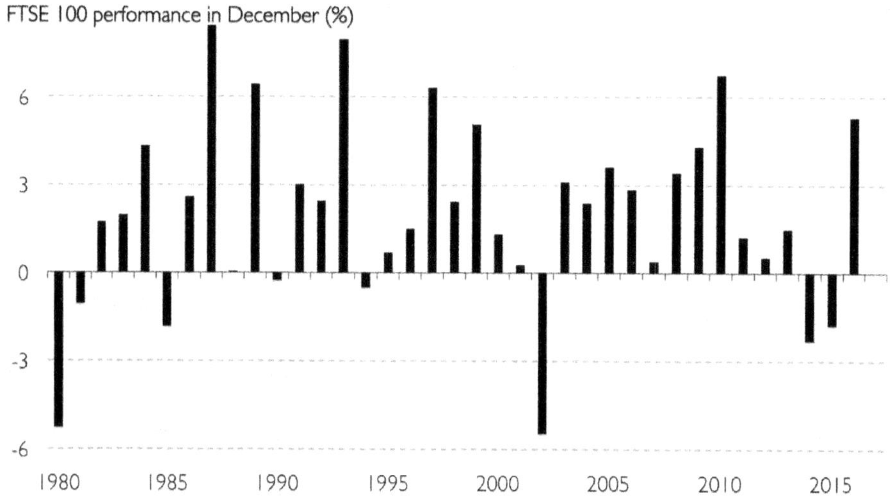

## December summary

<table>
<tr><td>Market performance</td><td>Avg change (%): 2.0%</td><td>Positive (%): 78%</td><td>Ranking: 1st</td></tr>
<tr><td>Sector performance</td><td>Strong<br>Electronic & Electrical Equipment, Construction & Materials, Media</td><td colspan="2">Weak<br>Banks, General Retailers, Fixed Line Telecommunications</td></tr>
<tr><td>Share performance</td><td>Strong<br>Ashtead Group [AHT], Taylor Wimpey [TW.], Spectris [SXS], Paddy Power Betfair [PPB], Ferguson [FERG]</td><td colspan="2">Weak<br>Marks & Spencer Group [MKS], Assura [AGR], Halfords Group [HFD], Clarkson [CKN], Barclays [BARC]</td></tr>
<tr><td>Main features</td><td colspan="3">Strongest month of the year for shares<br>FTSE 100 often outperforms the S&P 500 in December<br>Worst month for FTSE 100 dividend payments<br>First trading day average return: -0.06%; positive: 46% (year's weakest)<br>Last trading day average return: 0.04%; positive: 52%<br>Consider Bounceback Portfolio<br>Santa Rally starts on 9th trading day<br>GBPUSD historically strong this month</td></tr>
<tr><td>Significant dates</td><td colspan="3">03 Dec: MSCI semi-annual index review [effective date]<br>05 Dec: FTSE quarterly reviews announced<br>07 Dec: US Nonfarm payroll report<br>13 Dec: ECB Governing Council Meeting (monetary policy)<br>18 Dec: Two-day FOMC meeting starts<br>20 Dec: MPC interest rate announcement at 12 noon<br>21 Dec: Triple Witching<br>21 Dec: FTSE Index series quarterly changes effective today<br>24 Dec: Christmas Eve – LSE closed<br>25 Dec: Christmas Day – LSE, NYSE, HKSE closed<br>26 Dec: Boxing day – LSE, HKSE closed<br>31 Dec: LSE closed</td></tr>
<tr><td>Average chart of the month</td><td colspan="3">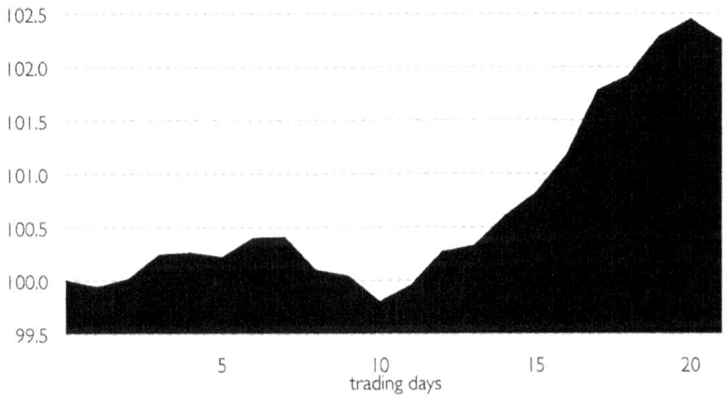
</td></tr>
</table>

# 2.
# STRATEGIES

# CONTENTS

# BOUNCEBACK PORTFOLIO

The *Bounceback Portfolio* invests in the ten worst performing FTSE 350 index stocks of the previous year and holds them for the three-month period, January–March.

Let's see how the Bounceback Portfolio fared in 2017.

### Performance in 2017

The following table lists the ten worst performing FTSE 350 stocks in 2016. These ten stocks were picked to form the 2017 Bounceback Portfolio.

The final column in the table also gives the returns for each stock for the period January–March 2017. For example, Capita shares fell 56.0% in 2016, and then rose (*bounced back*) 6.3% in the first three months of 2017.

| Company | TIDM | 2016 (%) | 2017 Jan–Mar (%) |
|---|---|---:|---:|
| Capita | CPI | −56.0 | 6.3 |
| Restaurant Group (The) | RTN | −52.7 | 2.8 |
| Sports Direct International | SPD | −51.7 | 10.6 |
| Essentra | ESNT | −44.3 | 13.9 |
| easyJet | EZJ | −42.2 | 2.1 |
| International Personal Finance | IPF | −40.4 | -5.0 |
| IG Group Holdings | IGG | −38.4 | 0.6 |
| McCarthy & Stone | MCS | −36.6 | 17.4 |
| Inmarsat | ISAT | −33.9 | 13.2 |
| Man Group | EMG | −32.6 | 24.5 |
| FTSE 350 | NMX | 12.5 | 2.9 |

For reference, the performance of the FTSE 350 is also shown for the same periods.

As can be seen, the majority of the bounceback stocks outperformed the index in the first quarter of 2017.

The performance of the ten Bounceback Portfolio stocks for January–March 2017 is shown in the following chart.

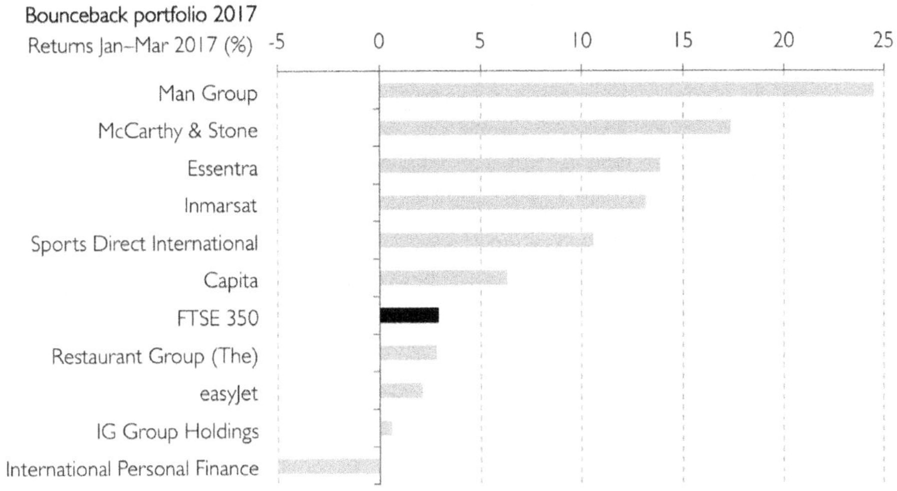


On average, the Bounceback Portfolio stocks had a three-month return of 8.6%, compared with a FTSE 350 return of 2.9% for the same period.

So, an equally-weighted portfolio of the ten bounceback stocks would have outperformed the FTSE 350 by 5.7 percentage points over the target first three months of 2017.

## Bounceback portfolio performance 2003–2017

The Bounceback strategy has been tracked since 2003. The following chart shows the comparative performance of the portfolio and the FTSE 350 for each year since 2003.

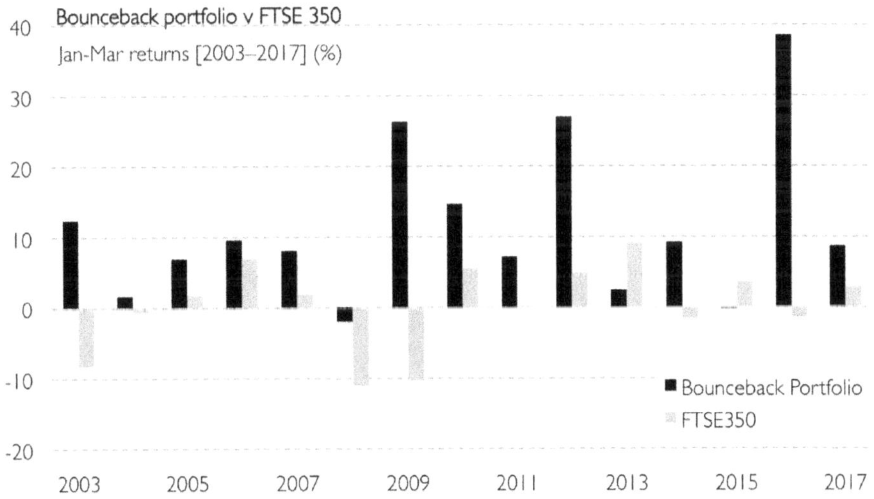


The Bounceback Portfolio has outperformed the FTSE 350 by an average of 11.3 percentage points each year since 2003. And in that period has underperformed the index only twice (in 2013 and 2015).

The following chart plots the cumulative performance of two portfolios that invested in the market only over the January–March period for the years 2003–2017; one portfolio invests in the FTSE 350, the other in that year's Bounceback Portfolio.

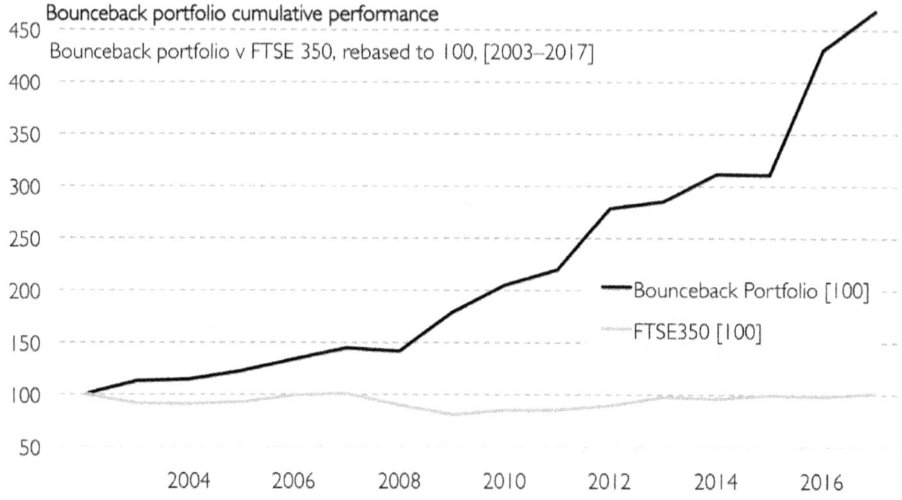


By 2017 the FTSE 350 portfolio value would have gained 1.2%, while the Bounceback Portfolio would have risen 367.5%.

# CONSTRUCTION SECTOR 4M STRATEGY

Elsewhere in this edition we look at seasonality of various cycle lengths, for example, monthly, quarterly and annual. Here we look at an interesting seasonality effect of four months.

The following two charts analyse the monthly seasonality of the FTSE 350 Construction & Material sector. The charts plot the outperformance of the sector over the FTSE 100 index.

The chart below plots the average outperformance for each month since 1999. For example, the construction sector has outperformed the FTSE 100 in January by any average 2.4 percentage points over the 18 years since 1999. The value for April is negative (−1.3), indicating that on average the construction sector has underperformed the market in that month.

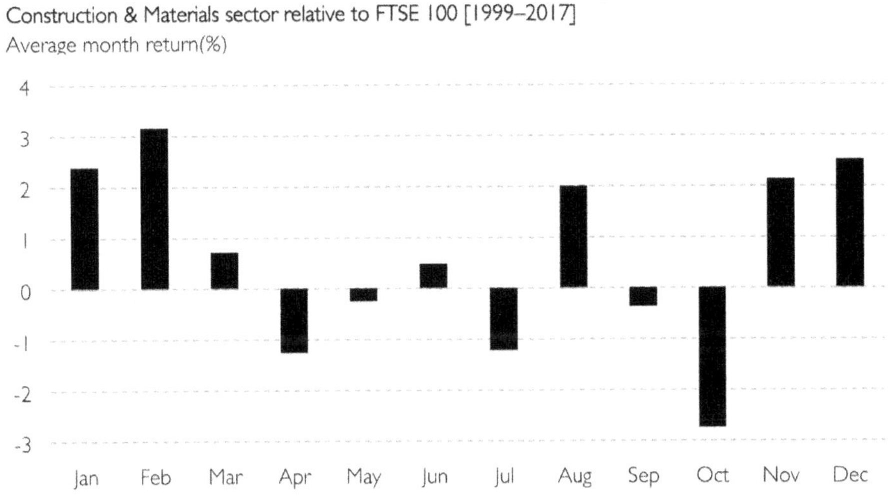


The following chart plots the proportion of years that have seen a positive outperformance by the construction sector in each month. For example, the sector has outperformed the market in January in 13 of the last 18 years (i.e. 72%).

The characteristic that jumps out from this analysis is the relative strength of the construction sector in the four months: January, February, November and December.

Construction & Materials sector relative to FTSE 100 [1999–2017]
Months with positive returns(%)

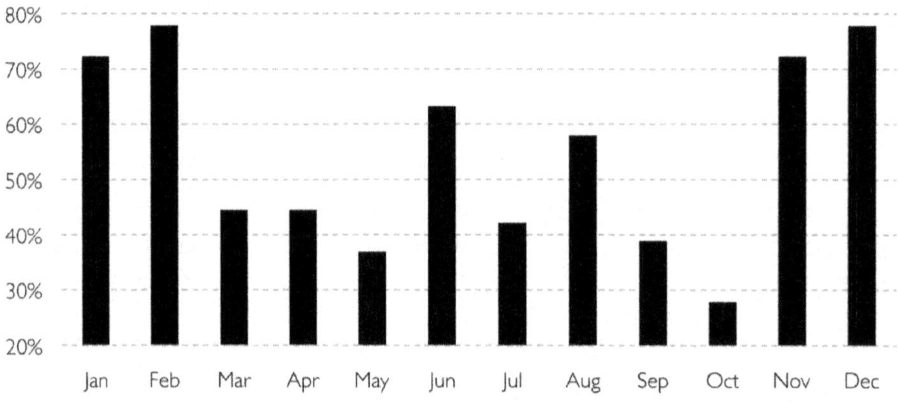


## Strategy

The above analysis suggests a simple strategy (*Construction Sector 4M Strategy*) that invests in the Construction sector continuously in the four months from November through to February of the following year and is in cash for the rest of the year (i.e. the remaining eight months).

The following chart plots the value of this strategy if it had been set up in 1999 and run through to today. For comparison, also plotted is the value of a buy-and-hold FTSE 100 portfolio (both series are rebased to start with values of 100).

Construction Sector 4M Strategy [1999–2017]

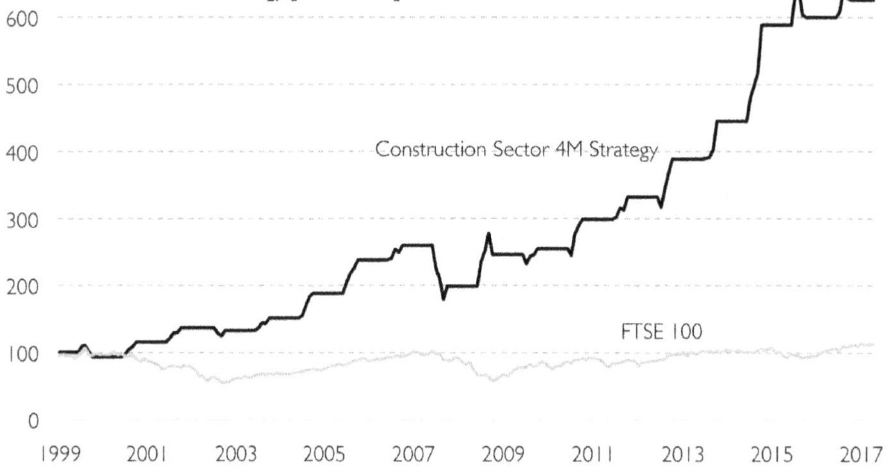


By mid-2017 the FTSE 100 portfolio would have had a value of 113, while the Construction Sector 4M Strategy portfolio would have a value of 625.

A good way to build value!

# SELL IN MAY STRATEGY

Elsewhere in the *Almanac* we have looked at the characteristics of the Sell in May anomaly. We'll consider here how to exploit it.

First, let's consider two portfolios:

- **Summer Portfolio**: this portfolio only invests in the UK stock market in the summer period (1 May–31 October) and is in cash for the rest of the time.
- **Winter Portfolio**: does the reverse of the above portfolio – it invests in shares only in the winter period (1 November–30 April), and for the other six months of the year the portfolio is all in cash.

For the purposes of this simple study, we'll assume that the portfolios' investments track the FTSE All-Share index. The chart below shows the comparative performance of the two portfolios, each starting with £100, from 1994.

Summer v Winter Portfolios [1994–2016]

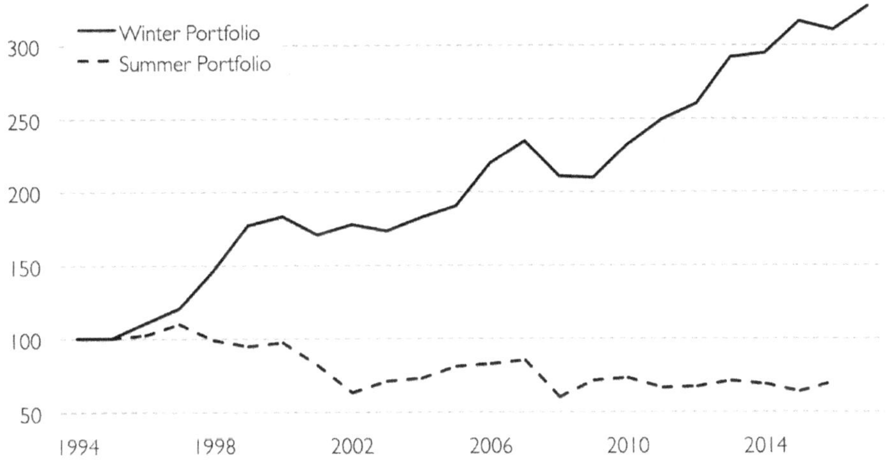


Starting with £100 in 1994, the:

- *summer portfolio* would be worth £70 by 2016; but the
- *winter portfolio* would be worth £326.

This is a striking result and should be very profitable to exploit. However, it's not quite that easy...

### Exploiting the Sell in May anomaly

An obvious strategy would be to simply follow the instructions on the tin – i.e. sell in May.

It is certainly the case that equities over the six-month period May to October tend to underperform the November to April period. However, just because the market underperforms May–October doesn't necessarily mean that the market experiences negative returns over these summer months.

As we see elsewhere in the *Almanac*, since 1982 the market has actually risen more often than it has fallen over the May to October period.

So, the case is not necessarily looking strong to sell in May. Especially if one adds in the argument that being out of the market an investor will forgo any dividend payments over the May–October period (and at a time when interest rates are very low).

An argument in favour of selling might be that, although the market often sees positive returns in the period, when the market does fall, the falls tend to be quite large. So, since 2000, the average return for May–October has been −0.9%. Admittedly, this is quite heavily influenced by the fall in 2008, which might be regarded as something of an outlier. But over the longer periods, the average returns are negative as well (−0.1% from 1982, and −0.7% from 1972).

Let's investigate what a Sell in May strategy would look like.

The strategy **invests** in the stock market (e.g. a FTSE 100 tracker) during the period 1 November–30 April, and then liquidates the portfolio and puts the cash in a deposit account or buys sterling T-bills for the other six months of the year.

The following chart illustrates the result of doing this methodically since 1994, and compares the performance of this strategy to the FTSE 100 Total Return index (i.e. compares it to being fully invested in the market all year and receiving dividends).

Starting in 1994 with £100 the strategy would have increased in value to £656 by 2017; over the same period a portfolio tracking the FTSE 100 Total Return index year-round would have increased to £513 (incl. dividends).

It can be seen that the strategy benefited from being out of the market for the steep market declines in 2002 and October 2008. This largely accounts for its outperformance.

So, one of the principal attractions of the Sell in May strategy is that it keeps investors out of the market during periods of historically high volatility.

The above does not take into account transaction costs, but these would not significantly impact a reasonably-sized portfolio.

There is evidence that the profitability of the strategy can be further enhanced by using an indicator like the MACD (as explained in the 2013 edition of the *Almanac*) to time the exact entry and exit points for the equity investment.

In summary, while Sell in May is a significant and persistent anomaly, it is not that easy to exploit it. Of course, its very persistence is also a strong signal that the anomaly is difficult to arbitrage (i.e. exploit).

# SELL IN MAY SECTOR STRATEGY (SIMSS)

This is another strategy to exploit the Sell in May anomaly.

The idea is to stay in the market throughout the year but to rebalance a stock portfolio according to which sectors perform the best in the two six-month periods as defined by the Sell in May Effect.

First, the performance of the respective FTSE 350 index sectors is analysed for the two periods in recent years. Then some filters are applied:

1. Sectors with less than four component stocks were not considered.

2. Sectors must have a minimum 13-year track record.

3. Standard deviation (i.e. volatility) of a sector's returns must be below the average standard deviation.

4. Positive returns must be over 50%.

From this, the sector portfolios selected were:

| Summer Portfolio | Winter Portfolio |
|---|---|
| Gas, Water & Multiutilities | Construction & Materials |
| Beverages | Industrial Engineering |
| Personal Goods | Chemicals |

The Sell in May Sector Strategy (SIMSS) is therefore:

- in the **summer period**: equal long sectors Gas, Water & Multiutilities, Beverages, and Personal Goods, and then switch to...
- in the **winter period**: equal long sectors Construction & Materials, Industrial Engineering, and Chemicals.

Just to reiterate, the portfolio is fully invested in the market year round, it never holds cash.

### Performance of SIMSS

The following chart shows the simulated performance of the Sell in May Sector Strategy backdated to 1999 benchmarked to the FTSE 350.

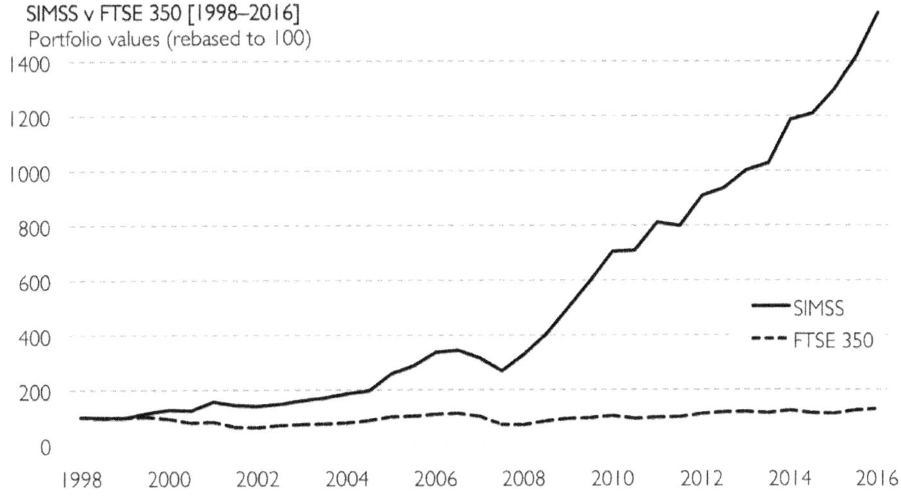


After 17 years the SIMSS portfolio would have grown in value to 1575 (from a starting value of 100), while the FTSE 350 (buy and hold) portfolio would have grown to 128.

This simulation does not include transaction costs, but as the strategy only trades twice a year these would not significantly affect the above results.

# SUMMER SHARE PORTFOLIO

*How do shares behave in the summer?*

A simple question perhaps, but first it is necessary to define "summer".

*When do you think summer begins and ends?*

The summer solstice marks the date when the earth's axis is most inclined towards the sun – this results in the longest day of the year (and occurs between 20 June and 22 June in the northern hemisphere). Strictly, this should mark the *middle* of the summer season in the astronomical calendar. However, due to seasonal lag the warmest days of the year tend to occur after this date, and so in the meteorological calendar summer extends for the whole months of June, July and August. But in some countries (e.g. the UK) where the temperature lag can be up to half a season, then summer is taken to *start* with the summer solstice and *end* with the autumn equinox (22 September), when the earth is tilted neither towards nor away from the sun).

For the purposes of the analysis here we will take the dates of summer as being 21 June–22 September. The following analysis looked at the performance of the share prices of the 350 companies in the FTSE 350 index over summer for the ten years 2008–17.

### Stocks that like summer

The table below shows eight companies whose share prices have risen in at least eight summers in the past ten years. For example, Next shares rose 27.7% in the summer of 2017, and the shares had an average summer return of 11.1% for the years 2008–17.

| Company | TIDM | 2008 | 2009 | 2010 | 2011 | 2012 | 2013 | 2014 | 2015 | 2016 | 2017 | Avg |
|---|---|---|---|---|---|---|---|---|---|---|---|---|
| Galliford Try | GFRD | 35.8 | 36.7 | 0.4 | -2.8 | 19.4 | 12.5 | 13.1 | -6.2 | 3.9 | 15.4 | 12.8 |
| Renishaw | RSW | 2.0 | 44.9 | 40.2 | -37.3 | 12.1 | 8.0 | 4.5 | -15.7 | 26.5 | 28.4 | 11.4 |
| Next | NXT | 19.7 | 25.7 | 1.3 | 15.7 | 8.1 | 13.5 | 9.0 | 0.3 | -10.2 | 27.7 | 11.1 |
| Randgold Resources | RRS | 16.5 | 12.4 | 0.9 | 43.7 | 25.4 | 8.9 | -11.4 | -16.9 | 23.0 | 5.5 | 10.8 |
| Booker Group | BOK | 9.5 | 19.0 | 15.6 | 7.3 | 4.0 | 14.5 | -5.0 | 2.6 | 2.7 | 8.9 | 7.9 |
| TR Property IT | TRY | 5.2 | 38.3 | 7.8 | -17.4 | 10.5 | 9.5 | 3.0 | -1.5 | 6.7 | 4.4 | 6.7 |
| Rotork | ROR | -17.2 | 30.9 | 22.1 | 2.4 | 20.4 | 6.6 | 5.2 | -27.8 | 10.7 | 10.6 | 6.4 |
| TP ICAP | TCAP | -30.5 | 22.7 | 12.6 | 4.3 | 1.2 | 15.6 | 8.7 | 3.7 | 14.9 | 1.3 | 5.4 |
| | *average:* | 5.1 | 28.8 | 12.6 | 2.0 | 12.6 | 11.1 | 3.4 | -7.7 | 9.8 | 12.8 | 9.1 |
| | *FTSE 350:* | -6.8 | 19.3 | 5.6 | -11.8 | 4.7 | 7.5 | -0.7 | -10.7 | 10.5 | -2.0 | 1.5 |
| | *diff:* | 11.9 | 9.6 | 7.0 | 13.8 | 8.0 | 3.6 | 4.1 | 3.0 | -0.7 | 14.8 | 7.5 |

On average over the last ten years the market (FTSE 350) has risen 1.5% over the summer, but an equally-weighted portfolio of these eight stocks rose an average of 9.1% in each summer and would have outperformed the index in nine of the past ten years.

### Stocks that don't like summer

The following table is similar to the above, but this time shows four companies whose share prices have *fallen* in at least seven summers in the past ten years.

| Company | TIDM | 2008 | 2009 | 2010 | 2011 | 2012 | 2013 | 2014 | 2015 | 2016 | 2017 | Avg |
|---|---|---|---|---|---|---|---|---|---|---|---|---|
| Carillion | CLLN | -2.2 | 10.3 | -4.6 | -8.6 | 1.2 | 21.4 | -1.6 | -10.3 | -3.3 | -77.8 | -7.6 |
| Mitie Group | MTO | -8.7 | 19.7 | -11.0 | -2.5 | 5.3 | 14.2 | -6.4 | -14.0 | -30.9 | -15.4 | -5.0 |
| Serco Group | SRP | -16.2 | 23.1 | -0.1 | -12.5 | 6.5 | -6.8 | -22.6 | -15.0 | 20.9 | -4.6 | -2.7 |
| NEX Group | NXG | -24.8 | -6.8 | -0.4 | -0.6 | -9.3 | 7.1 | 6.7 | -15.8 | 19.3 | -1.4 | -2.6 |
| | *average:* | -13.0 | 11.6 | -4.0 | -6.0 | 0.9 | 9.0 | -6.0 | -13.8 | 1.5 | -24.8 | -4.5 |
| | *FTSE 350:* | -6.8 | 19.3 | 5.6 | -11.8 | 4.7 | 7.5 | -0.7 | -10.7 | 10.5 | -2.0 | 1.5 |
| | *diff:* | -6.2 | -7.7 | -9.6 | 5.8 | -3.7 | 1.5 | -5.3 | -3.1 | -9.0 | -22.8 | -6.0 |

An equally-weighted portfolio of the above four stocks fell an average of −4.5% in each summer and would have underperformed the index in eight of the past ten years by an average 6.0 percentage points each summer.

An equally-weighted portfolio of the eight strong summer stocks would have outperformed an equally-weighted portfolio of the four weak summer stocks every summer for the past ten years by an average of 13.5 percentage points each summer.

# SELL ROSH HASHANAH, BUY YOM KIPPUR

In 1935, the Pennsylvania Mirror referred to a Wall Street adage, "Sell before Rosh Hashanah; buy before Yom Kippur". Recently an academic paper[1] quoted this article and set out to establish if the adage was true and still valid today.

The theory is that the market is weak during the approximately seven trading-day gap between the Jewish New Year (Rosh Hashanah ) and the Day of Atonement (Yom Kippur). To test this theory the authors studied the results of short selling the Dow Jones Industrial Average on one of the three days before Rosh Hashanah and buying back on one of the three days following Yom Kippur. They analysed the nine different combinations of trade dates, i.e. selling on the third day before Rosh Hashanah (R-3) and buying back on the day after Yom Kippur (Y+1), R-3 and Y+2, R-3 and Y+3, R-2 and Y+1, etc. The period tested was 1907 to 2008.

The paper found that the mean returns for the DJIA for the nine trade dates considered ranged from -0.47% for R-3/Y+2 (i.e. shorting three days before Rosh Hashanah and covering two days after Yom Kippur) , to −1.01 for R-2/Y+1.

In other words, they found that the market had indeed been weak between the two Jewish holidays, and that five of the nine scenarios yielded statistically significant results. They checked to see if this *Jewish Holiday Effect* might have diminished in recent years and found that the effect over 1998–2008 was actually stronger for six of the nine trade scenarios than for the prior period 1907–1998.

*So, what's the reason for this?*

The authors of the paper found that this was not a result of the influence of other anomalies (e.g. the Weekend Effect), nor was it the result of data outliers. One Wall Street trader gave the traditional explanation that people of the Jewish religion "wished to be free (as much as possible) of the distraction of worldly goods during a period of reflection and self-appraisal." Of course, Jewish traders are only a small part of the market, but at the margin their withdrawal from the market over this period may increase volatility and risk, and thus discourage others from trading, and then the arbitrage traders exploiting the effect can make it self-fulfilling.

*Is this a peculiarity of just the US market, or is the effect present in other markets?*

The above cited paper starts by quoting a 9 September 1915 *New York Times* article titled "The London Market Quiet – Jewish Holiday Causes Small Attendance on the Exchange". The newspaper reported that money and discount rates on the London Stock Exchange were "easy today" and attendance at the exchange was low due to the Jewish holiday of Rosh Hashanah.

*So, might this effect still be in force in the London market today?*

The following chart shows the mean returns for the FTSE 100 index for the nine combinations of trade dates (as above) for the period 1984–2017.

1. Pan Yaktrakis and Albert Williams, 'The Jewish Holiday Effect: Sell Rosh Hashanah, Buy Yom Kippur', *Advances in Business Research*, 2010, Vol 1(1).

Average FTSE 100 returns for period between Rosh Hashanah and Yom Kippur [1984–2017]

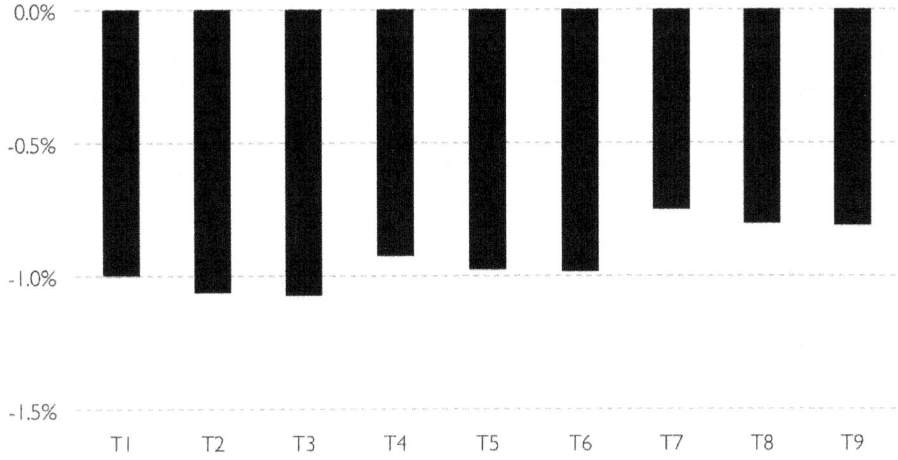


The X-axis labels are explained in the following table.

| Label | Parameters |
|---|---|
| T1 | R-3/Y+1 |
| T2 | R-3/Y+2 |
| T3 | R-3/Y+3 |
| T4 | R-2/Y+1 |
| T5 | R-2/Y+2 |
| T6 | R-2/Y+3 |
| T7 | R-1/Y+1 |
| T8 | R-1/Y+2 |
| T9 | R-1/Y+3 |

So, for example, T1 refers to the period three days before Rosh Hashanah to one day after Yom Kippur.

As can be seen, the market was weak for all nine combinations of trade dates over the Rosh Hashanah to Yom Kippur period. The weakest combination was for T5 (i.e. selling on the third day before Rosh Hashanah and buying back on the second day after Yom Kippur), when the mean return has been −1.2%.

The Jewish Holiday Effect would therefore seem to be as strong in the London market as it is in New York.

# SANTA RALLY

The *Santa Rally* is a term often used to refer to the strength of equities at the end of the year. We look here at whether a Santa Rally actually exists for shares and, if so, when it starts each year.

The following chart plots an index of average daily returns for the FTSE 100 index for the trading days from the beginning of November to the end of December for all the years since 2000. The values are rebased to start at 100.

For example, for the 17 years since 2000, the mean return for the FTSE 100 on the first trading day of November has been 0.7%. So, the first value plotted on the chart is 100.7.

NB. The X-axis labels refer to the trading days of respectively November and December.

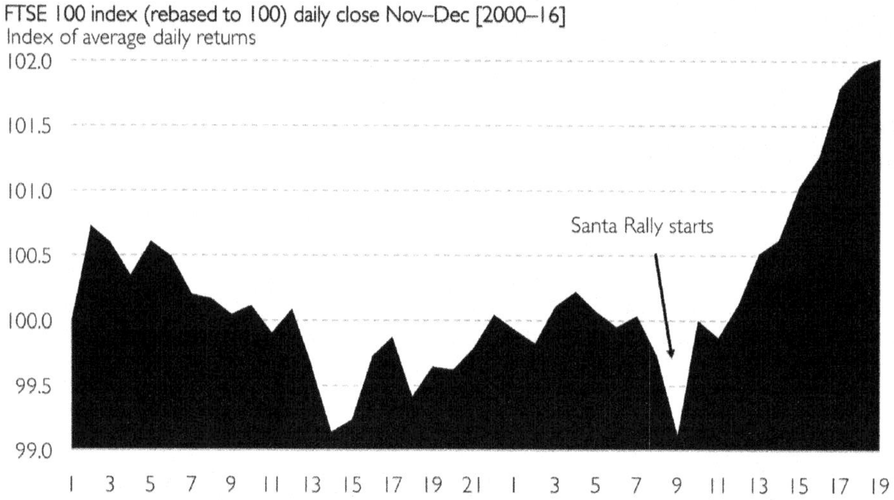


We can see from the chart that since 2000 the equity market has tended to be flat, or even weak, from the start of November through into December. But from the ninth trading day of December the market experiences a surge in prices – this is the Santa Rally!

As just remarked, up to the ninth trading day of December share prices can actually be quite weak, which often prompts market commentators to ask "Where's Santa?" and "Is the Santa Rally no more?"

There is no definitive explanation for this Santa Effect, although various possible causes have been proposed, including: fund managers window dressing their portfolios, positive sentiment in the market caused by the festive season which is accentuated by low trading volumes, anticipation of the January Effect, and tax reasons (NB. "tax reasons" are often cited in the absence of any definitive explanation).

In 2018 the tenth trading day of December will be on 14 December.

# DAY OF THE WEEK STRATEGY

*Previous editions have been tracking the performance of the Day of Week (DOTW) Strategy. This is an update on that strategy.*

[You may like to refer to the Statistics section in this edition, where you will find an analysis of the returns for the FTSE 100 index by days of the week.]

Since 2012, the FTSE 100 has had negative average returns on Monday and Wednesday, and positive average returns on Tuesday, Thursday and Friday.

This suggested a strategy of shorting the market for Monday (i.e. shorting at the close the previous Friday), switching to long on Tuesday, back to short on Wednesday, and then long on Thursday and Friday (and back to short at the close of Friday).

The following chart updates the results of implementing this strategy every week from January 2015 to mid-2017 (the time of writing). For comparison, a simple long-only FTSE 100 portfolio is also shown. The portfolios values are rebased to start at 100.

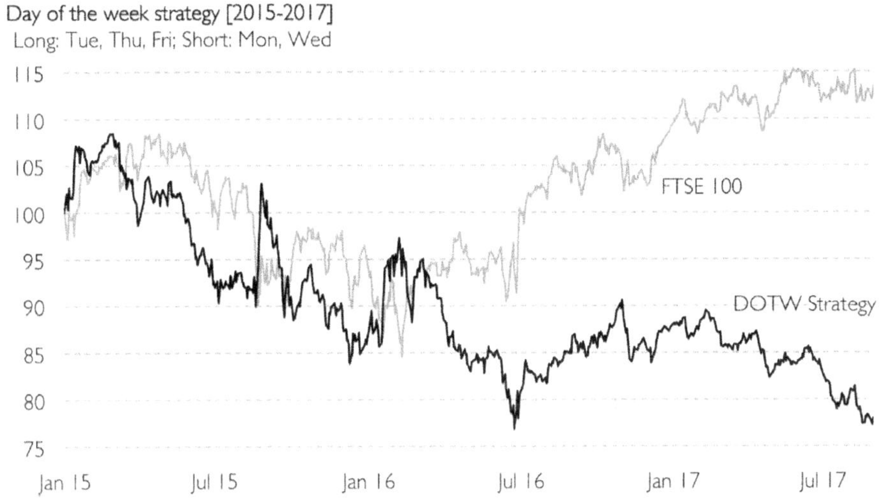


Woops! For three years from 2012 this strategy worked well, but as the chart above shows this has not been the case from 2015 (and the above does not take into account transaction costs, which would negatively impact the strategy's performance even further). One reason for this poor performance is that in the last couple of years Wednesday no longer has relatively weak returns.

So, we could consider a variant of the strategy which replaces Wednesday with Thursday (which has been weaker than Wednesday since 2015). The following chart plots the performance of such a strategy (i.e. Long: Tuesday, Wednesday, Friday; Short: Monday, Thursday).

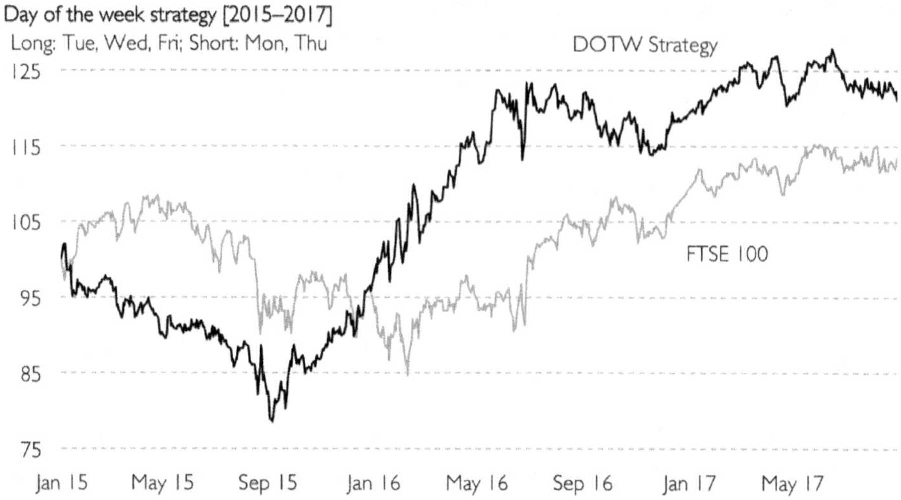


This strategy has performed better (and was particularly strong for about a year from September 2015). But so far in 2017 the strategy returns have merely tracked the index.

Let's look now at a simplified strategy that just goes long on Mondays, short on Fridays and is in cash for the rest of the time.

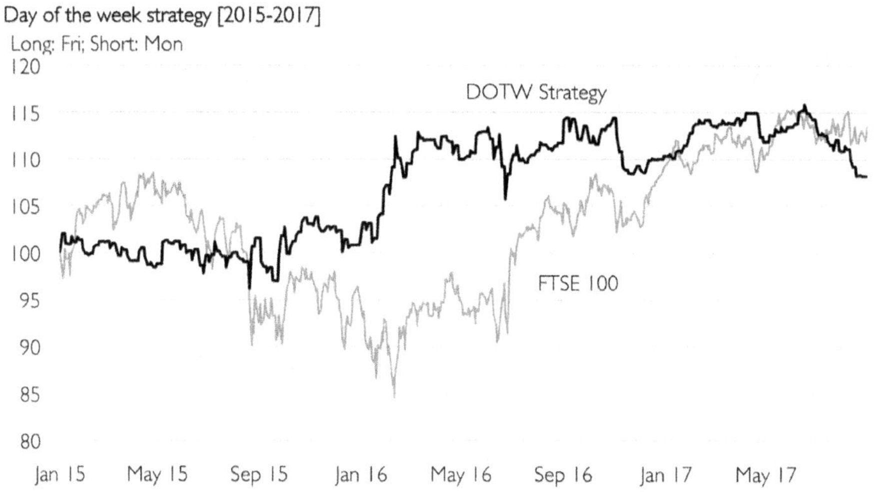


As can be seen, this strategy had a brief period when it outperformed the index, but is currently underperforming. The reason can be found in the recent analysis of the daily returns of the index (see Statistics section): in 2017 the index has seen relatively strong returns on Mondays (and recently returns on Friday have been weak).

The lesson here is that the persistency of anomalies needs to be monitored closely. And this is especially the case with this Day of the Week Strategy; it *is* possible to identify periods of abnormal returns on specific days of the week, but history show us that these periods do not persist over the long term. The DOTW Strategy is obviously a strategy that needs to be closely monitored and adjusted as the relative strengths of the days of the week change.

# TUESDAY REVERSES MONDAY

*Do market returns on Tuesdays reverse those on Monday?*

We first looked at this in the 2013 edition of the *Almanac* and it is now time to see if anything has changed.

The following updates the chart to 2017 plotting Tuesday returns for the FTSE 100 index split by whether the previous day's returns were positive or negative. Two time periods are considered: 1984–2017 and 2000–2017.

For example, for the longer period, the average return on Tuesday when Monday was up is 0.03%, while the average Tuesday return when Monday was down is 0.09%.

FTSE 100 returns on Tuesdays when Monday was up/down

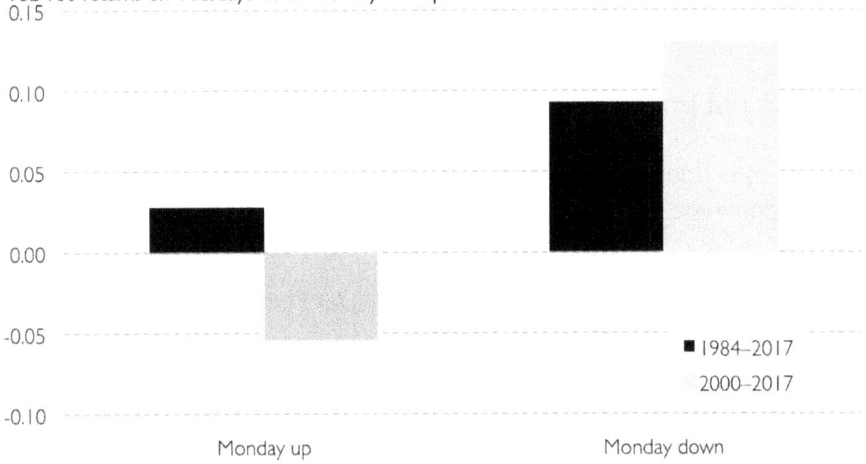


While the figures have marginally changed from the previous study in 2013, the overall finding is the same: namely that the theory that Tuesday reverses Monday does not seem to hold. Since 1984 the theory holds when Monday returns have been negative, but not when they have been positive.

But, as in the 2013 study, the theory *has* been valid for the market since 2000.

The previous study suggested that further analysis might include a filter on the size of the Monday returns. This is done in the following chart, where Tuesday returns are only considered if Monday's returns were beyond a certain threshold (i.e. of a certain size). The (arbitrary) threshold chosen was Monday's returns being more than 1 standard deviation away from the mean of Monday returns.

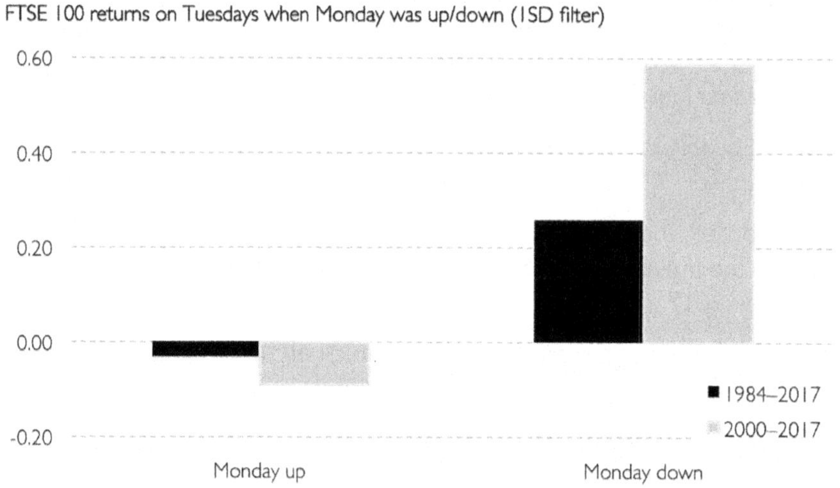


It can be seen that limiting the analysis of Tuesday returns to just large movements on Monday (i.e. beyond 1 standard deviation) does help the reversal theory. In this case, if the market rises on Monday, then on average it falls the following day (albeit a pretty small average fall), and if the market falls on Monday, the market rises (fairly strongly) on the Tuesday.

Let's now look at how the theory has been holding up in recent years.

## Recent years

The following chart is similar in design to the previous charts, but this time it plots the reversal results for the discrete years 2014–2017.

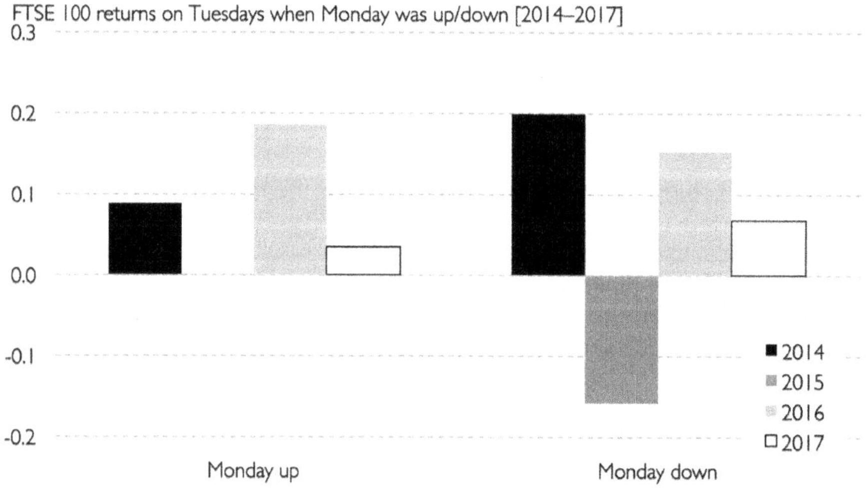


First, when the market is up on Monday, all four of the past four years has failed to support the reversal theory as Tuesday has followed with positive returns as well. When Mondays are down, in three of the past four years Tuesdays have seen positive average returns (the exception being 2015).

## Exploiting the reversal effect

*OK, so how to exploit this?*

The following chart plots the value of a portfolio that invests in the FTSE 100 just on Tuesdays when the previous day saw negative returns. For the rest of the time it is in cash.

In the 2013 study a variant portfolio was also considered that, as well as going long Tuesdays following negative Mondays, also went short Tuesdays following positive return Mondays. There's currently not much point in considering this as the reversal effect is not working for positive Mondays.

So, instead, the variant second strategy studied here is as above (i.e. long Tuesday following a negative Monday) but with a 1 standard deviation filter applied to the Monday return (i.e. the strategy only goes long on Tuesday if the Monday negative return is a greater than 1 standard deviation return).

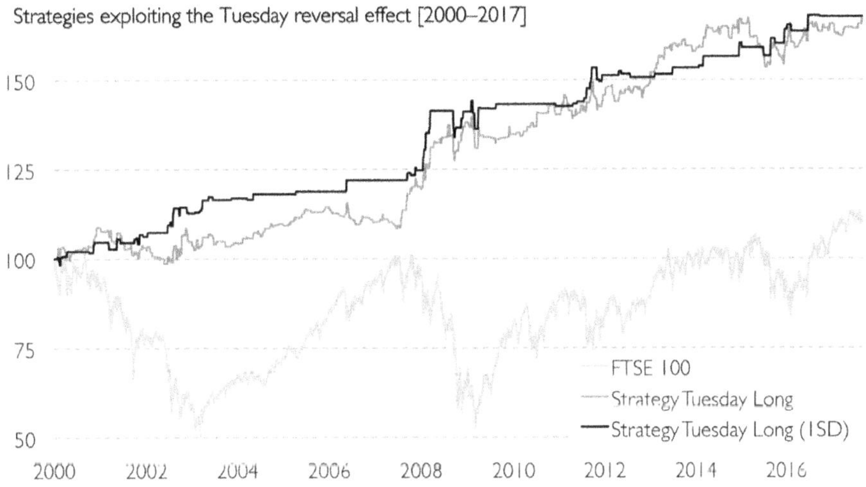


Since 2000 it can be seen that the simple long Tuesday strategy outperforms the benchmark buy-and-hold FTSE 100 portfolio. The variant 1SD strategy only marginally outperforms the simple long Tuesday strategy, but does so with a greatly reduced volatility.

# TURN OF THE MONTH STRATEGY

*A strategy that exploits the Turn of the Month anomaly.*

The *Almanac* has previously investigated the Turn of the Month anomaly (whereby the market sees abnormally high returns around the turn of the month). An update of the analysis can be seen elsewhere in this edition.

A recent academic paper[1] addresses the same topic. The paper makes the rather remarkable claim that:

> "since July 1926, one could have held the US value-weighted stock index (CRSP) for only seven days a month and pocketed the entire market excess return with nearly fifty percent lower volatility compared to a buy and hold strategy."

These seven days straddle the turn of the month.

*What might cause this behaviour?*

The paper argues that it is the month-end liquidity needs of US institutions, such as pension funds and mutual funds, that have month-end distributions. For example, the first chart below from the paper shows the proportion of US pension payment dates around the turn of the month (day T denotes the last trading day of the month). And because settlement in the US is T+3, institutions have to sell at least three days in advance to ensure they have the necessary liquidity for the end of the month. Then, at the beginning of the month, institutions look to invest recently received dividends, which puts demand pressure on stocks over the first few days. (And, yes, some pension funds are now changing their distribution dates to get out of synchronisation with their peers!)

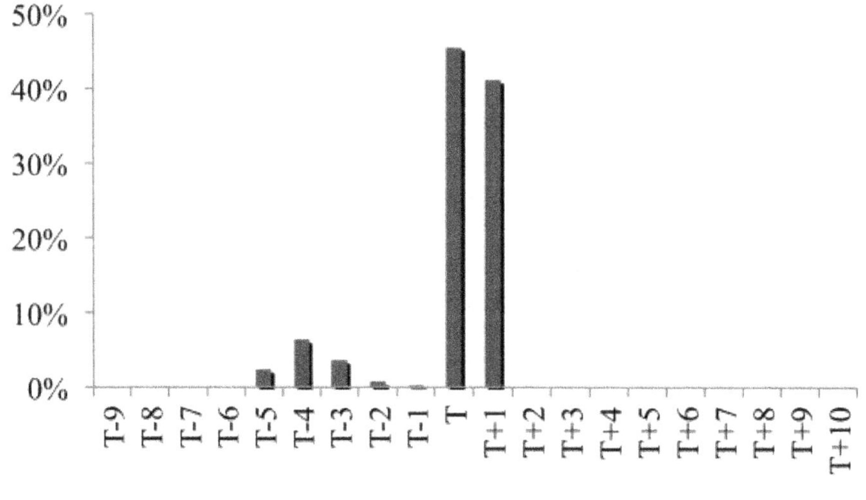


1. Erkko Etula, Kalle Rinne, Matti Suominen and Lauri Vaittinen, 'Dash for Cash: Month-End Liquidity Needs and the Predictability of Stock Returns' (17 May 2016).

Generally, the paper found that the turn of the month anomaly has become more pronounced as mutual funds' AUM as a proportion of the overall stock market has increased. The paper's authors also found that the anomaly exists in other developed markets and was more pronounced in countries with larger mutual fund sectors.

*Is such behaviour seen in the UK?*

As mentioned above, the *Almanac* has already previously documented the strength of the market around the turn of the month. But the following chart replicates (for the UK market) the one found in the Etula paper: it plots the cumulative returns of the FTSE All-Share index for the six days around the turn of the month (TOM: T-3 to T+3) against the cumulative returns of the index for the rest of the month (X-TOM) for the period 2003–17. The FTSE All-Share is added as a benchmark. All series are rebased to start at 100.

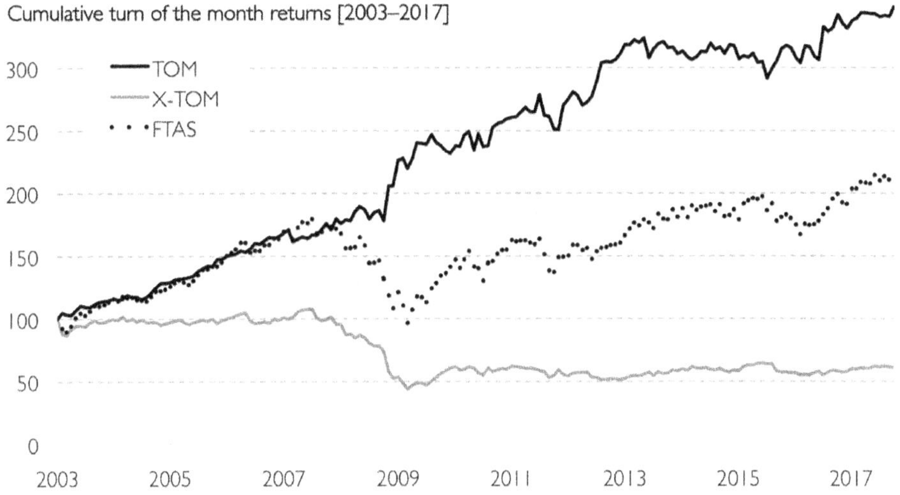


By 2017, a TOM portfolio would have had a value of 349, and an X-TOM portfolio a value of 61. Which does suggest (as the paper found for the US market) that all the market's gains come in just a few days around the turn of the month.

For comparison, the buy-and-hold FTSE All-Share portfolio would have had a value of 213 by the end of the period. So the TOM would have significantly outperformed the index, because on average the market had negative returns during the X-TOM part of the month. Which is quite a result!

In addition, the TOM portfolio would have had 50% less volatility than the index.

# FTSE 100/250 MONTHLY SWITCHING STRATEGY

Analysis of the historic data shows that although the FTSE 250 index has greatly outperformed the FTSE 100 index in the medium and long term (since 2000 the FTSE 100 has risen 7% compared with an increase of 207% for the FTSE 250) there are certain months for which the large-cap index on average outperforms the mid-cap index.

A previous edition of the *Almanac* presented a strategy that exploited this feature; this is updated here with the performance of the strategy in the last year.

The following chart shows the average outperformance of the FTSE 100 over the FTSE 250 by month for the period 2000–2017. For example, on average the FTSE 100 has outperformed the FTSE 250 by -1.7 percentage points in January since year 2000.

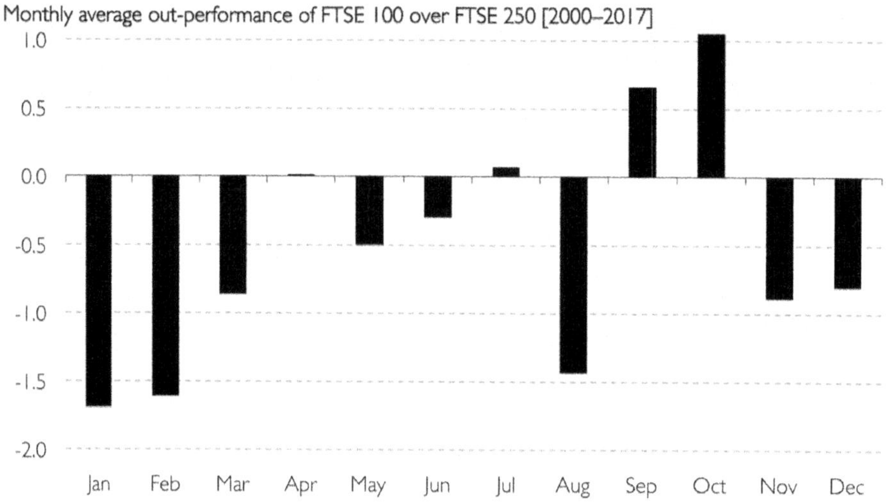


As can be seen, there are only two months, September and October, in which the FTSE 100 significantly outperforms the FTSE 250.

## The FTSE 100/FTSE 250 monthly switching strategy

The above analysis suggests a strategy of investing in the FTSE 250 for the year but switching into the FTSE 100 for just the two-month period September–October. In other words, the portfolio would be invested in the FTSE 250 from January to August, at the end of August it switches out of the FTSE 250 into the FTSE 100 for two months, then back into the FTSE 250 until the end of August the following year.

The following chart shows the result of operating such a strategy from 2000. For comparison, the chart also includes the portfolio returns from continuous investments in the FTSE 100 and FTSE 250. All the data series have been rebased to start at 100.

FTSE 100/250 monthly switching strategy [2000-2017]

The result: from 2000–2017 the FTSE 100 portfolio would have grown +7%, the FTSE 250 +207%, but the FTSE 100/FTSE 250 monthly switching portfolio would have increased 325%.

Switching between the indices each year would have incurred transactions costs which have not been included here, but these would have been relatively negligible relative to the overall returns.

In the last year (since the previous edition of the *Almanac*), the strategy portfolio would have gained 16%, compared with gains of 4% and 10% respectively for the FTSE 100 and FTSE 250. So, for the moment, this strategy still seems to be working well.

# FTSE 100/S&P 500 MONTHLY SWITCHING STRATEGY

*An update on a strategy to exploit the monthly comparative returns of the FTSE 100 and S&P 500 indices.*

Although since 1984 the S&P 500 has greatly outperformed the FTSE 100 (+1379% against +643%), there are months in the year when the FTSE 100 fairly consistently outperforms the S&P 500.

The following chart shows the average monthly outperformance of the FTSE 100 over the S&P 500 since 1984.

Comparative average monthly returns of FTSE 100 v S&P 500 [1984–2017]

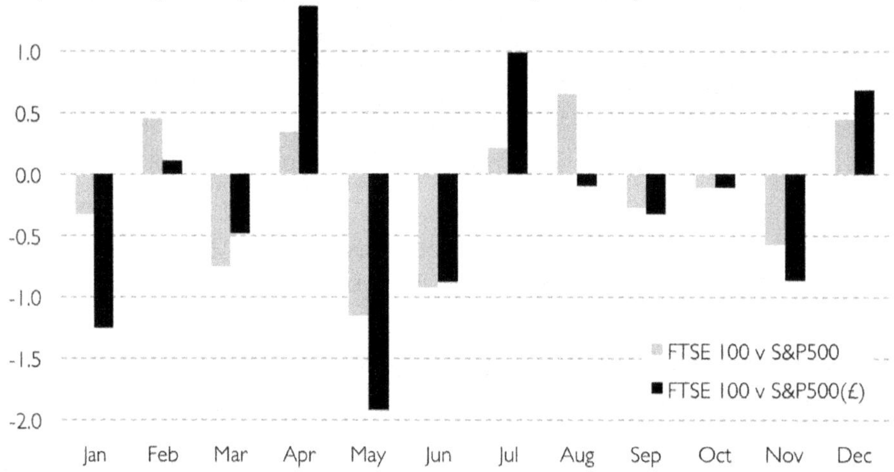


Looking first at the light grey bars in the chart, this shows, for example, that on average in January the FTSE 100 has outperformed the S&P 500 by −0.3 percentage points (i.e. the UK index has underperformed the US index). From the chart we can see that the five months that are relatively strong for the FTSE 100 are: February, April, July, August and December. For example, the FTSE 100 has outperformed the S&P 500 in February in 13 of the past 15 years.

Now, turning to the black bars, these display the same average monthly outperformance of the FTSE 100 over the S&P 500, except this time the S&P 500 has been sterling-adjusted. One effect of adjusting for currency moves is to amplify the outperformance of the FTSE 100 in certain months (April, July, and December). Conversely, the FTSE 100 underperformance is amplified in January, May and November.

Whereas, before, the relatively strong FTSE 100 months were February, April, July, August and December, we can see that the currency-adjusted strong months are just April, July, and December.

## The FTSE 100/S&P 500 Monthly Switching Strategy (FSMSP)

The above analysis suggests a strategy of investing in the UK market (i.e. the FTSE 100) in the months April, July and December and in the US market (i.e. the S&P 500) for the rest of the year. In other words, the portfolio would be invested in the S&P 500 from January to March, then at the end of March it switches out of the S&P500 into the FTSE 100 for one month, then back into the S&P 500 for two months, into the FTSE 100 for July, back into the S&P 500 for four months, then back into the FTSE 100 for December, and finally back into the S&P 500 to start the next year.

The following chart shows the result of operating such a strategy from 2000 to 2017. For comparison, the chart also includes the portfolio returns from continuous investments in the FTSE 100 and S&P 500 (in GB pounds).

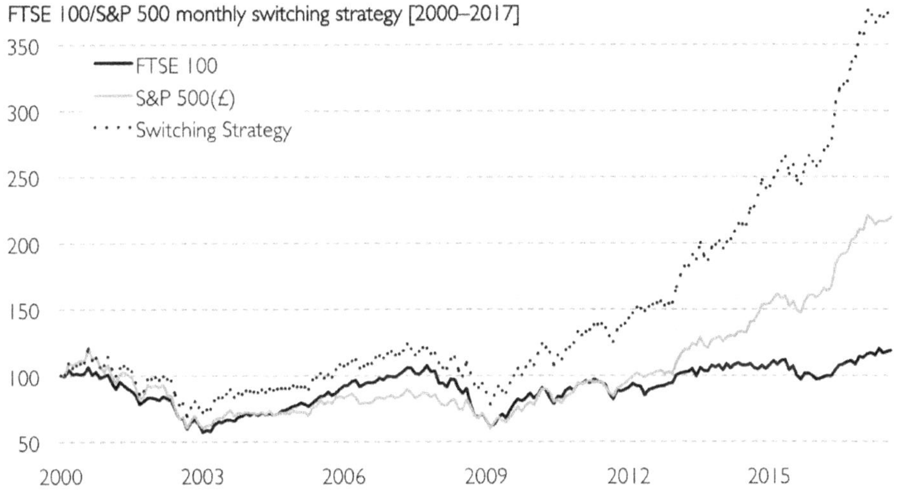


The final result: since 2000, the FTSE 100 portfolio would have grown 19%, the S&P 500(£) would have risen 120%, but the FTSE 100/S&P 500 monthly switching portfolio (FSMSP) would have increased 278%. Switching six times a year would have incurred some commission costs, but these would not have dented performance significantly.

In the last year (since the previous edition of the *Almanac*), the portfolio would have gained 18%, compared with gains of 10% and 14% for the FTSE 100 and S&P 500 respectively. So, for the moment, this strategy still seems to be working well.

# MONTHLY SEASONALITY OF OIL

*Does the price of oil display a monthly seasonality pattern?*

A previous study in the *Almanac* found that since 1986 the price of oil has displayed a seasonality pattern defined by two parts of the year:

1. *March–September* when WTI is strong, and
2. *October–February* when the WTI price has been relatively weak.

Let's see if this is still the case.

## Mean returns

The following chart plots the average monthly returns of the price of WTI (West Texas Intermediate) for the period 2000–17.

A two-part pattern for the year is still observable, but the periods have shifted slightly.

As can be seen, since 2000, WTI monthly returns have tended to be high in the period February to June. The strongest month of the year in this period has been February, with an average return in the month of 4.7%.

The weak part of the year has also shifted: it is now September to January. The weakest month has been November, with an average price return of −2.7%.

## Positive returns

The following chart plots the proportion of monthly returns that were positive over the same period.

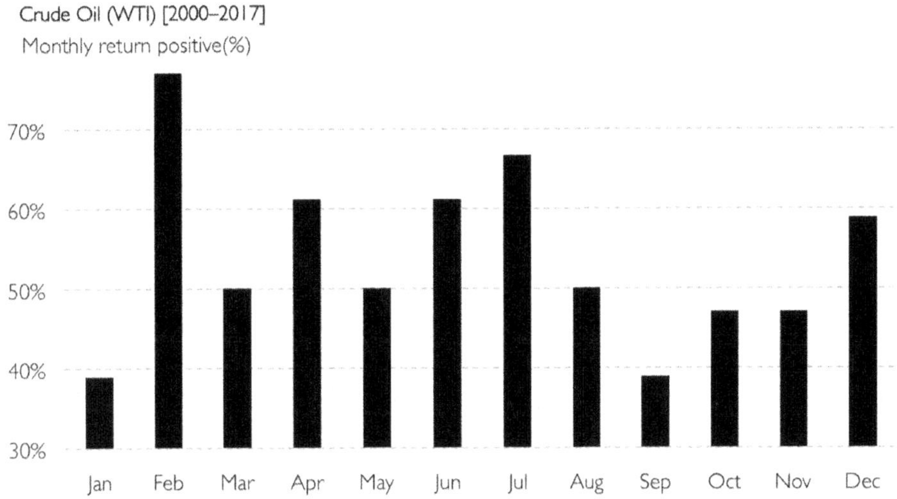


This pattern of positive returns largely supports the preceding analysis. Since 2002 WTI has seen negative returns in February in only three years. By contrast, January has seen only one positive return in the last 11 years.

The new seasonality pattern can thus be summarised as:

1. *February–June* when WTI is **strong**, and
2. *September–January* when the WTI price has been relatively **weak**.

## Cumulative performance

The following chart plots the cumulative performance of WTI for two portfolios:

1. *WTI (Strong Months)* – this holds WTI in just the strong months identified above (February–June), and is in cash for the rest of the year.

2. *WTI (Weak Months)* – this holds WTI in just the weak months (September–January), and is in cash for the rest of the year.

For benchmarking purposes WTI (continuous holding) and the S&P 500 index are also plotted. All series are rebased to start at 100.

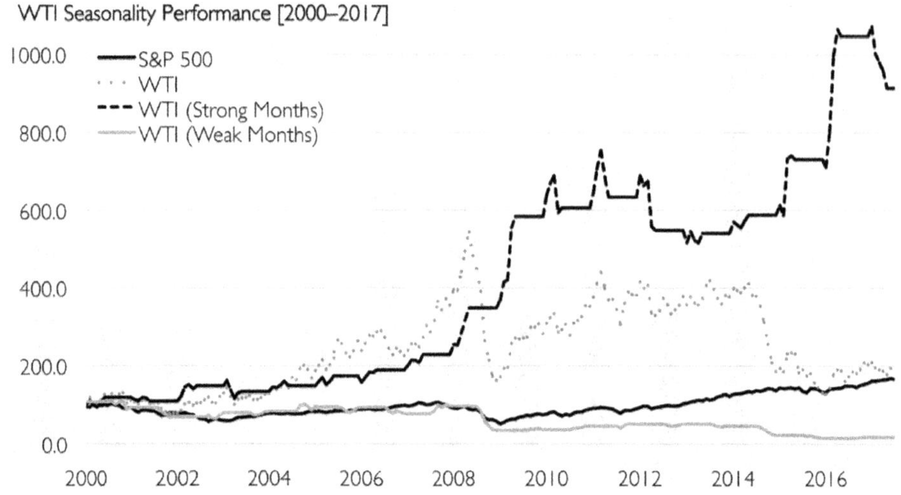


Starting at 100 in 2000, the WTI (Weak Months) portfolio would have fallen to a value of 18 by 2017. The S&P 500 would have a value of 166, and a continuous holding in WTI a value of 184. But the WTI (Strong Months) portfolio would today have a value of 914 (albeit 2017 was a weak year for the strategy).

# MONTHLY SHARE MOMENTUM

*Do shares exhibit a momentum effect from one month to the next?*

## Momentum portfolios

If we selected the best performing shares in one month and created an equally-weighted portfolio of those shares to hold for the following month and then repeated this every month, would that portfolio outperform the market index?

Previous editions of the *Almanac* analysed this for the companies in the FTSE 100 index; here that study is updated, comparing momentum portfolios comprising each month five and ten shares of the best performing shares from the previous month.

The following chart shows the results of operating such momentum portfolios from 2010 to 2017 and, for comparison, the FTSE 100 (all three series have been rebased to start at 100). So, to summarise, the two portfolios in the chart are:

1. **MSMP(5)**: a portfolio rebalanced at the end of each month comprising the *five* best performing FTSE 100 shares of the previous month
2. **MSMP(10)**: as above, but this portfolio contains the *ten* best performing FTSE 100 shares of the previous month

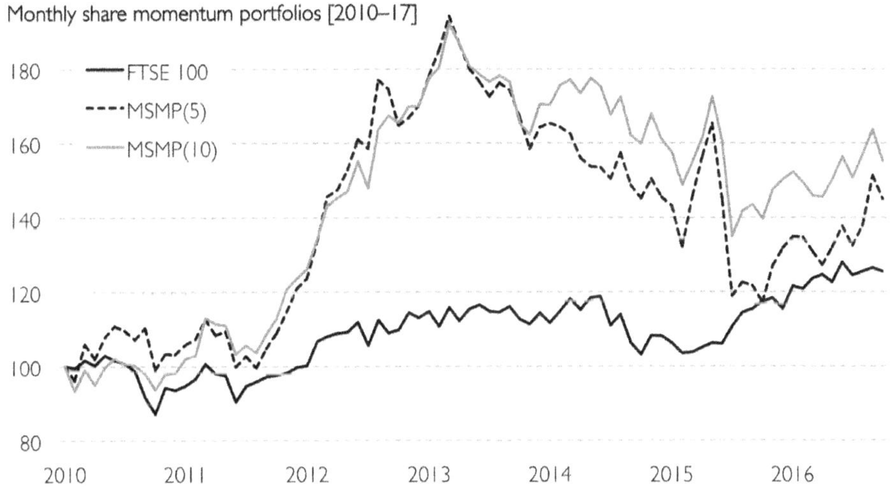


As can be seen in the chart, the ten-stock portfolio only marginally outperforms the five-stock portfolio, suggesting the latter may be adequate for this strategy. But the big story is the decline in momentum profitability from 2014. The strategy's performance has improved slightly in the last year, but the situation needs close monitoring.

## Reversal portfolios

Let's look now at what would happen if, instead of selecting the best performing shares from the previous month, we chose the worst performing shares.

So, the two portfolios in this case will be:

1. **MSRP(5)**: a portfolio rebalanced at the end of each month comprising the *five* worst performing FTSE 100 shares of the previous month
2. **MSRP(10)**: as above, but this portfolio contains the *ten* worst performing FTSE 100 shares of the previous month

The following chart plots the performance of these portfolios from 2010, and adds a buy and hold FTSE 100 portfolio as a benchmark. All portfolios are rebased to start at 100.

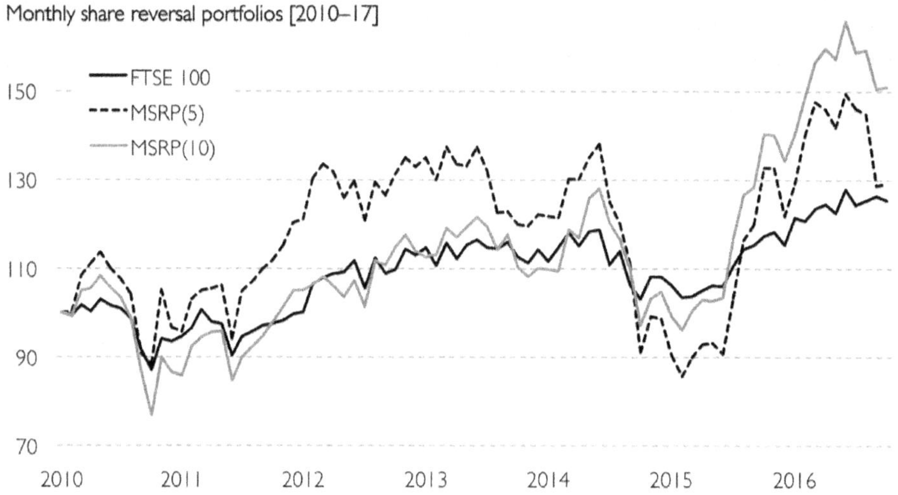


For around a year from May 2016, the portfolios performed strongly. But over the longer term, this strategy has never convincingly outperformed the FTSE 100.

# QUARTERLY SECTOR STRATEGY

*A previous edition of the* Almanac *proposed a simple quarterly trading strategy for FTSE 350 index sectors. This page updates the results of the strategy's performance since the last edition.*

## Quarterly Sector Strategy (QS strategy)

To recap, in the Statistics section of this *Almanac* the performance of the FTSE 350 sectors in each quarter can be found. From this data, the sectors that have been consistently strong in each quarter over the past ten years can be identified.

The four strongest sectors selected for each quarter with this analysis are given in the table.

| Quarter | Strong |
|---|---|
| 1st | Industrial Engineering |
| 2nd | Personal Goods |
| 3rd | Software & Comp Srvs |
| 4th | Chemicals |

NB. The compilers of the FTSE 350 sector indices discontinued the Technology Hardware & Equipment (NMX9570) sector in December 2016. This sector was the constituent strong sector for the third quarter in the original QSS. So, it has been replaced by the Software & Computing Services (NMX9530) sector, and all the performance results have been back-calculated using this new set of four strong sectors for each respective quarter.

*OK, so how does this strategy work?*

The Quarterly Sector Strategy cycles a portfolio through the four strong sectors throughout the year. In other words, the portfolio is 100% invested in the Industrial Engineering sector from 31 December to 31 March, then switches into Personal Goods to 30 June, then switches into Software and Computing Services to 30 September, then switches into Chemicals to 31 December, and then switches back into Industrial Engineering and starts the cycle again.

Obviously, a more sophisticated strategy would be to run the analysis again each year to see if the strongest sectors in each quarter have changed. Another variation would be to hold the top three strongest sectors for each quarter – which would likely reduce the portfolio volatility. However, the purpose of this strategy is to keep things as simple as possible and to see how far such a simple strategy can go without any further analysis and modification.

The following chart plots the performance of such a strategy for the period Q3 2007 to Q2 2017, with a benchmark of the FTSE All-Share (both data series have been rebased to start at 100).

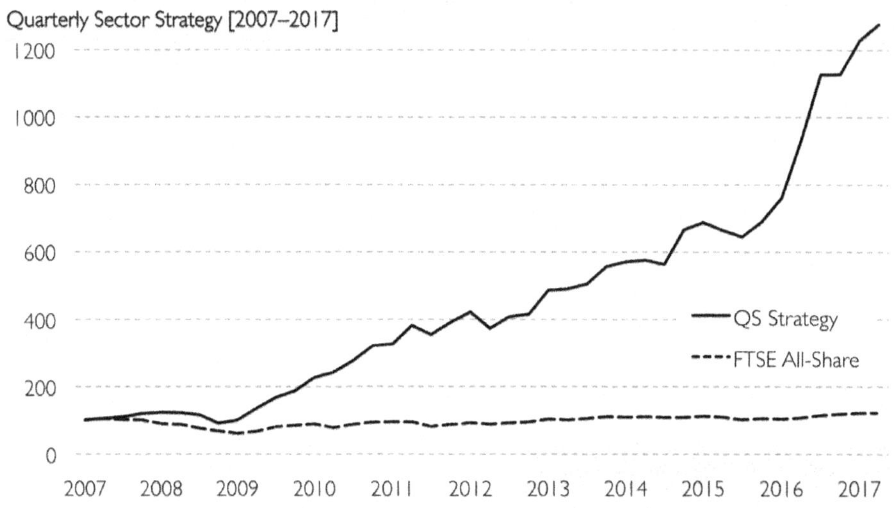


1. Starting in 2007, by the end of Q2 2017 the strategy would have grown £1000 into £12,750; while a £1000 investment in the FTSE All-Share would have become just £1220.

2. Elsewhere in this edition of the *Almanac* there is featured a moving average trading system that we have somewhat hyperbolically called the 'World's Simplest Trading System'. It must be said, however, that the trading system outlined above could also challenge for the title of simplest trading system.

## Hedged Quarterly Sector Strategy (HQS strategy)

We will now look at enhancing the above strategy by, in each quarter, going long of the strong sector and hedging that by shorting the quarter's weak sector.

First, the weak sectors for each quarter are shown in the table (with a recap of the strong sectors).

| Quarter | Strong | Weak |
|---|---|---|
| 1st | Industrial Engineering | Banks |
| 2nd | Personal Goods | Construction & Materials |
| 3rd | Software & Comp Srvs | Oil & Gas Producers |
| 4th | Chemicals | Industrial Transportation |

The following chart shows the outperformance of the strong sector over the weak sector for each respective quarter for the period 2007–17.

As can be seen, the selected strong sector in each respective quarter fairly consistently outperforms the corresponding weak sector.

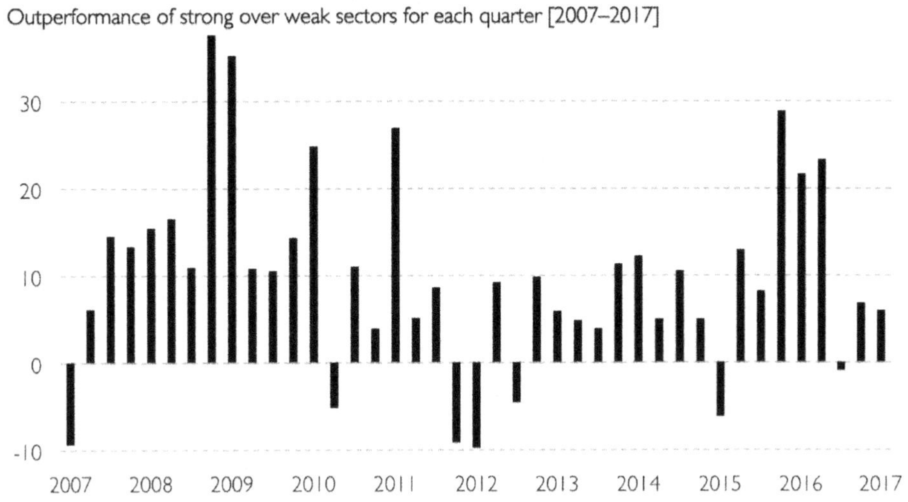


As before, the Hedged Quarterly Sector (HQS) Strategy trades just four times a year. For example, in Q1 the strategy would be long the Industrial Engineering sector and short the Banks sector.

The following chart shows the performance of the HQS Strategy compared to the simple Quarterly Sector (QS) Strategy (from above), and the FTSE All-Share – with all series rebased to start at 100.

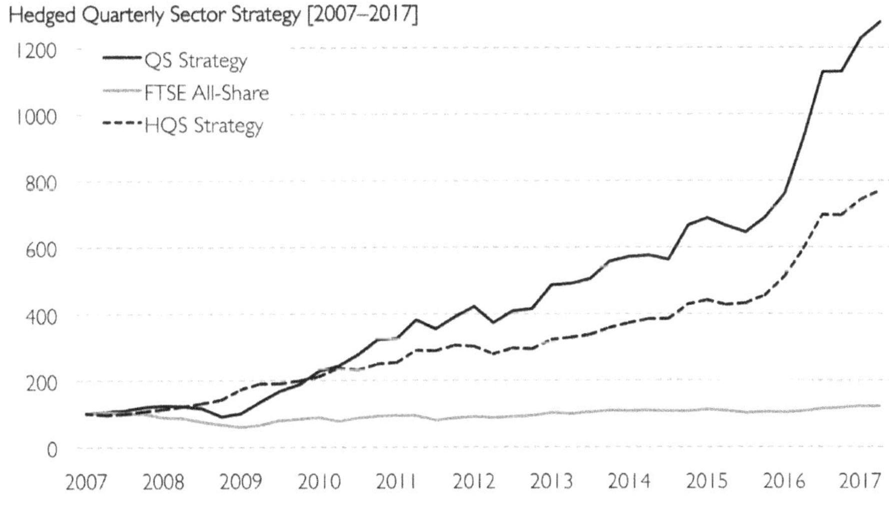


Although the hedge strategy underperforms the simple long strategy, the volatility of the former is less than that of the latter (the standard deviation of the hedge strategy is 0.08 compared to 0.14 for the simple long strategy).

Again, a more sophisticated variation would be to re-analyse the data annually to identify any changes in the strongest/weakest sectors; but this strategy keeps things simple and sticks with the same sectors each year.

# QUARTERLY SECTOR MOMENTUM STRATEGY

*Do FTSE 350 index sectors display a quarterly momentum behaviour that can be exploited?*

This analysis updates the performance of two strategies, defined as:

1. **Strong Sector Momentum Strategy (Strong SMS)** – The portfolio comprises just one FTSE 350 sector, that being the sector with the strongest performance in the previous quarter. So at the end of each quarter, the portfolio is liquidated and a 100% holding established in the strongest sector of the quarter just finished. This is held for three months, when the portfolio is liquidated and re-invested in the newly strong sector. Therefore the strategy will trade four times a year.

2. **Weak Sector Momentum Strategy (Weak SMS)** – As above, but in this case it is the weakest sector of the previous quarter that is held by the portfolio. (This could be called a *bounceback*, or *reversal*, strategy.)

Only FTSE 350 sectors with at least three component companies are considered. The period studied was from 2005 to the second quarter 2017.

The accompanying chart compares the performance of the two strategies, and adds the FTSE All-Share as a benchmark. All series are rebased to start at 100.

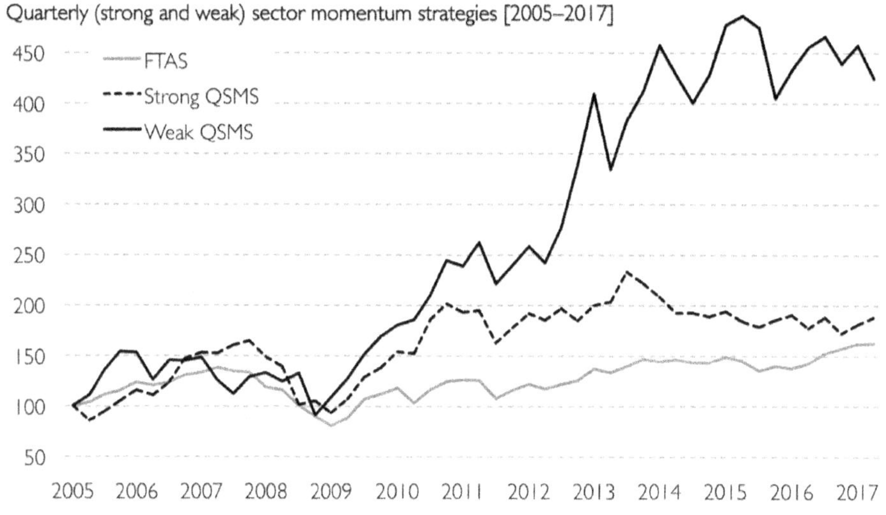


## Notes

1. As can be seen, both the SMS strategies outperformed the index over the period of the study. However, they did so with greater volatility (the standard deviation of the Strong SMS quarterly returns was 0.09, against comparable figures of 0.12 for the Weak SMS and 0.07 for the FTSE All-Share).

2. From 2012, the reversal portfolio (Weak SMS) started strongly outperforming the Strong SMS and the index. And overall the Weak SMS has greatly outperformed the Strong SMS.

3. From 2014, performance of both the Strong and Weak SMS has declined (in common with other momentum strategies recently).

4. A refinement of the strategy would be to hold the two or three best/worst performing sectors from the previous quarter instead of just the one (which would likely have the effect of reducing volatility).

5. Costs were not taken into account in the study. But given that the portfolio only traded four times a year costs would not have had a significant impact on the overall performance.

# THE LOW-HIGH PRICE PORTFOLIO

*Do investors like low share prices?*

Investors liking low share prices is the reason often given for companies having share splits or bonus issues. But surely rational investors understand that price is independent of value?

Apparently not.

Previous editions of the *Almanac* have compared the historic performance of low-priced shares against high-priced ones. Here, the study is updated to include the most recent data.

To recap, an academic paper[1] in 2008 found that in the US equity market share returns are inversely proportional to share price (i.e. the lower the share price, the higher the future return). In addition, the paper found that a portfolio that was long of stocks under $5 and short of stocks over $20 and rebalanced annually generated average monthly returns of 0.53%. Lengthening the rebalancing period to two years increased the returns and reduced the costs.

## Portfolio definition

To test whether this applies also to the UK market the performance of two portfolios is compared; the two portfolios are:

1. **LowPrice**: this portfolio buys equal amounts of the 20 lowest priced shares in the FTSE All-Share index at close on 31 December, holds the same portfolio for one year, and then rebalances the next 31 December.
2. **HighPrice**: as above, but this portfolio buys the 20 highest priced shares.

The following table lists the component shares in the 2017 LowPrice portfolio and 2017 HighPrice portfolio (i.e. these were determined by the level of share prices at 31 December 2016).

| 2017 HighPrice portfolio | 2017 LowPrice portfolio |
|---|---|
| Lindsell Train Investment Trust (The) | Oxford BioMedica |
| Personal Assets Trust | Petropavlovsk |
| Paddy Power Betfair | Sirius Minerals |
| Reckitt Benckiser Group | Pendragon |
| Randgold Resources Ltd | Huntsworth |
| Daejan Holdings | Redefine International |
| DCC | EnQuest |
| Next | Communisis |
| Ferguson | Renold |

1. Soosung Hwang and Chensheng Lu, 'Is Share Price Relevant?' (25 September 2008).

| 2017 HighPrice portfolio | 2017 LowPrice portfolio |
|---|---|
| Electra Private Equity | Raven Russia Ltd |
| Shire | Nanoco Group |
| British American Tobacco | Premier Foods |
| AstraZeneca | Gulf Marine Services |
| Spirax-Sarco Engineering | Speedy Hire |
| Carnival | Sirius Real Estate Ltd |
| Rightmove | Coats Group |
| InterContinental Hotels Group | Capital & Regional |
| Whitbread | Assura |
| Capital Gearing Trust | Schroder Real Estate Investment Trust Ltd |
| Imperial Brands | Debenhams |

## Comparative performance

The following chart plots the outperformance of the LowPrice portfolio over the HighPrice portfolio for the period 2005–17. For example, in 2005 the LowPrice portfolio had an annual return of 45% and the HighPrice portfolio a return of 19%, so the difference was 26 percentage points (and that is the first bar plotted in the chart).

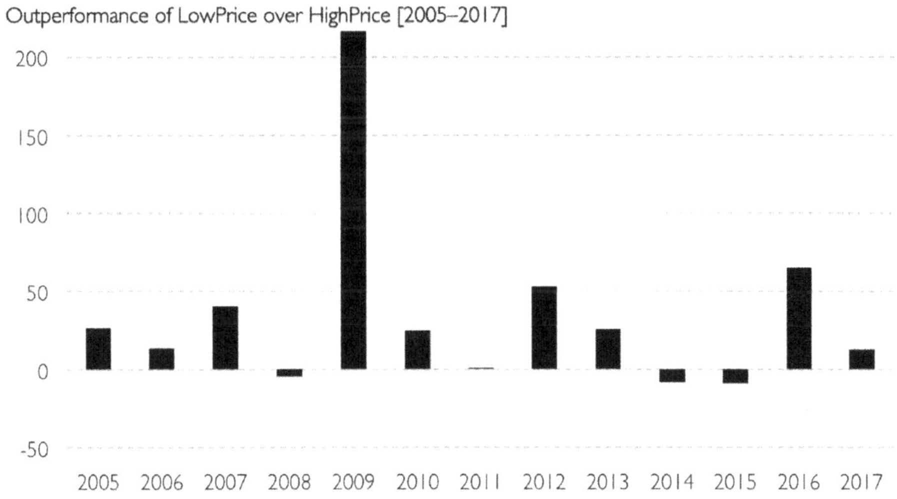


We can see from the chart that the LowPrice portfolio outperforms the HighPrice portfolio in most years. In fact, since 2005 it underperformed in just three years and then by only small amounts.

The following chart plots the performance of the LowPrice and HighPrice portfolios for the period 2005–17. The portfolios were both rebased to start at 100, and the FTSE All-Share was added as a benchmark.

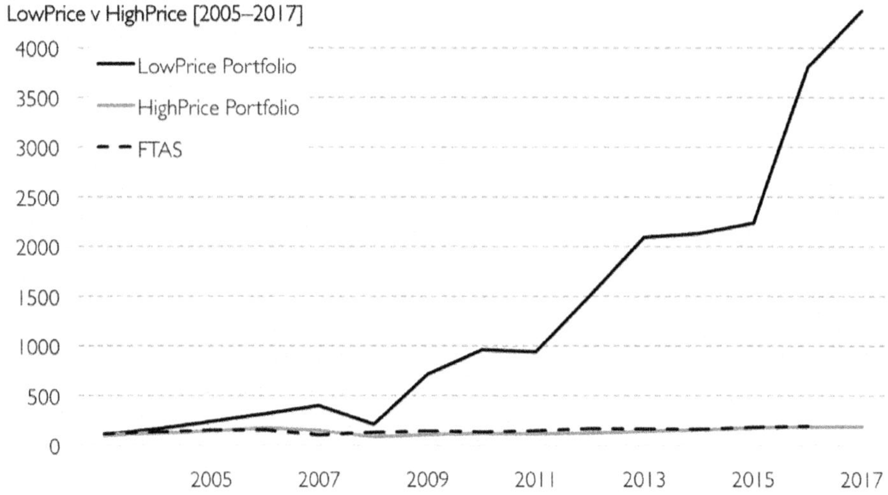


The HighPrice portfolio performed very closely in line with the benchmark (the FTSE All-Share). After 12 years, the HighPrice portfolio has a value of 190, while the benchmark a value of 188. Such a close correlation of performance is somewhat surprising, seeing as the HighPrice portfolio is a fairly arbitrary portfolio of stocks (reminder: it contains merely the 20 highest priced stocks – not the highest capitalised stocks).

However, the standout result is the stellar performance of the LowPrice portfolio. Since 2005 it has had a CAGR of 31.0%, compared with a CAGR for the HighPrice portfolio of 4.7%.

Of course the performance of the LowPrice portfolio would be reduced somewhat by the high bid-offer spread common with low-priced shares, but the portfolio only trades once a year.

## Share price frequency distribution

While we're on the topic, let's look at the distribution of prices.

The following bar chart shows the frequency distribution of prices for shares in the FTSE All-Share at mid-2017.

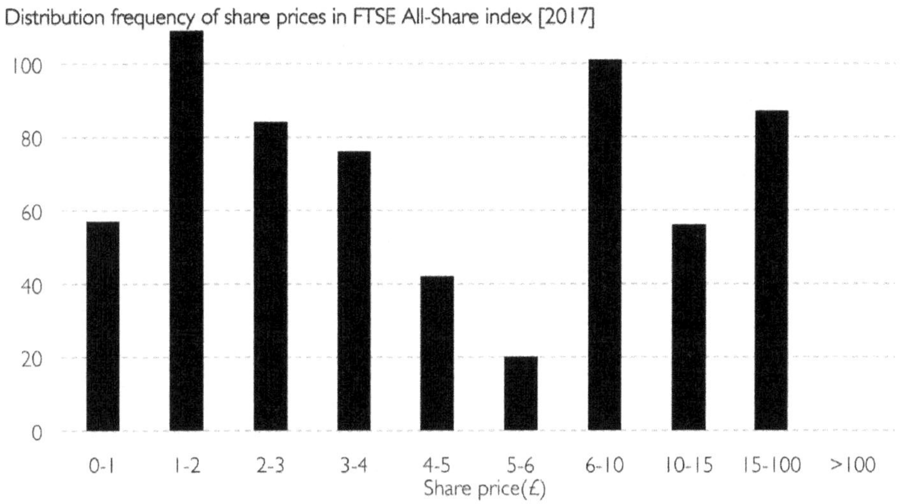


The chart shows that, for example, there are 57 companies with share prices below £1, 109 companies with share prices £1–£2 and 87 companies with share prices £15–£100.

The median share price of the 634 shares in the FTSE All-Share is £3.85, while the mean is £8.06.

## Portfolio definition

Here's the system:

At the end of every month:

- if the index is *above* its ten-month simple moving average, the portfolio is 100% in the market.
- if the index is *below* its ten-month simple moving average, the portfolio is 100% in cash.

And that's it.

So, if we take the FTSE 100 index as an example, if at the end of a month the FTSE 100 is above its ten-month simple moving average then either:

- the portfolio moves into the market by buying, say FTSE 100 ETFs (these will be the easiest instrument for most investors, but equally futures, CFDs or spread bets could be used), or
- nothing needs to be done if the portfolio is already in the market.

Conversely, if at the end of a month the FTSE 100 is below its ten-month simple moving average then the portfolio sells the ETFs and moves 100% to cash; if it is already in cash then nothing is done.

NB. It's possible that this isn't absolutely the simplest trading system imaginable, but apart from buy and hold it is unlikely there are many systems much simpler than this one!

The first chart below illustrates such a portfolio for the FTSE 100 since 1995. The markers indicate the decisions made at the end of each month whether to be in the market (circles) or in cash (triangles).

One can see that the system roughly kept the portfolio in the market in uptrends and out of the market (in cash) when the market fell.

This trading system is well-known in the US. What we will look at here is:

1. If the trading system can be profitably applied to the FTSE 100.
2. Whether ten months is the optimum parameter for the moving average (or would a five-month, or 15-month, moving average produce superior results?)

### Terminology

SMATS(10) will be used to refer to the ten-month simple moving average trading system. And SMATS(5) for the trading system using the five-month simple moving average, etc. Below we will analyse the trading system for 14 different parameters of the simple moving average, i.e. from SMATS(4) to SMATS(16).

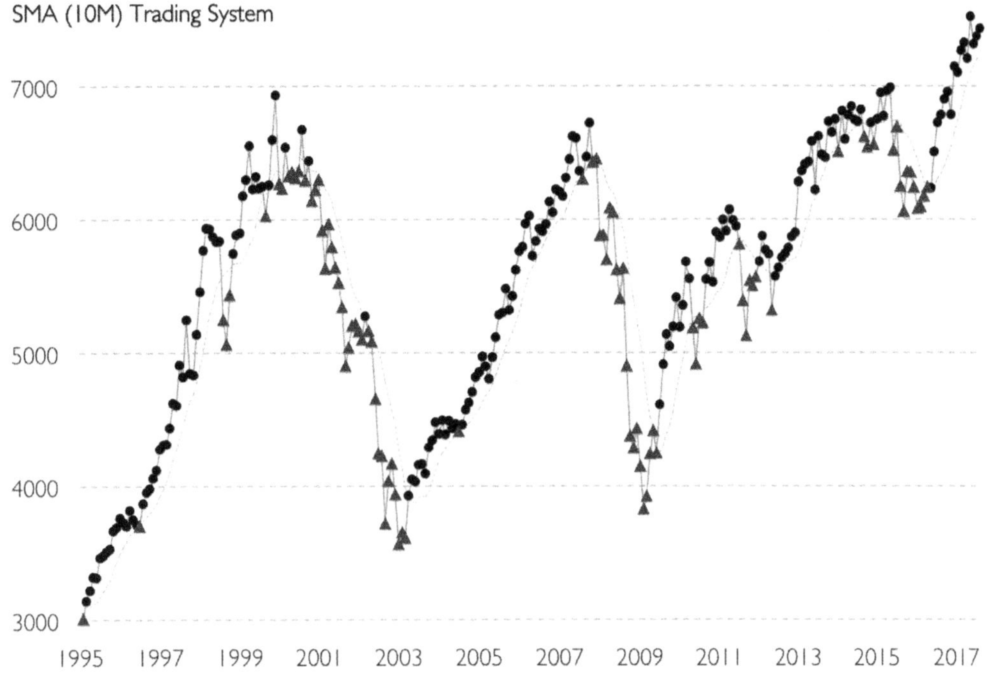


## Performance analysis

The analysis carried out here can be used as a rough template for the type of scrutiny that should be applied to any prospective trading system.

First, let's look at the overall profitability of SMATS.

### Profitability

The following chart plots the values of the SMATS portfolios for the 14 different simple moving averages (i.e. four-month to 16-month). As a benchmark the FTSE 100 is added (i.e. this is the value of a buy and hold FTSE 100 portfolio). All values were rebased to start at 100.

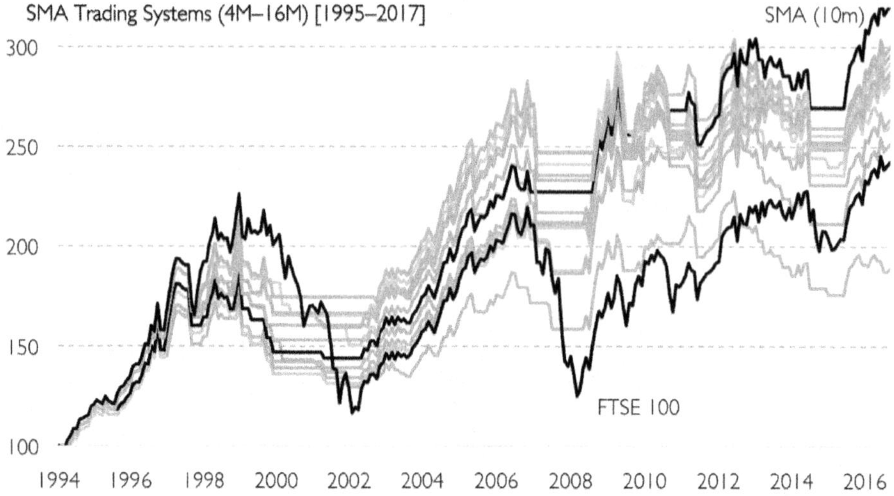


*Some observations:*

1. By the end of the 20-year period all the SMATS portfolios had outperformed the FTSE 100 – except SMATS(5).

2. By the end of the period, SMATS(10) had the highest value; although it can be seen that it wasn't consistently the most profitable throughout the whole period.

3. For the first six years (up to August 2001) all SMATS underperformed the FTSE 100. This was caused by the market volatility in 1998 and 2001, which caused the portfolios to be whipsawed in and out of the market.

The following chart summarises the final portfolio values in 2017 after running the trading system from 1995.

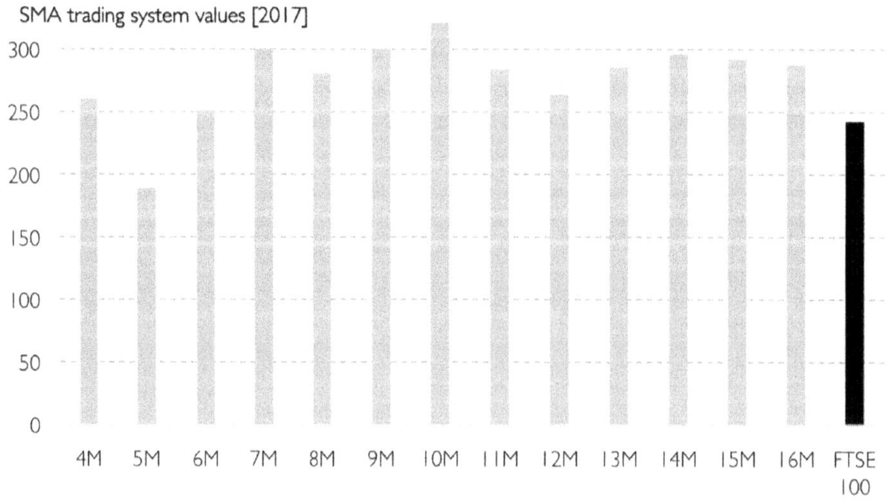

By 2017 the STATS(10) portfolio had the highest value of all portfolios at 321; the FTSE 100 buy and hold portfolio a value of 242.

### Risk

We've looked at profitability, let's now consider the risk incurred by each portfolio. We'll use volatility as a (fairly standard) proxy for risk.

The following chart shows the volatility of the portfolios over the 20-year period.

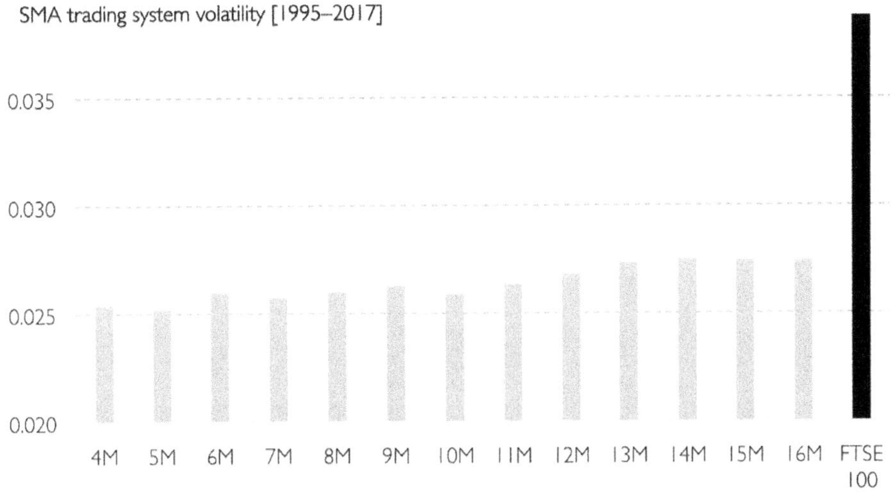


Not surprisingly the FTSE 100 had the highest volatility. The volatilities of the SMATS portfolios were less due to the fact they were in cash for part of the time; generally their respective volatilities increase as the moving average month parameter increases.

The *Sharpe Ratio* combines returns with volatility to provide a comparative measure of profitability per unit of risk incurred. The ratio's purpose is to answer questions of the form: is the profitability of a strategy justified by the risk incurred, compared to another strategy?

The following chart plots the Sharpe Ratio for the 14 portfolios. (The benchmark for the Sharpe Ratio calculation was the FTSE 100.)

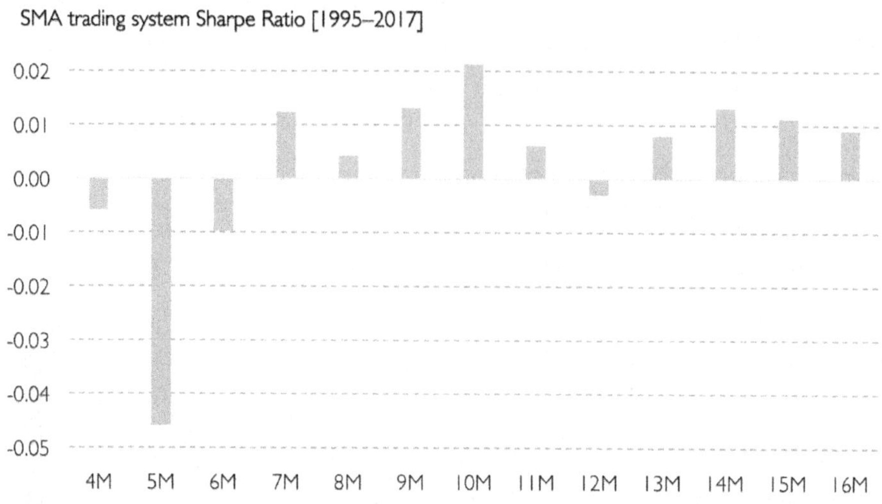


SMATS(10) had the highest (i.e. the best) Sharpe Ratio, followed by SMATS(9), SMATS(14), and SMATS(7).

## Max drawdown

Maximum drawdown describes the maximum loss a portfolio suffered from a previous high value. For example, in this test SMATS(10) had a max drawdown value of 22.8%. This means that over the 21-year test period the portfolio was at most 22.8% under water (from a previous high).

Frankly, max drawdown has more significance for strategies that employ leveraged products (e.g. futures), where drawdowns incur *realised* losses as margins have to be paid. By contrast, in the case of unleveraged equities or ETFs, drawdowns incur *unrealised* losses. Having said that, unrealised losses can still be uncomfortable and can have a major adverse psychological impact on the investor or trader.

The following chart shows the max drawdown values for the 14 SMATS portfolios and the FTSE 100.

SMA trading system max drawdown [1995–2017]

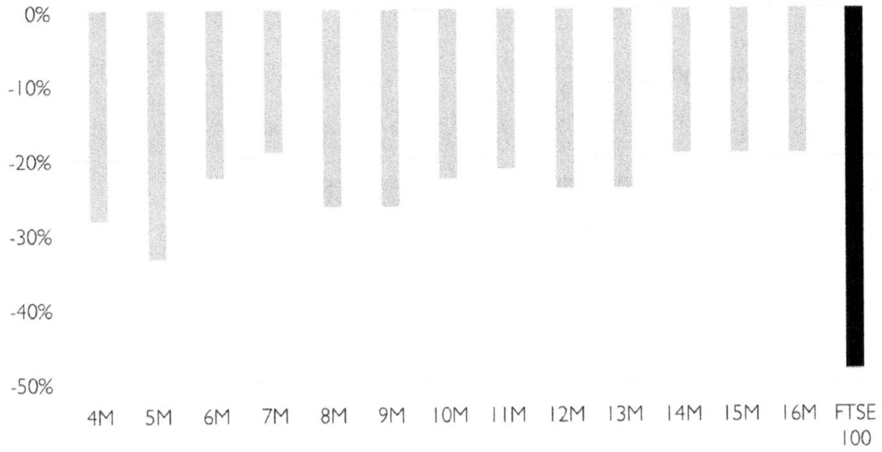


Here the SMATS(10) portfolio only had a middling relative score. The best portfolios (i.e. those with the lowest max drawdowns) were: SMATS(7), SMATS(14), SMATS(15) and SMATS(16).

### Trade frequency

The following chart shows the average number of trades for the year for each portfolio. For example, over the 21-year test period SMATS(10) portfolio traded 37 times, which is an average of 1.6 times a year.

SMA trading system average trades/yr [1995–2017]

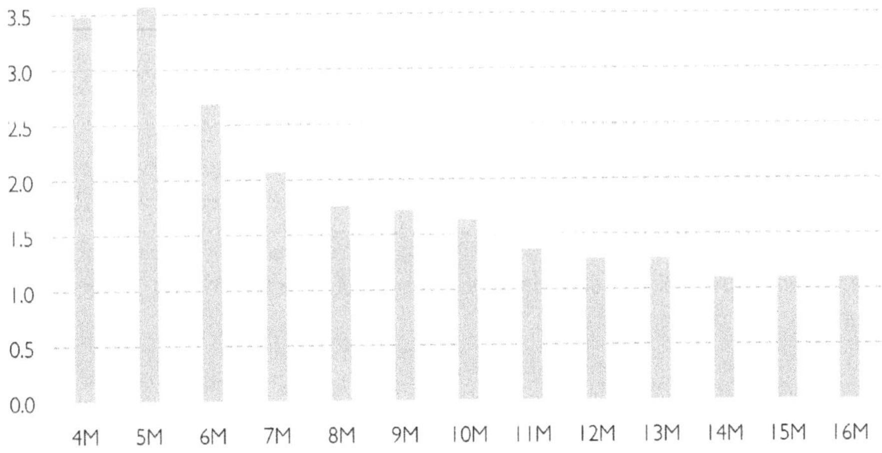


As would be expected the number of trades decreases as the length of the moving average month parameter increases. In other words, systems get whipsawed less with longer moving averages.

The profitability figures above did not include transaction costs, but with the systems averaging under two trades per year the transaction costs would not be significant.

## Summary of analysis

The following tables summarise the results of the above analysis.

| SMA period | 4M | 5M | 6M | 7M | 8M | 9M | 10M |
|---|---|---|---|---|---|---|---|
| Portfolio Value 2017 | 261 | 189 | 252 | 300 | 281 | 300 | 321 |
| CAGR | 3.110% | 2.847% | 3.103% | 3.099% | 3.111% | 3.098% | 3.074% |
| Volatility (StdDev) | 0.025 | 0.025 | 0.026 | 0.026 | 0.026 | 0.026 | 0.026 |
| Sharpe Ratio | −0.006 | −0.046 | −0.010 | 0.012 | 0.004 | 0.013 | 0.021 |
| Max drawdown | −28.3% | −33.5% | −22.6% | −19.2% | −26.6% | −26.6% | −22.8% |
| Average trades/yr | 3.5 | 3.6 | 2.7 | 2.1 | 1.8 | 1.7 | 1.6 |

| SMA period | 11M | 12M | 13M | 14M | 15M | 16M | FTSE 100 |
|---|---|---|---|---|---|---|---|
| Portfolio Value 2017 | 284 | 264 | 286 | 296 | 292 | 287 | 242 |
| CAGR | 3.110% | 3.112% | 3.109% | 3.102% | 3.105% | 3.108% | 3.091% |
| Volatility (StdDev) | 0.026 | 0.027 | 0.027 | 0.028 | 0.027 | 0.027 | 0.039 |
| Sharpe Ratio | 0.006 | −0.003 | 0.008 | 0.013 | 0.011 | 0.009 | |
| Max drawdown | −21.6% | −24.2% | −24.2% | −19.5% | −19.5% | −19.5% | −48.5% |
| Average trades/yr | 1.4 | 1.3 | 1.3 | 1.1 | 1.1 | 1.1 | |

## Conclusion

This simple moving average trading system did work for the FTSE 100 (i.e. the system outperformed the FTSE 100) over the 21-year period.

The best performing system was indeed SMATS(10), i.e. using the ten-month simple moving average. It had the highest absolute profitability and also the highest Sharpe Ratio.

This trading system is not strictly exploiting a market anomaly, it is just a standard moving average system. However, the superiority of, specifically, the ten-month parameter, and its persistency, is fairly anomalous!

# 3.
# ANALYSIS

# CONTENTS

# MARKET INDICES

# DAYS OF THE WEEK

*Is the performance of the FTSE 100 index influenced by the day of the week?*

First, let's review how the index has performed on the different days of the week over a range of periods.

## Longer-term analysis

The following chart shows the average returns of the FTSE 100 for the five days of the week over the periods 1984–2017, 2000–2017 and 2012–2017. For example, since 1984 the index has fallen by an average 0.02% on Mondays.

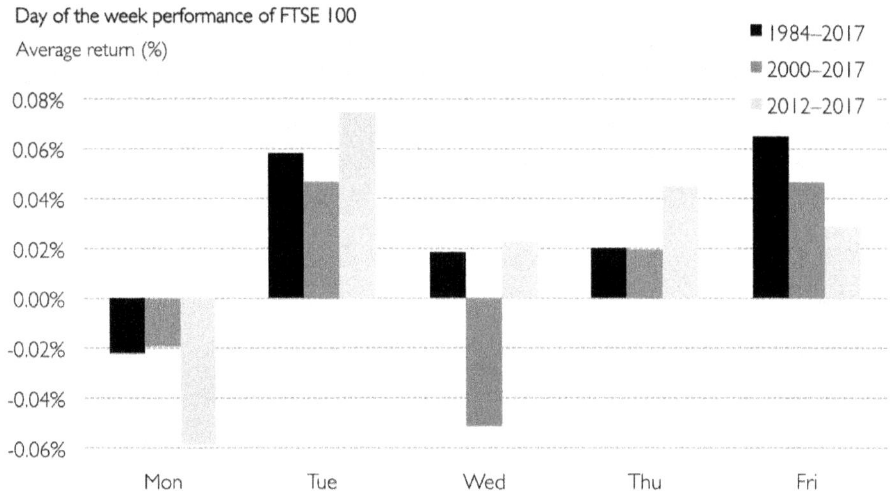


Broadly, a similar profile of behaviour can be seen over the three periods. Namely, the index is weak on Mondays and relatively strong on Tuesdays, Thursdays and Fridays. The weakest day is obviously Monday, while the strongest day is Tuesday (this profile has been particularly strong in the last four years).

It is one thing to observe this behaviour, it is another to explain it. The weakness on Mondays might be a result of a reversal of the strength on Fridays, and the strong Tuesdays a reversal of Monday's weakness. Obviously, this sequence of causal price reversals can only be taken so far!

It can be observed that the strength of the market on Fridays has been steadily declining in the three periods shown here.

The following chart is similar to the above except instead of average returns it shows the proportion of days seeing positive returns. For example, since 1984 the index has risen on 55% of Fridays.

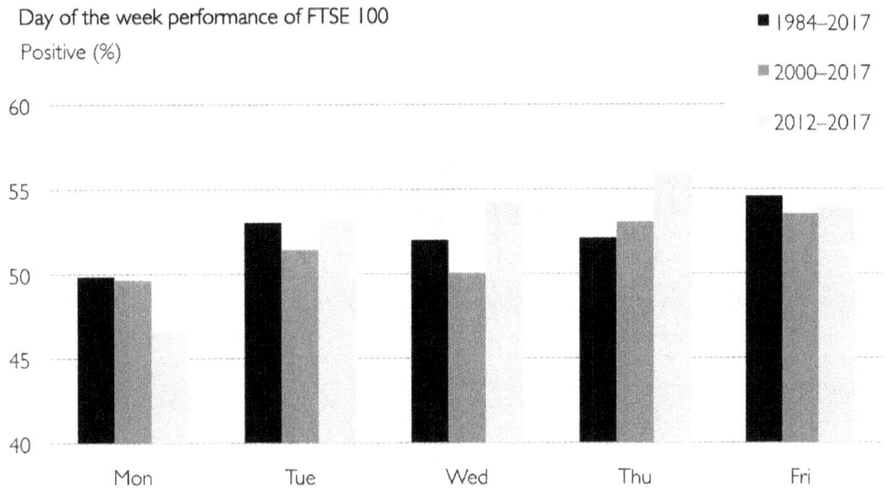


The profile seen here is similar to that seen in the first chart. The weak day again is Monday, and Tuesday and Friday are relatively strong.

*So, that's the longer term, let's look now at recent behaviour.*

## 2017

The following chart shows the average returns of the FTSE 100 index for the five days of the week over the period Jan–Aug 2017 (the time of writing).

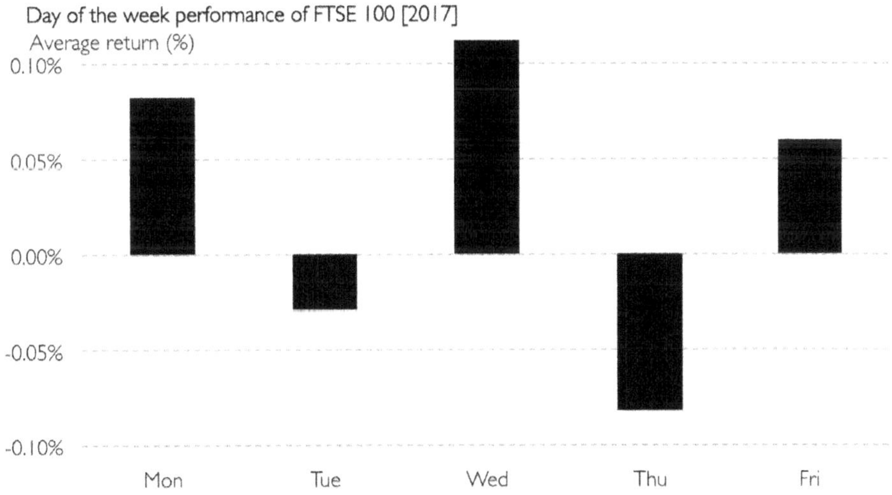


As can be seen, recently the pattern has changed a fair bit. Wednesday and Friday are still relatively strong, but now so is Monday, and Tuesday and Thursday are weak days.

So far in 2017 it is Wednesday that has seen the highest average day returns.

The following chart shows the proportion of positive return days for each day of the week.

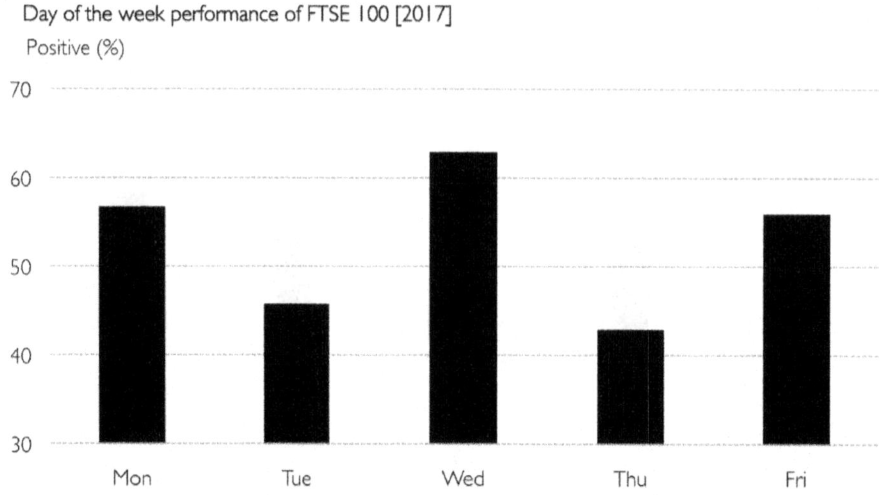


This chart reinforces the observation that Monday has recently been a relatively strong day, while Tuesday and Thursday have been weak.

The following chart shows the cumulative performance of the Index for each respective day of the week. For example, the FTSE 100 has a cumulative return of 11.1% for all Fridays so far in 2017.

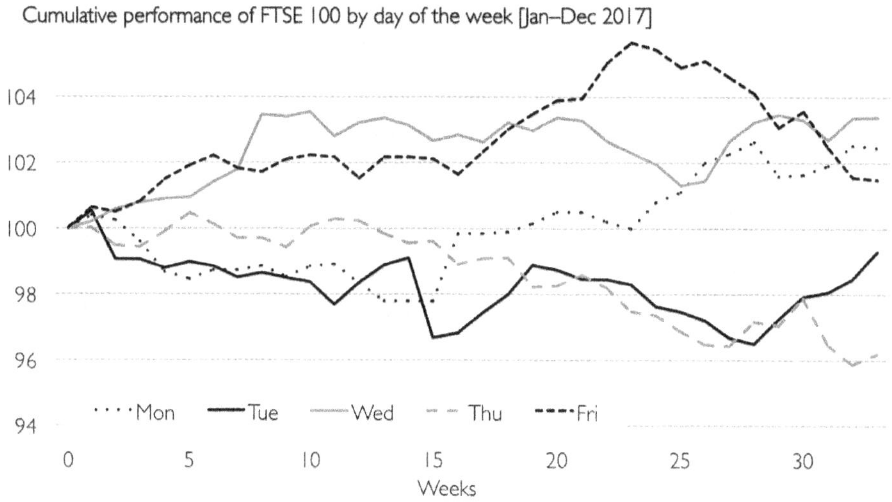


The above chart supports the view that the majority of the positive performance in shares in 2017 has been due to price strength on Wednesdays and Fridays, with Mondays also increasing in strength recently.

While certain days of the week obviously do display periods of strength or weakness, this is not a strong effect and the behaviour does change over time. So this is an effect that needs to be monitored closely.

# TURN OF THE MONTH

This study analyses the behaviour of the market on the ten days around each turn of the month (ToM). The days studied are the five last trading days of the month, from ToM(−5) to ToM(−1) (the latter being the last trading day of the month), and the first five trading days of the following month, from ToM(+1) to ToM(+5). The index analysed is the FTSE All-Share.

## From 1970

The charts below analyse the 572 ToMs since 1970. The first chart shows the average return on the day, and the next chart is the percentage number of positive days. For example, on ToM(−5) the market has on average risen 49.8% of the time with an average return of −0.04.

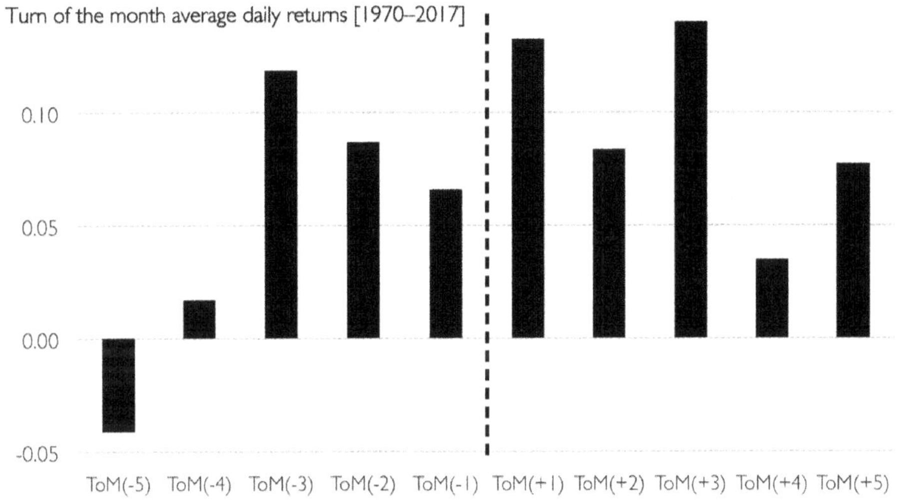


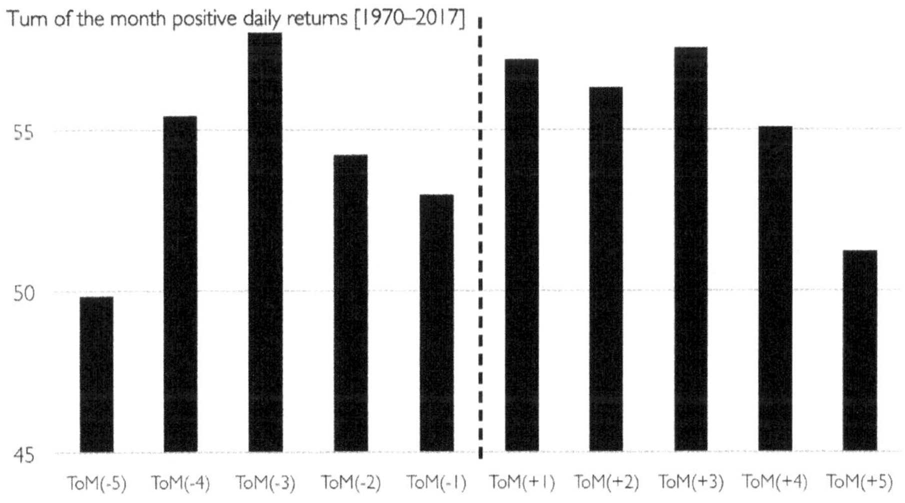

We can see that there is a definite trend for the market to be weak at the beginning of the ten-day period, to then strengthen on the third day before the end of the month, then weaken in the final two days, before starting strong in the new month.

*Does this behaviour persist in more recent years?*

## From 2000

The charts below are the same configuration as above, except they look at a shorter time period: the 212 ToMs since the year 2000.

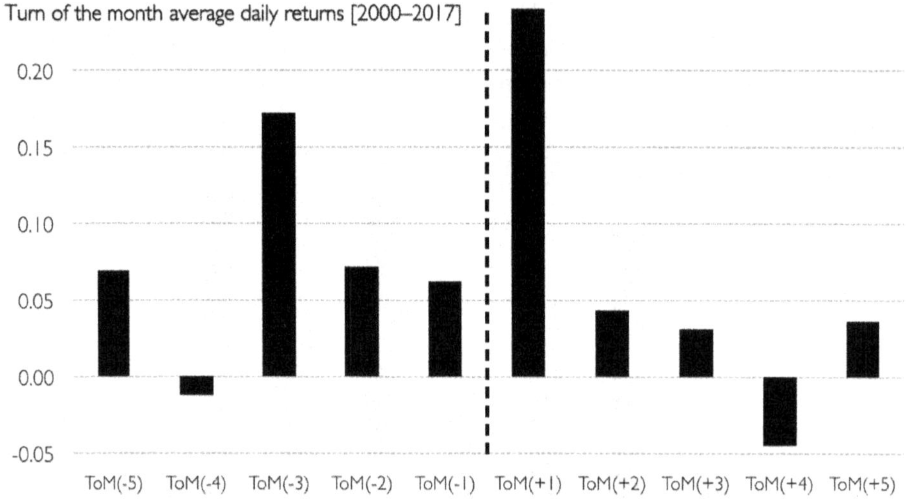


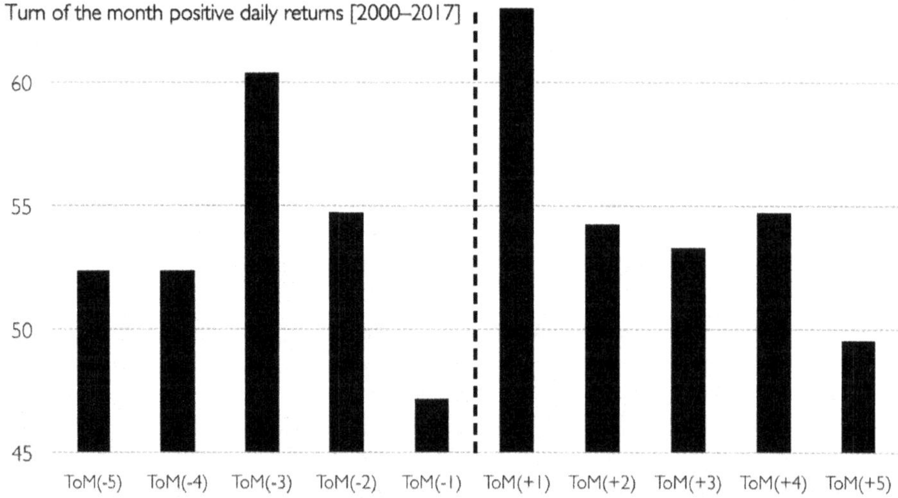


Broadly, the behaviour for the last few years has been the same as the behaviour since 1970. The main observation is that the strength of the first trading day of the month, ToM(0), has become ever more pronounced. On average since 2000, the market rises 63% of all ToM(+1) with an average change of 0.25% (which is eight times the average change on all trading days).

# FIRST TRADING DAYS OF THE MONTH

*Does the market display any special effect on the first trading day of each month?*

FTSE 100 index daily data was analysed from 1984 to discover if the UK equity market displayed abnormal returns on the first trading day (FTD) of each month. The results are shown in the table below.

| | Days | Positive | Positive(%) | Avg Rtn(%) |
|---|---|---|---|---|
| All days | 8441 | 4281 | 50.7 | 0.03% |
| First trading day of each month | 400 | 238 | 59.5 | 0.20% |
| First trading day of each month (from 2000) | 212 | 131 | 61.8 | 0.24% |

Of the 400 months since 1984, the market has had positive returns 230 times (59.5%) on the FTD of each month, with an average daily return of 0.20%. These figures are significantly greater than the average for all days, where the market has risen 50.7% of the time with an average return of 0.03%.

The FTD effect seems to have been marginally stronger in recent years. Since 2000, the market has increased 61.8% on months' FTDs with an average rise of 0.24% (eight times greater than the average return for all days in the period).

## Analysis by month

The following charts break down the performance of the market on the first trading days by month since 1984.

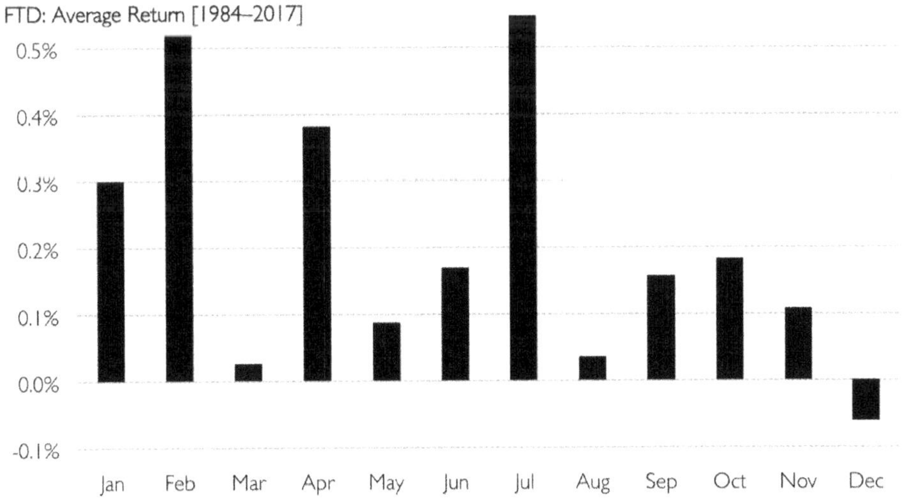

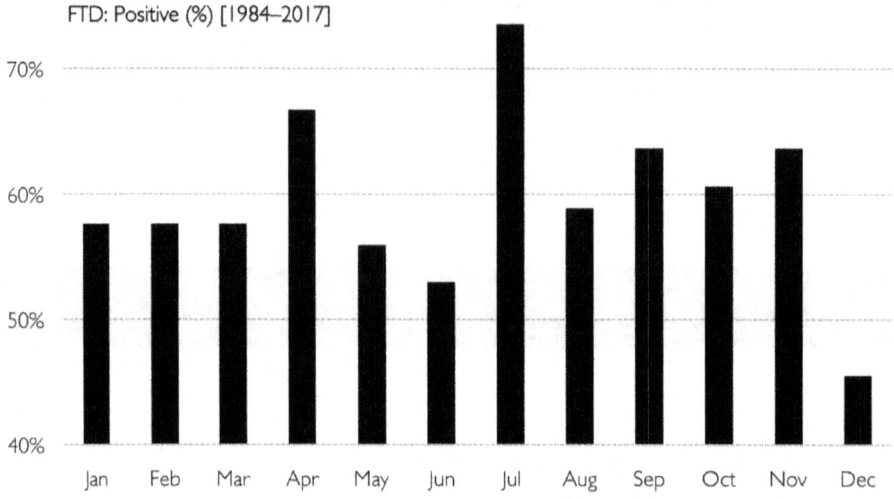


The average returns on the FTDs have been strongest for the months of February, April and July. The average return on the FTD of July has been 0.55% (18 times greater than the average return for all days of the month). In addition, returns have been positive for 74% of all July FTDs.

The weakest month FTD is December – the only month when the market has fallen more often than it has risen on the first trading day since 1984. This is an unexpected result as December as a whole is one of the stronger months for the market.

# LAST TRADING DAYS OF THE MONTH

*In the previous article we looked at the first trading day of each month; here we will look at the last trading days.*

The following table shows the results of analysing the performance of the FTSE 100 index on the last trading day (LTD) of each month since 1984 and compares this to the average performance on all days in the month.

| | Days | Positive | Positive(%) | Avg Rtn(%) |
|---|---|---|---|---|
| All days | 8441 | 4416 | 52.3 | 0.03% |
| Last trading day of each month | 401 | 208 | 51.9 | 0.09% |
| Last trading day of each month (from 2000) | 212 | 92 | 43.4 | 0.03% |

Overall, since 1984, the market has a tendency to increase above the average on the LTD of each month. On average, the market has risen 0.09% on months' last trading days, against a rise of 0.03% for all days in the month; and the market has had a positive return in 51.9% on all LTDs since 1984. However, in recent years (since 2000), the effect has somewhat reversed, with the majority of last trading days seeing falls in the market (when the market only rises on 43.4% of month LTDs).

This behaviour is very different from that of the first trading days in the month, which strongly outperform the average for all days, and where the effect has strengthened in recent years.

## Analysis by month

The following charts break down the performance of the market on the last trading days by month since 1984.

LTD: Average Return [1984–2017]

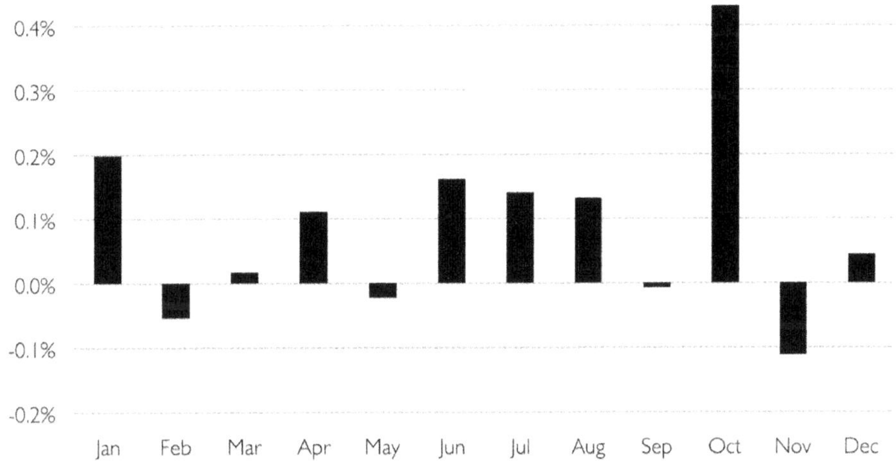

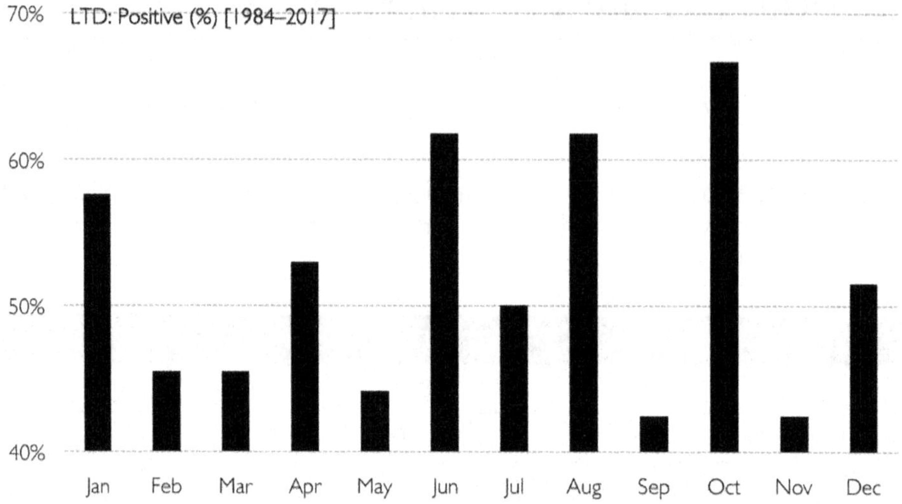


The difference in performance between the months is quite striking. Since 1984, the last trading days in January, June, August and October are all abnormally strong. By contrast, the last trading days of February, September and November are very weak. In recent years, since 2000, the pattern has changed somewhat: the strong months are June and August; the weak months are February and September.

# HOLIDAYS AND THE MARKET

*How does the market behave around holidays?*

In 1990 an academic paper[1] was published with the finding that the trading day prior to holidays in the US market had an average return 14 times greater than the average for the other days in the year. This, and other papers, found that the day immediately before holidays had the highest returns (in the period around holidays), with the third day before the holidays having the next highest return, while the day following the holiday had negative returns.

*Does such a holiday effect exist in the UK market?*

The following charts show the results of research on the daily returns of the FTSE 100 index around holidays. The three trading days immediately prior to holidays, H(-3) to H(-1), and the three trading days after holidays, H(+1) to H(+3), were analysed. A holiday was defined as a three-day (or longer) period with no trading.

The bars in the first chart show the mean return for each of the six days around holidays for the period 1984–2017. For example, since 1984 the mean return for the third day before a holiday, H(-3), is 0.1%.

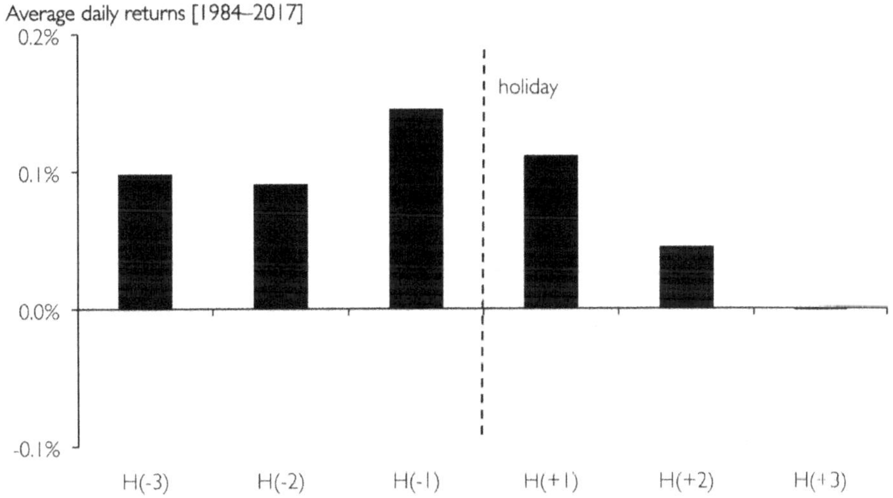


The following chart plots the proportion of daily returns that were positive. For example, since 1984 the third day before a holiday has had a positive return in 58% of cases.

1. R. A. Ariel, 'High stock returns before holidays: existence and evidence on possible causes', *Journal of Finance* (1990).

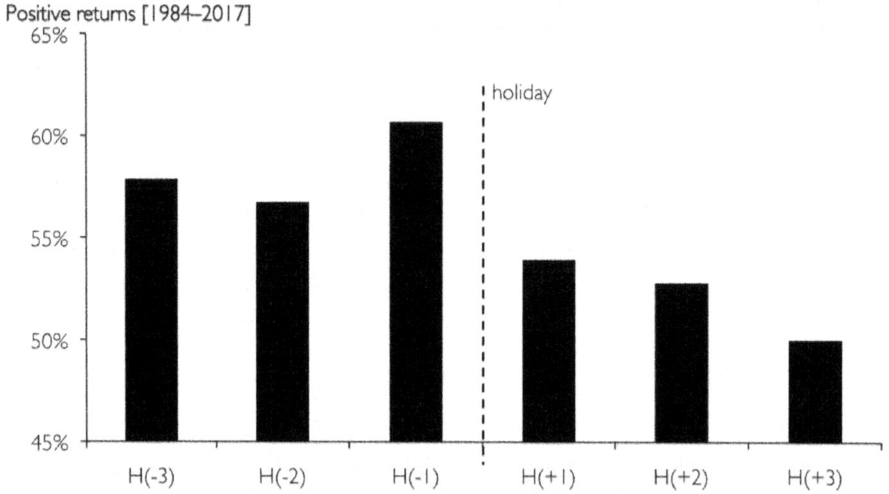


From the charts we can see that, as with the US studies, H(-3) and H(-1) were strong during the holiday periods. Although, unlike the US studies, the day after a holiday, H(+1), was also found to be strong – this day has an average return of 0.11% (four times greater than the average return for all days in the year). After the holiday, returns drop off steadily, with the weakest day in the six-day period being the third day after the holiday.

Let's look at the period from 2000, to see if anything has changed recently.

The following chart plots the mean returns as above, but this time for the period 2000–17.

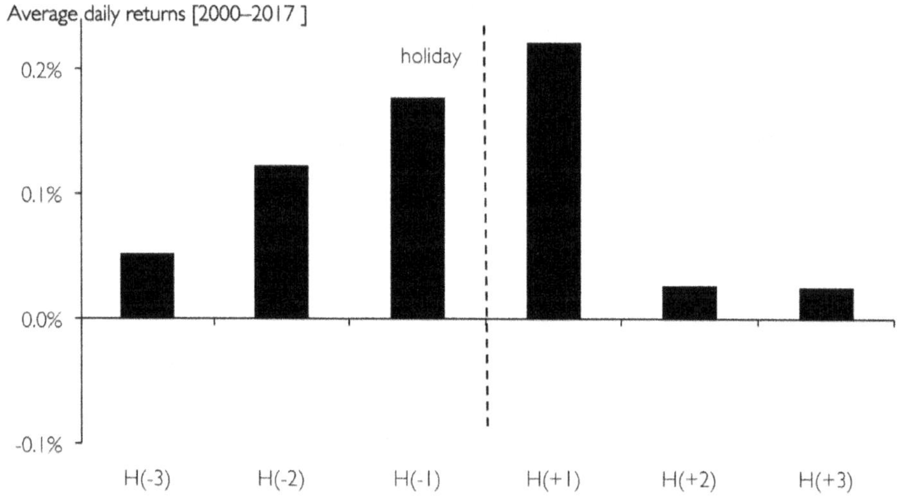


It can be seen that the UK holiday effect has changed slightly in recent years. Since 2000 the market has still been significantly strong on the days immediately before holidays, but weaker on the third day before. And the strongest day in the period is now the day immediately following a holiday, H(+1); this has a mean return of 0.22% – seven times the mean daily return for all days in the year.

## Easter

The strongest holiday effect is often seen around Easter, so let's take a quick look at that.

As above, the following charts analyse the market behaviour around holidays, but this time the data is restricted to just Easter holidays. The following chart plots the daily returns for the six trading days around Easter each year since 1984.

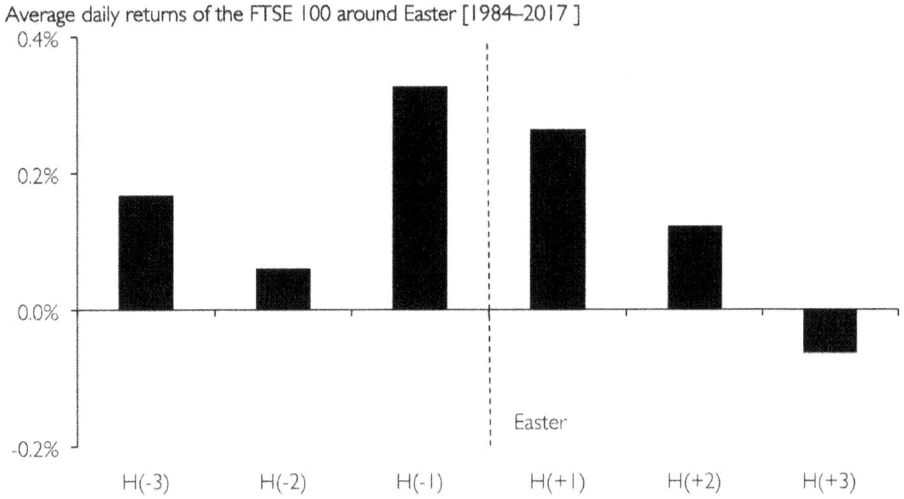


From the chart, the general profile of behaviour around Easter can be seen to be similar to that for all holidays. The main difference is that the average returns for the day immediately before, and after, Easter are significantly higher than for all holidays. For example, the average return for H(-1) is 0.33% (11 times greater than the average return for all days in the year). The second day before Easter is relatively weaker than the comparable day before other holidays.

*Let's look at the situation more recently.*

The following chart is the same as the above, but plotted for the period 2000–17.

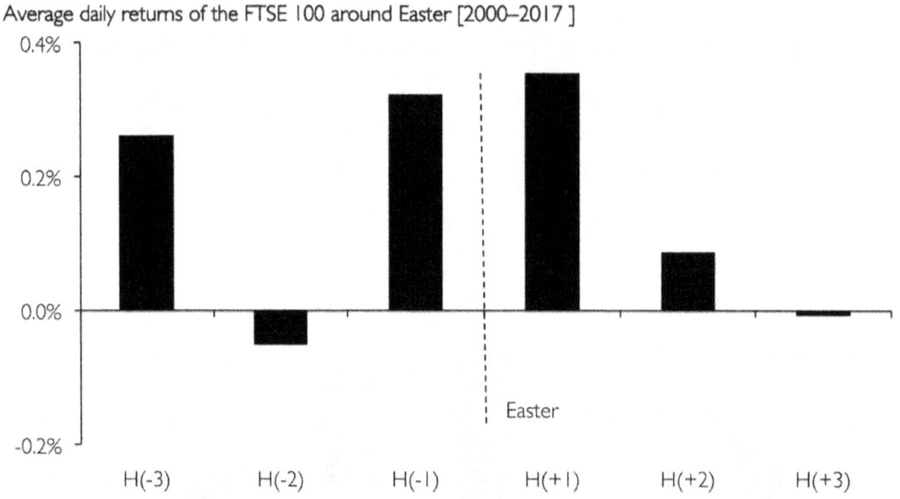


We can see that recently the main characteristics of behaviour are similar to the longer term. The weakness of the second day before Easter has become more pronounced. And, as for all holidays, recently the strongest day of the six-day period is now the day after Easter, with a mean daily return since 2000 of 0.35%.

# TRADING AROUND CHRISTMAS AND NEW YEAR

This page updates the analysis of the historical behaviour of the FTSE 100 index since 1984 for the nine days around Christmas and New Year. The days studied are:

- **Days 1–3**: the three trading days leading up to Christmas.
- **Days 4–6**: the three trading days between Christmas and New Year.
- **Days 7–9**: the first three trading days of the year.

## Mean returns

The following chart plots the average daily returns for these nine days for two time ranges: 1984–2017 and 2000–17.

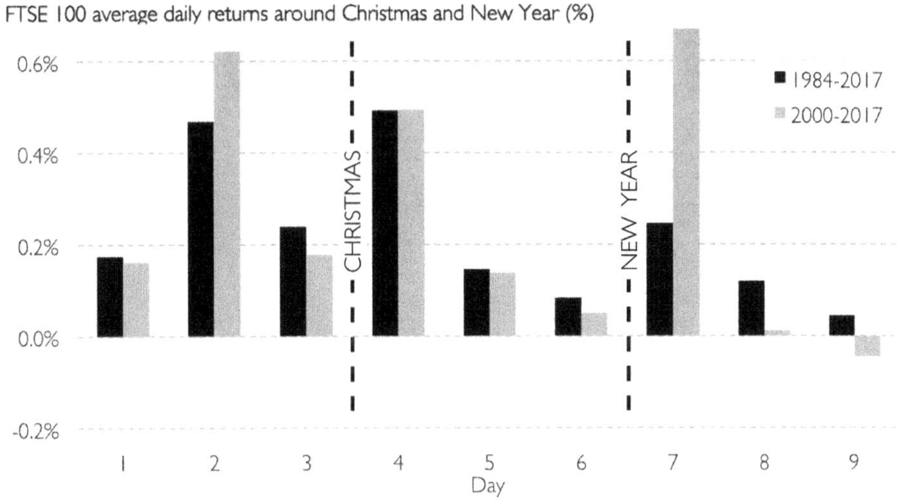


## Analysis

1. The market strength increases to the fourth day (the trading day immediately after Christmas). Since 1984 this has been the strongest day of the whole period, with an average daily return of 0.49% (albeit the volatility of returns on this day is high).

2. Generally the profile of returns for the shorter time range (2000–17) is similar to that for the whole period from 1984. The one significant difference is that since 2000 the strongest day of the period has been the first trading day of the new year. The new year generally starts strongly on the first day, with performance trailing off in the following two days.

3. The weakest day in the period is the third day of the new year, followed by the last trading day of the year.

## Positive returns

The following chart plots the proportion of the respective days that saw positive returns since 1984. For example, for 84% of the years since 1984 the returns on the day after Christmas were positive.

FTSE 100 positive daily returns around Christmas and New Year (%) [1984–2017]

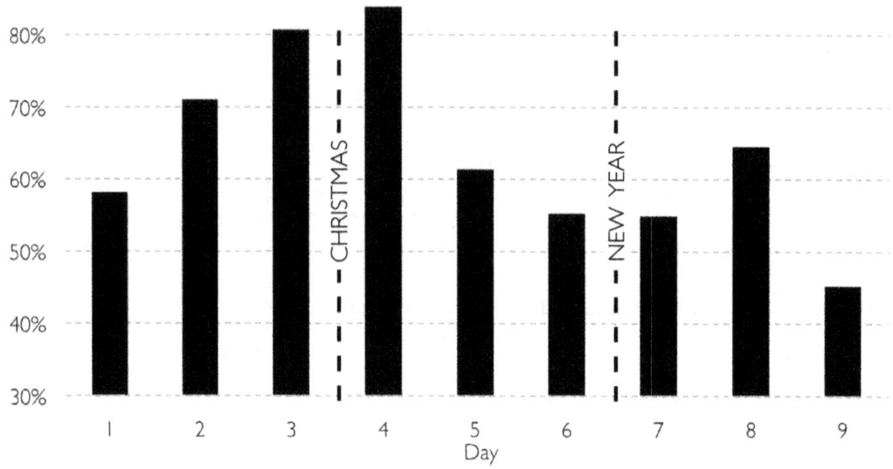


The profile of behaviour demonstrated by the positive returns is similar to that for the mean returns above.

# INTRA-DAY VOLATILITY

*Study of market volatility during the day by analysing the high and low index values of the day.*

Since 1985, the average daily Hi-Lo range of the FTSE 100 index has been 1.23% (expressing the Hi-Lo difference as a percentage of the close). This means that when the index is at, say, 6000, the average daily difference between the high and low levels of the index is 74 points. The standard deviation of this daily range is 0.9. We could define a very volatile day as one where the day's Hi-Lo range is 2 standard deviations above the average (i.e. above 3.03%).

The table below plots the Hi-Lo range for the 322 days since 1985 when the range has been over 3.03%.

FTSE 100 daily returns > 2 standard deviations (%)

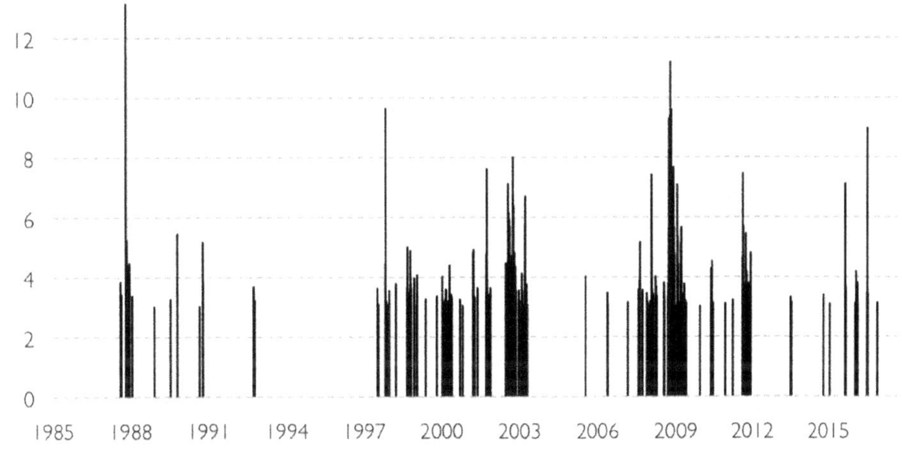


As can be seen, the index has experienced periods of heightened intra-day volatility, notably 1997–2003 and 2007–2009. The record for the greatest Hi-Lo range in a day is still 13.1% seen on 20 October 1987.

After a greater than 2SD (two standard deviation) daily return, the average return on the following day is 0.14%, and the average return over the following five-day period is 0.54%.

# HI-LO CLOSE

*Analysis of the relationship between the closing level of the market and the Hi-Lo range during the day.*

The chart below shows the frequency with which the index closes near to the high (or low) of the day. The data analysed is FTSE 100 index daily data since 1985. The analysis first takes the day's hi-lo range, and then calculates three threshold levels (1%, 5%, and 10%).

For example, if a day's low is 50 and high is 70, then the Hi-Lo range would be 20. And the 1%, 5%, and 10% thresholds would 0.2, 1 and 2. The day would be said to close within 10% of the low of the day if the closing price was below 52. The day would be said to close within 5% of the high if the closing value was above 69.

For example, since 1985 the FTSE 100 has closed within 10% of its daily high on 20.8% of all days, and it has closed within 1% of its low on 5.6% of all days.

Frequency of FTSE 100 Index closing near high or low of the day (%)

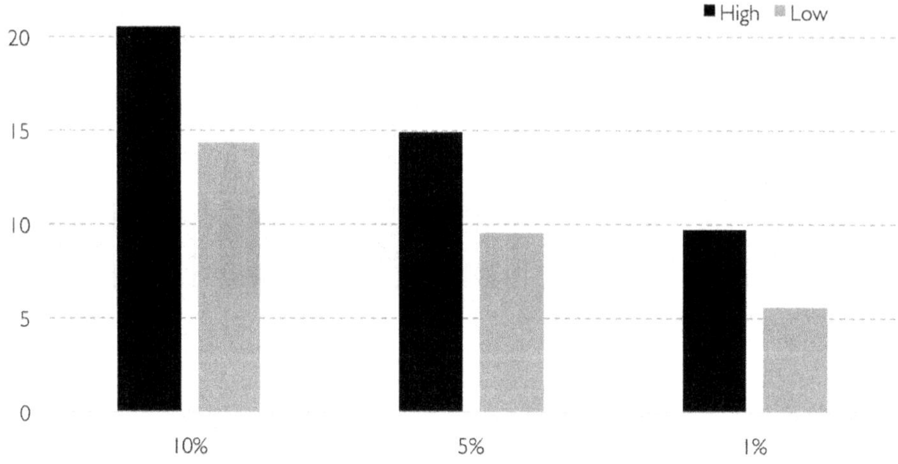


An obvious observation to make is that the index closes more often near its high of the day than the low. In nearly one-in-ten days, the index closes within 1% of the high.

## The effect on returns the following day

Continuing this analysis of where the index closes relative to the Hi-Lo range of the day, the following chart shows the performance of the FTSE 100 on the following day, split by where the index closed the previous day relative to that day's Hi-Lo range.

For example, on the days when the index closes within 10% of its low for the day, on average the index return is −0.005% the following day; and when the index closes within 1% of its high for the day, on average the index return is 0.167% the following day.

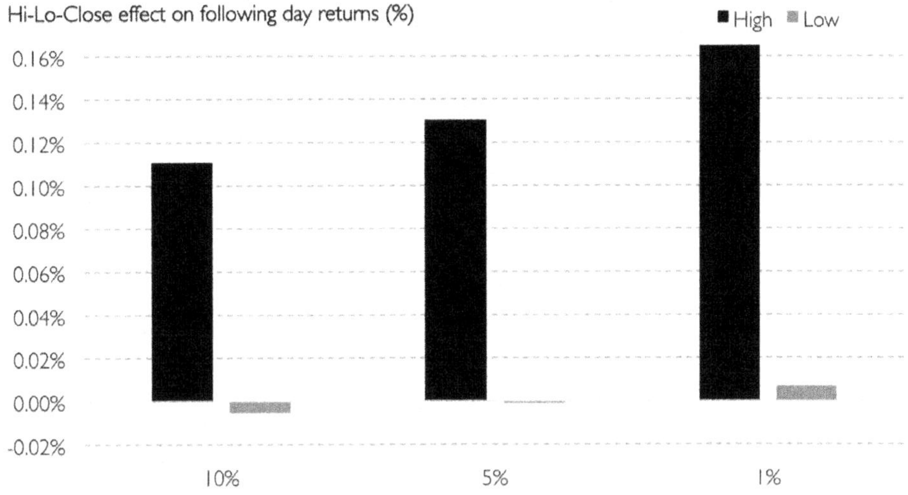


As can be seen, the nearer the index closes to its high of the day, the higher the following day's return. The other striking observation is that, whereas a close near the day's high is associated with relatively strong returns the following day, a close near the day's low has little effect on the average return the following day.

# VERY LARGE ONE-DAY MARKET FALLS

*Analysis of the behaviour of the FTSE 100 index for very large one-day falls.*

On 20 October 1987, the FTSE 100 fell 12.2% in one day. This is the largest one-day fall in the index since its inception in 1984. The accompanying table shows the ten largest one-day falls in the index since 1984.

| Date | Change(%) |
|---|---|
| 20 Oct 87 | −12.2 |
| 10 Oct 08 | −8.8 |
| 06 Oct 08 | −7.9 |
| 15 Oct 08 | −7.2 |
| 26 Oct 87 | −6.2 |
| 19 Oct 87 | −5.7 |
| 06 Nov 08 | −5.7 |
| 22 Oct 87 | −5.7 |
| 21 Jan 08 | −5.5 |
| 15 Jul 02 | −5.4 |

Judging by the table it would seem that many of the largest one-day falls have occurred in recent years.

*Is the FTSE 100 becoming increasingly volatile?*

Since 1984 there have been 230 very large one-day falls, where 'very large fall' is defined as a move more than two standard deviations beyond the average daily change in the index. In other words, a very large fall is any decrease over −2.16%. These falls are plotted on the chart below.

As can be seen in the chart, the periods 1997–2003 and 2007–2010 saw an increased frequency of large one-day falls.

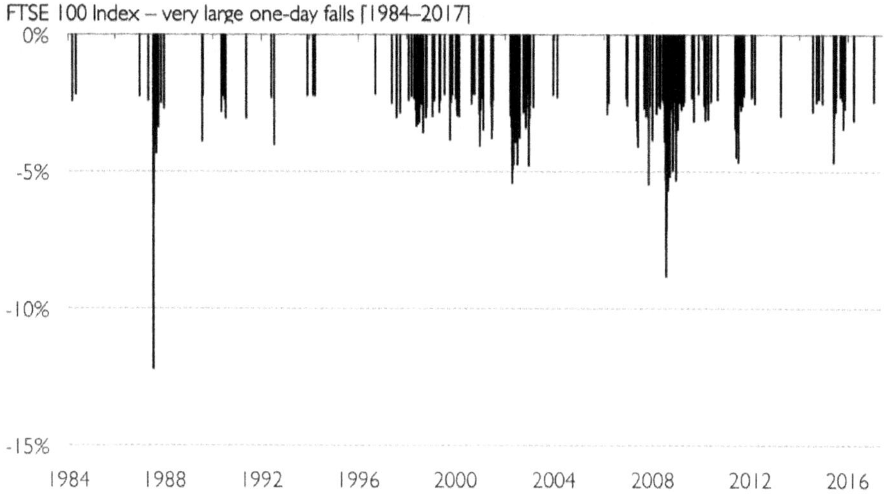


## After the fall

The following chart shows how on average the index behaves in the days immediately following a very large fall. The Y-axis is the percentage move from the close of the index on the day of the large fall. For example, by day 5 the index has risen 0.9% above the index close on the day of the large fall.

FTSE 100 average returns in the days after a large one-day fall [1984–2017]

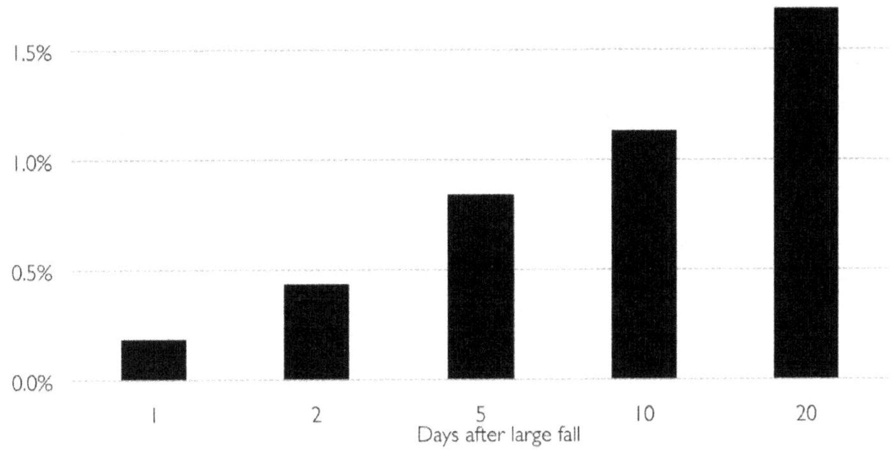


As can be seen, the index steadily recovers in the days following a very large fall, such that by the 20th day after the fall the index has bounced back 1.7%.

# AN AVERAGE MONTH

*What does an average month for the FTSE 100 index look like?*

A previous article described how to plot a chart of average cumulative price returns of the market day-by-day (see page 148). The chart is produced by calculating the daily mean return for each day in the trading year over a specific period (in this case from 1984). These charts then show the average behaviour of the market for the 12 calendar months for each day of the month.

The following chart plots the average daily returns for each day in the month for the FTSE 100 over the period 1984–2017. For example, since 1984 the market has traded 252 times on the first calendar day of all the months, and the average return of the FTSE 100 on those 252 days has been 0.23%.

Note: the chart here plots the average returns on the *calendar days* of the months, whereas in the previous article we looked at just the trading days.

Average daily returns for the FTSE 100 index for the calendar days in a month [1984–2017]

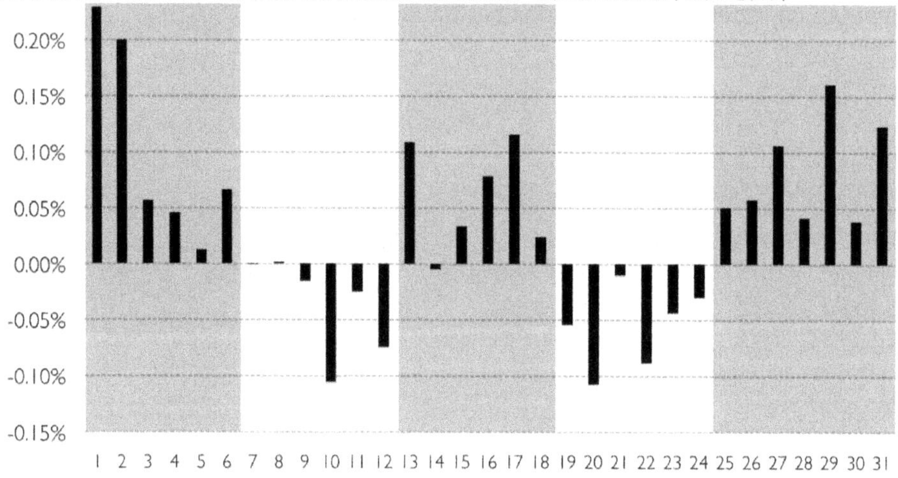


Some observations:

1. The first day of each month has the highest average daily return for the FTSE 100. Followed closely by the second day of the month.

2. The worst average daily return has been on the 20th of the month.

3. As can be seen in the chart, the periods of strongest daily returns occur in the first and final weeks of months.

4. The pattern of daily returns in months divides into five (rather surprisingly precise) phases:

- **Phase 1** (1st–6th): the index sees positive average daily returns
- **Phase 2** (7th–12th): the index sees negative average daily returns

- **Phase 3** (13th–18th): the index sees positive average daily returns
- **Phase 4** (19th–24th): the index sees negative average daily returns
- **Phase 5** (25th–31st): the index sees positive average daily returns

NB. The chart above highlights the positive daily return phases of a month.

## Cumulative average month performance

From this data we can calculate the average cumulative performance of the FTSE 100 in a month based on each day's average gain/loss (see following chart). The cumulative average performance is indexed to start at 100.

Cumulative performance of the FTSE 100 index in an average month

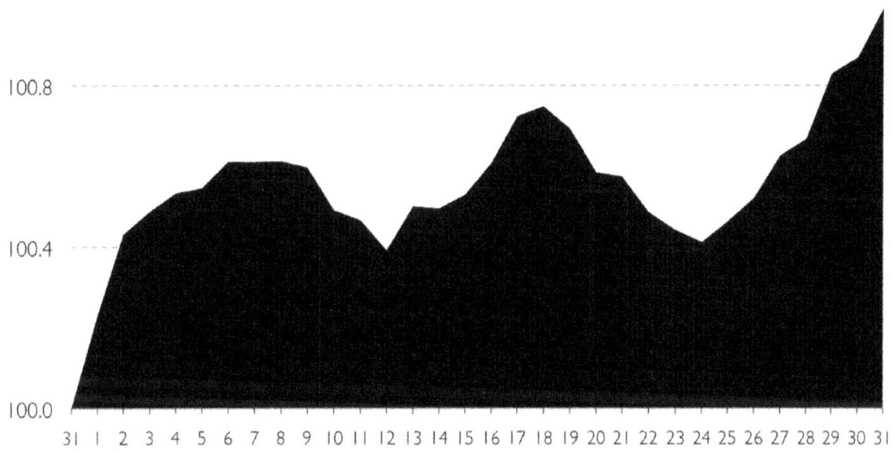


So, in an average month the FTSE 100 rises to the 5th of the month, then falls back until the 12th, before it increases again briefly to the 18th. It then falls back – finally bottoming on the 24th – and then rises quite strongly from there to the end of the month.

In conclusion, we have the rather remarkable fact that 76% of all the index gains in a month come from the first and last six days of the month. For more on this, see the 'Turn of the Month Effect' elsewhere in this volume.

# THE JANUARY EFFECT

In 1976 an academic paper[1] found that equally weighted indices of all the stocks on the NYSE had significantly higher returns in January than in the other 11 months over the period 1904–74. This indicated that small capitalisation stocks outperformed larger stocks in January. Over the following years many further papers were written confirming this finding. In 2006 a paper[2] tested this effect (now called the *January Effect*) on data from 1802 and found the effect was consistent up to the present time.

*Does the January Effect work for UK stocks?*

To analyse this we will look at the relative performance of the following four UK stock indices in January:

1. FTSE 100 [UKX]
2. FTSE 250 [MCX]
3. FTSE Small Cap [SMX]
4. FTSE Fledgling [NSX]

The following bar chart shows the average returns of the four indices in January for the years 1996–2017.

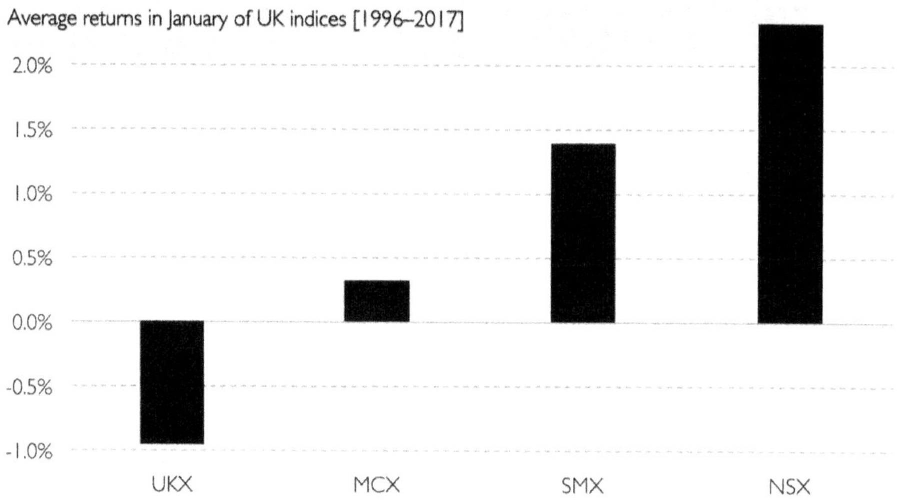


The above chart shows that the January Effect *is* apparent in the UK market – i.e. that small-cap stocks outperform large-cap stocks in January.

As can be seen, not only do the smaller cap indices have greater January average returns than the large-cap FTSE 100, but the latter actually has a negative average return in January.

1. Rozeff and Kinney, 'Capital market seasonality: The case of stock returns', *Journal of Financial Economics* 3, 379–402 (1976).
2. M. Haug and M. Hirschey, 'The January effect', *Financial Analysts Journal* 62 (5), 78–88 (2006).

In the 22 years since 1996, the FTSE Fledgling has only seen negative January returns in three years.

The following chart plots the outperformance of the FTSE Fledgling over the FTSE 100 for each January for the period 1996–2017. For example, in January 2017 the returns for the FTSE 100 and Fledgling indices were 1.9% and 3.0% respectively, giving an outperformance of 1.1 percentage points (and this is the last value plotted in the chart).

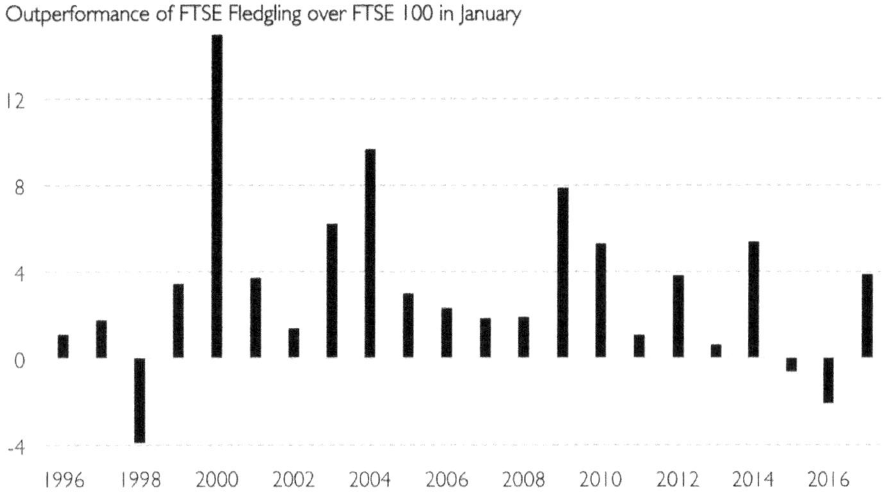


That is quite an impressive record!

To illustrate the extent of the outperformance of the smaller-cap indices over the FTSE 100 in January, the following chart plots the cumulative performance from 1995 to 2017 of the four stock indices in the month of January.

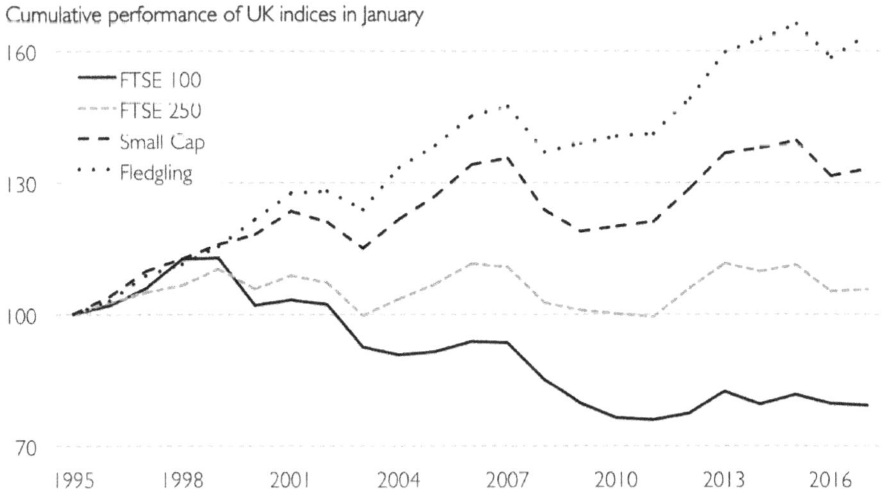

A portfolio investing in the FTSE 100 in just the Januaries since 1995 would have fallen 21% in value by 2017. By contrast, similar portfolios investing in the FTSE 250, Small Cap and Fledgling indices would have returned 6%, 33% and 64% respectively.

This suggests that not only does the January Effect hold for UK equities but also that, to a certain extent, performance in January is inversely proportional to company size (down to the level of Fledgling companies at least).

## Other January Effects

In academic literature the term *January Effect* usually refers to the anomaly described above; however the term is occasionally used in another couple of cases.

1. The returns in January indicate the returns for the rest of the year. If January market returns are positive, then returns for the whole year will be positive (and vice versa). This is sometimes called the *January Predictor* or *January Barometer*. A variant of this effect has it that returns for the whole year can be predicted by the direction of the market in just the first five days of the year.

2. In 1942 Sidney B. Wachtel wrote a paper, 'Certain Observations on Seasonal Movements in Stock Prices', in which he proposed that stocks rose in January as investors began buying again after the year-end tax-induced sell-off. As we see above, this observation may be valid in the UK for small-cap stocks, but it is not true for large-caps.

# JANUARY BAROMETER

The *January Barometer* holds that the direction of the market in January predicts the direction of the market for the whole year. The saying is:

> as January goes, so goes the year

The January Barometer was first mentioned by Yale Hirsch of the *Stock Trader's Almanac* in 1972.

[NB. The January Barometer is sometimes confused with the *January Effect*, which is explained in the previous article.]

*So, does the January Barometer work?*

According to John Dorfman in an article in January 2016:

> the barometer has been correct in 38 of the past 54 years for a success rate of 70 percent.

70% accuracy is not bad. Although Dorfman does point out that this underperforms a naive model (which forecasts the market will be up every year) which has an accuracy of 74% over the same period.

### How does the January Barometer fair in the UK market?

Let's jump straight in with a long-term view. The following chart plots the January and same-year full-year returns for the FTSE All-Share index since 1800 on a scatter chart.

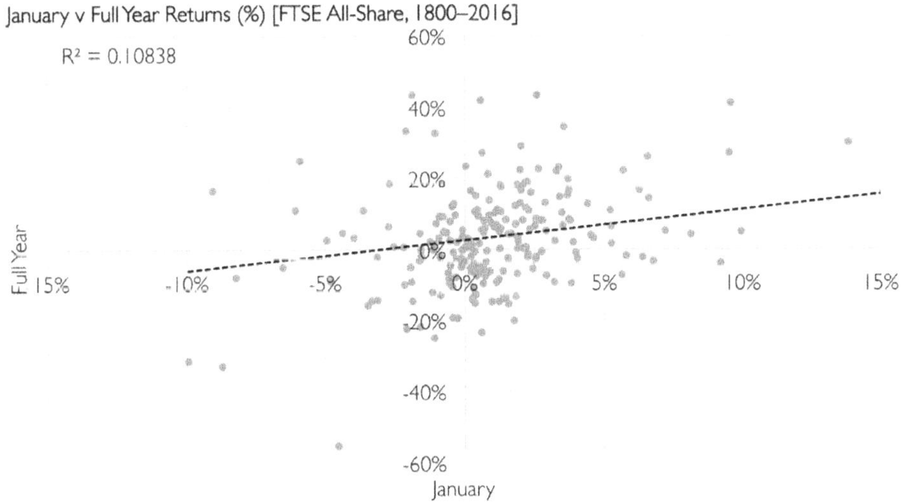


To support the January Barometer there needs to be a majority of points in the top-right and bottom-left sectors (i.e. both positive returns for January and the full year, or both negative for January and the full year). And, yes, broadly that does seem to be the case. The line of best fit has a positive slope which agrees with our visual inspection. The correlation

(R2 = 0.108) is very low, but to be fair the January Barometer does not claim there is a close correlation in (January and full-year) returns, just that the sign (i.e. the direction) is the same.

We'll now look at a shorter period to see how the relationship changes over time.

The following chart is as above except the time period is from 1900 to the present day.

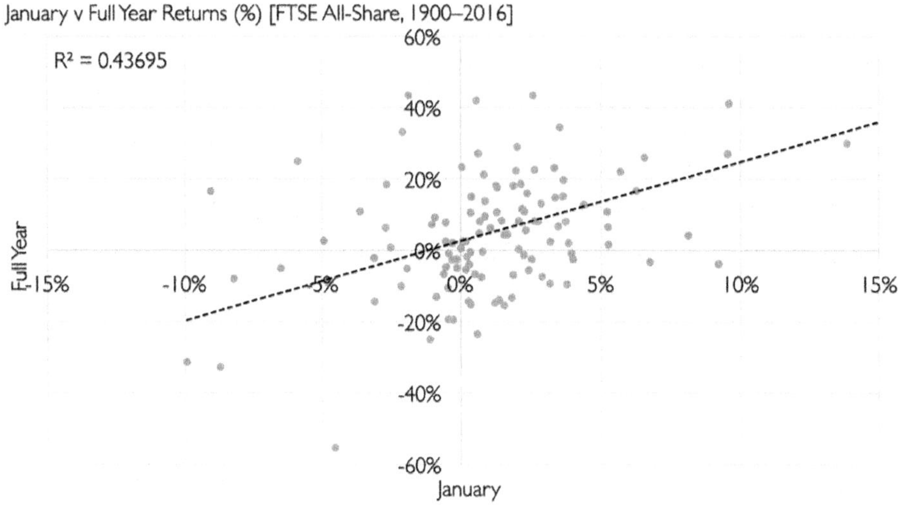


Since 1900 the relationship has remained largely the same, i.e. the January Barometer broadly holds. And we might also observe that the correlation coefficient has greatly increased (R2 = 0.437), albeit it is still low.

Finally, we look at the relatively short term; the chart below shows the relationship since 1980.

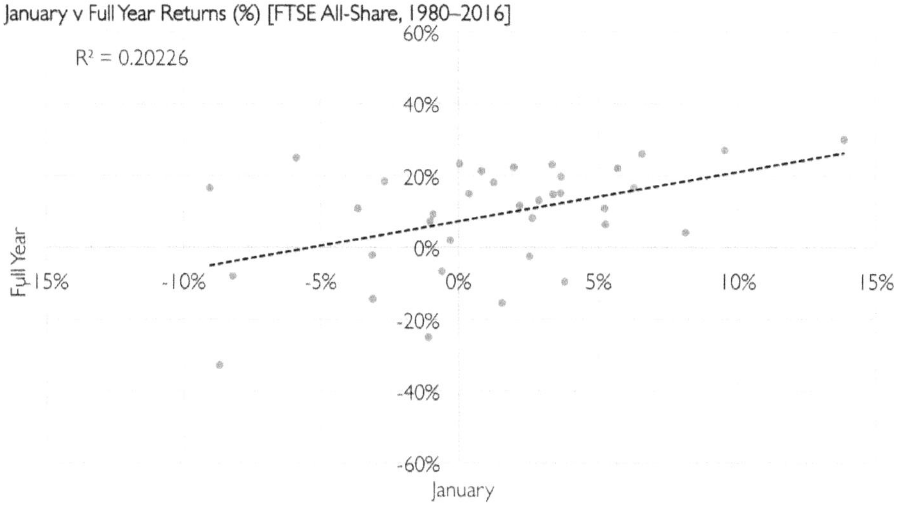

And, again, the January Barometer still seems to have broadly worked since 1980.

The following table summarises the success rate of the January Barometer over the three time periods. For example, since 1800, the Barometer has been correct for 61% of years.

The table also includes figures for the success rate for years in which the returns in January were respectively positive and negative. For example, since 1800 the Barometer was correct for 65% of years in which the market rose in January.

| | Jan (all) | Jan (up) | Jan (down) |
|---|---|---|---|
| 1800–2016 | 61% | 65% | 54% |
| 1900–2016 | 65% | 69% | 58% |
| 1980–2016 | 70% | 87% | 43% |

As can be seen, for all three periods the standard January Barometer had success rates of over 50% for all years – and so can be considered to have worked. Since 1980 the Barometer has been notably successful, with a success rate of 70%.

Restricting the January Barometer forecast to just those years when the market return in January was positive (and thereby forecasting a positive year), increases the success rate. Since 1980 this success rate has been 87% which is impressive. But the January Barometer is not so good when forecasting is restricted to just those years in which January returns were negative (final column); in this case, since 1980 the January Barometer has been more often wrong than right.

In summary, the Barometer works better in years with positive returns in January.

## The January Barometer since 1980

The following chart might help to visualise the behaviour of the Barometer in recent years. The chart plots the performance of the Barometer for each year from 1980; a 1 is plotted for years in which the Barometer worked, and a -1 in those years when it didn't.

Of late the performance has been patchy, but there was a remarkable run of 12 years from 1982 in which the Barometer worked every year. It should be noted perhaps that the market was strong in this period: annual returns were positive for every year except one year. And, as we saw above, the Barometer does seem to work better in years when the market rises.

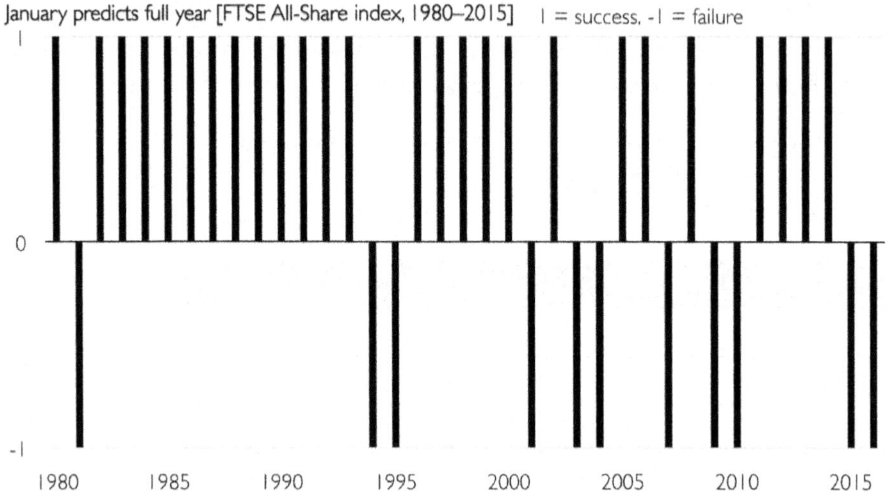


## Economic significance

*So, is the January Barometer economically significant – i.e. can you trade it profitably?*

The following chart plots the FTSE All-Share returns for January and the full-year for the period 1980–2016.

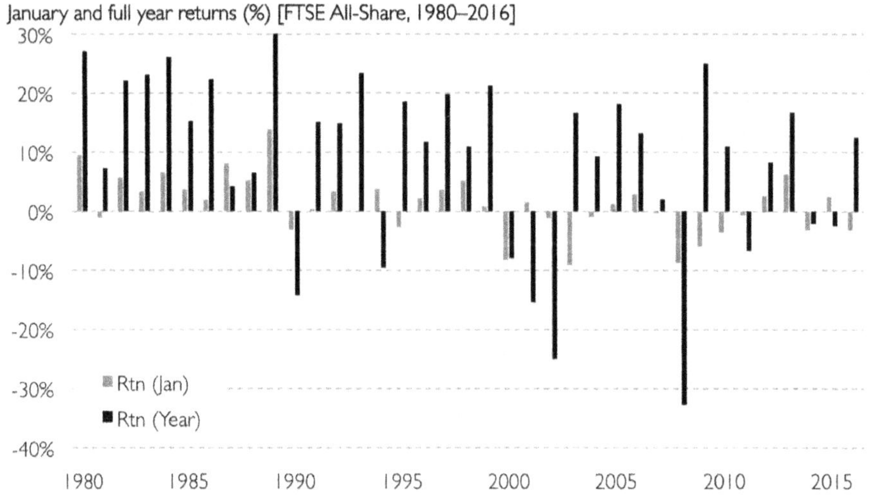


A concern might be that a significant portion of the full-year returns might be accounted for by the month of January itself. In other words, by the time one acts on a signal from the Barometer, the market has already moved significantly.

For example, if we look at 1980 (the first bar in the above chart), the annual return for the index that year was +27%; the January Barometer correctly forecast a positive year, but the return in January was itself +10%, so by the time one acted on the Barometer's signal (the end of January) over a third of the year's gain had already happened.

However, the chart shows that although a disproportionate part of the full-year returns are often accounted for in January, the remaining returns are still significant.

The following table summarises the results of the January Barometer (as before), but this time instead of assessing the Barometer on how accurately it forecasts the full-year performance, in this case it is used to forecast the return for the period from the start of February to the end of December. In other words, this is the period that one could effectively trade using a signal from the Barometer.

| | Jan (all) | Jan (up) | Jan (down) |
|---|---|---|---|
| 1800–2016 | 53% | 57% | 47% |
| 1900–2016 | 58% | 63% | 50% |
| 1980–2016 | 62% | 83% | 29% |

Comparing these results with those above (i.e. those forecasting the full year), we can see that the Barometer's accuracy falls significantly. In fact, recently, its accuracy is only good in years when January returns are positive.

Over this 1980–2016 period, if a strategy had invested in the market from February to year-end just in the years that the Barometer gave a signal for a positive market, the average annual strategy return in those years would have been 9.5%. This is (only) marginally better than the average market return for all years over the same period of 9.0%.

## Conclusion

The January Barometer has had a better than 50% success rate for the three periods studied here: 1800, 1900, and 1980 to the present day.

However, one should be wary about assigning a special relationship between January and the full-year. For example, since 1800 the month of February has been almost as good as January in predicting full year returns, and since 1900 February has had a higher success rate in positive return years.

*But we're not quite finished with the January Barometer…*

## Do the first five days predict the full year?

There is a variant of the January Barometer that references just the first five days of the new year instead of the full month of January. In other words:

> as the first five days of January go, so goes the year

We will call this variant of the January Barometer the *January Barometer (5D)*.

At first glance, the figures don't look too encouraging: in the 46 years since 1970, the January Barometer (5D) applied to the FTSE All-Share has been right in 26 years (57%). In other words in only just over half the years since 1970 the first five days of the year have accurately forecast the full year.

But let's look at this in more detail and see if we can tease anything out of the data.

The following is a scatter chart that plots the returns for the FTSE All-Share for the first five days of a year against the return for the full year, for the period 1970–2016.

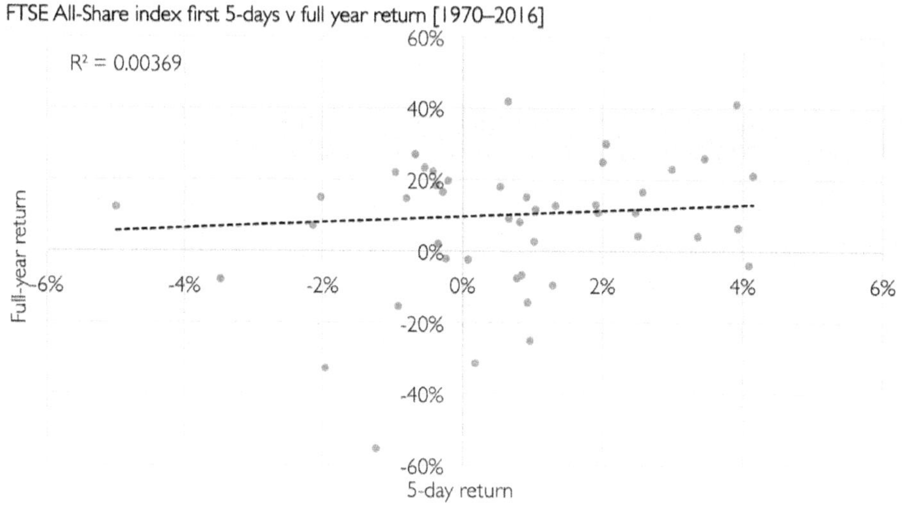


There is, just, a positive correlation here (given by the positive sloping trend line), however the measure of correlation (R2 = 0.004) is extremely low. But we don't need to refer to calculated correlation coefficients, just by looking at the chart we can see that there is very little relationship between the first five days and the full year. As a professional statistician may say, "the dots are all over the place".

In summary, the chart shows there is a very low level of correlation between first five-day returns and returns for the full year but it is far from being significant.

However, strictly, and as already mentioned above, the January Barometer only says the direction (i.e. positive or negative returns) can be forecast, not the size of returns. In which case the following chart may be more useful. This plots a binary value for each year:

- 1: if the sign on the full year return was the **same** as the sign for the return for the first five-days (i.e. either both positive returns or negative returns)
- -1: if the sign on the full year return was **different** to the sign for the return for the first five-days

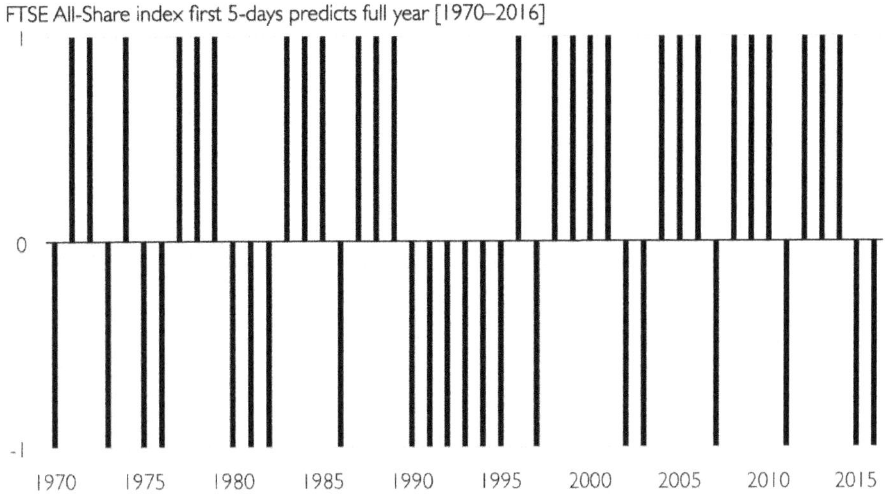


In this chart we can see the roughly even split between years when the January Barometer (5D) works and those years when it doesn't. However, the distribution of years when it works is interesting, as there does appear to be a certain clustering of years when the effect works and when it doesn't. For example, in the last 20 years the January Barometer (5D) has been accurate 14 times (a hit rate of 70%). And since 2004 there is this rather odd pattern of not working every fourth year – until it didn't work again last year (2016), so that's that mildly interesting observation knocked on the head.

To conclude (again), the January Barometer (5D) variant has nothing to recommend it. The standard January Barometer has been fairly accurate in recent years (i.e. since 1980), but it is safer to restrict its use to just those years when market returns in January are positive.

# FTSE 100 MONTH-END VALUES

The following table shows the month-end and year-end values of the FTSE 100.

NB. The FTSE 100 was launched on the first trading day of January 1984, but was given a starting value of 1000 assigned for the last trading day of 1983.

| | Jan | Feb | Mar | Apr | May | Jun | Jul | Aug | Sep | Oct | Nov | Dec |
|---|---|---|---|---|---|---|---|---|---|---|---|---|
| 1984 | 1063.0 | 1040.3 | 1112.5 | 1138.3 | 1021.0 | 1041.4 | 1010.1 | 1103.9 | 1140.3 | 1151.0 | 1181.3 | 1232.2 |
| 1985 | 1280.8 | 1259.7 | 1277.0 | 1291.0 | 1313.0 | 1234.9 | 1261.7 | 1341.1 | 1290.0 | 1377.2 | 1439.1 | 1412.6 |
| 1986 | 1435.0 | 1543.9 | 1668.8 | 1660.5 | 1602.8 | 1649.8 | 1558.1 | 1661.2 | 1555.8 | 1632.1 | 1636.7 | 1679.0 |
| 1987 | 1808.3 | 1979.2 | 1997.6 | 2050.5 | 2203.0 | 2284.1 | 2360.9 | 2249.7 | 2366.0 | 1749.8 | 1579.9 | 1712.7 |
| 1988 | 1790.8 | 1768.8 | 1742.5 | 1802.2 | 1784.4 | 1857.6 | 1853.6 | 1753.6 | 1826.5 | 1852.4 | 1792.4 | 1793.1 |
| 1989 | 2051.8 | 2002.4 | 2075.0 | 2118.0 | 2114.4 | 2151.0 | 2297.0 | 2387.9 | 2299.4 | 2142.6 | 2276.8 | 2422.7 |
| 1990 | 2337.3 | 2255.4 | 2247.9 | 2103.4 | 2345.1 | 2374.6 | 2326.2 | 2162.8 | 1990.2 | 2050.3 | 2149.4 | 2143.5 |
| 1991 | 2170.3 | 2380.9 | 2456.5 | 2486.2 | 2499.5 | 2414.8 | 2588.8 | 2645.7 | 2621.7 | 2566.0 | 2420.2 | 2493.1 |
| 1992 | 2571.2 | 2562.1 | 2440.1 | 2654.1 | 2707.6 | 2521.2 | 2399.6 | 2312.6 | 2553.0 | 2658.3 | 2778.8 | 2846.5 |
| 1993 | 2807.2 | 2868.0 | 2878.7 | 2813.1 | 2840.7 | 2900.0 | 2926.5 | 3100.0 | 3037.5 | 3171.0 | 3166.9 | 3418.4 |
| 1994 | 3491.8 | 3328.1 | 3086.4 | 3125.3 | 2970.5 | 2919.2 | 3082.6 | 3251.3 | 3026.3 | 3097.4 | 3081.4 | 3065.5 |
| 1995 | 2991.6 | 3009.3 | 3137.9 | 3216.7 | 3319.4 | 3314.6 | 3463.3 | 3477.8 | 3508.2 | 3529.1 | 3664.3 | 3689.3 |
| 1996 | 3759.3 | 3727.6 | 3699.7 | 3817.9 | 3747.8 | 3711.0 | 3703.2 | 3867.6 | 3953.7 | 3979.1 | 4058.0 | 4118.5 |
| 1997 | 4275.8 | 4308.3 | 4312.9 | 4436.0 | 4621.3 | 4604.6 | 4907.5 | 4817.5 | 5244.2 | 4842.3 | 4831.8 | 5135.5 |
| 1998 | 5458.5 | 5767.3 | 5932.2 | 5928.3 | 5870.7 | 5832.5 | 5837.0 | 5249.4 | 5064.4 | 5438.4 | 5743.9 | 5882.6 |
| 1999 | 5896.0 | 6175.1 | 6295.3 | 6552.2 | 6226.2 | 6318.5 | 6231.9 | 6246.4 | 6029.8 | 6255.7 | 6597.2 | 6930.2 |
| 2000 | 6268.5 | 6232.6 | 6540.2 | 6327.4 | 6359.3 | 6312.7 | 6365.3 | 6672.7 | 6294.2 | 6438.4 | 6142.2 | 6222.5 |
| 2001 | 6297.5 | 5917.9 | 5633.7 | 5966.9 | 5796.1 | 5642.5 | 5529.1 | 5345.0 | 4903.4 | 5039.7 | 5203.6 | 5217.4 |
| 2002 | 5164.8 | 5101.0 | 5271.8 | 5165.6 | 5085.1 | 4656.4 | 4246.2 | 4227.3 | 3721.8 | 4039.7 | 4169.4 | 3940.4 |
| 2003 | 3567.4 | 3655.6 | 3613.3 | 3926.0 | 4048.1 | 4031.2 | 4157.0 | 4161.1 | 4091.3 | 4287.6 | 4342.6 | 4476.9 |
| 2004 | 4390.7 | 4492.2 | 4385.7 | 4489.7 | 4430.7 | 4464.1 | 4413.1 | 4459.3 | 4570.8 | 4624.2 | 4703.2 | 4814.3 |
| 2005 | 4852.3 | 4968.5 | 4894.4 | 4801.7 | 4964.0 | 5113.2 | 5282.3 | 5296.9 | 5477.7 | 5317.3 | 5423.2 | 5618.8 |
| 2006 | 5760.3 | 5791.5 | 5964.6 | 6023.1 | 5723.8 | 5833.4 | 5928.3 | 5906.1 | 5960.8 | 6129.2 | 6048.8 | 6220.8 |
| 2007 | 6203.1 | 6171.5 | 6308.0 | 6449.2 | 6621.4 | 6607.9 | 6360.1 | 6303.3 | 6466.8 | 6721.6 | 6432.5 | 6456.9 |
| 2008 | 5879.8 | 5884.3 | 5702.1 | 6087.3 | 6053.5 | 5625.9 | 5411.9 | 5636.6 | 4902.5 | 4377.3 | 4288.0 | 4434.2 |
| 2009 | 4149.6 | 3830.1 | 3926.1 | 4243.7 | 4417.9 | 4249.2 | 4608.4 | 4908.9 | 5133.9 | 5044.5 | 5190.7 | 5412.9 |
| 2010 | 5188.5 | 5354.5 | 5679.6 | 5553.3 | 5188.4 | 4916.9 | 5258.0 | 5225.2 | 5548.6 | 5675.2 | 5528.3 | 5899.9 |
| 2011 | 5862.9 | 5994.0 | 5908.8 | 6069.9 | 5990.0 | 5945.7 | 5815.2 | 5394.5 | 5128.5 | 5544.2 | 5505.4 | 5572.3 |
| 2012 | 5681.6 | 5871.5 | 5768.5 | 5737.8 | 5320.9 | 5571.1 | 5635.3 | 5711.5 | 5742.1 | 5782.7 | 5866.8 | 5897.8 |
| 2013 | 6276.9 | 6360.8 | 6411.7 | 6430.1 | 6583.1 | 6215.5 | 6621.1 | 6483.0 | 6462.2 | 6731.4 | 6650.6 | 6749.1 |
| 2014 | 6510.4 | 6809.7 | 6598.4 | 6780.0 | 6844.5 | 6743.9 | 6730.1 | 6819.8 | 6622.7 | 6546.5 | 6722.6 | 6566.1 |
| 2015 | 6749.4 | 6946.7 | 6773.0 | 6960.6 | 6984.4 | 6521.0 | 6696.3 | 6247.9 | 6061.6 | 6361.1 | 6356.1 | 6242.3 |
| 2016 | 6083.8 | 6097.1 | 6174.9 | 6241.9 | 6230.8 | 6504.3 | 6724.4 | 6781.5 | 6899.3 | 6954.2 | 6783.8 | 7142.8 |
| 2017 | 7099.2 | 7263.4 | 7322.9 | 7203.9 | 7520.0 | 7312.7 | 7372.0 | 7430.6 | | | | |

# MONTHLY PERFORMANCE OF THE FTSE 100

The table below shows the percentage performance of the FTSE 100 for every month since 1986. The months where the index fell are highlighted. By scanning the columns it is possible to get a feel for how the market moves in certain months.

| | Jan | Feb | Mar | Apr | May | Jun | Jul | Aug | Sep | Oct | Nov | Dec |
|---|---|---|---|---|---|---|---|---|---|---|---|---|
| 1980 | 9.2 | 4.9 | -9.2 | 3.4 | -2.3 | 11.2 | 3.7 | 0.7 | 3.2 | 5.9 | 0.6 | -5.3 |
| 1981 | -1.5 | 4.3 | 0.4 | 6.9 | -5.0 | 1.9 | 0.4 | 5.0 | -16.6 | 3.2 | 10.5 | -1.1 |
| 1982 | 4.5 | -4.9 | 3.5 | 1.1 | 3.4 | -4.3 | 3.6 | 2.9 | 6.1 | 2.0 | 0.9 | 1.7 |
| 1983 | 3.1 | 0.6 | 1.8 | 8.1 | 0.2 | 2.8 | -2.1 | 2.6 | -2.6 | -3.4 | 5.7 | 1.9 |
| 1984 | 6.3 | -2.1 | 6.9 | 2.3 | -10.3 | 2.0 | -3.0 | 9.3 | 3.3 | 0.9 | 2.6 | 4.3 |
| 1985 | 3.9 | -1.6 | 1.4 | 1.1 | 1.7 | -5.9 | 2.2 | 6.3 | -3.8 | 6.8 | 4.5 | -1.8 |
| 1986 | 1.6 | 7.6 | 8.1 | -0.5 | -3.5 | 2.9 | -5.6 | 6.6 | -6.3 | 4.9 | 0.3 | 2.6 |
| 1987 | 7.7 | 9.5 | 0.9 | 2.6 | 7.4 | 3.7 | 3.4 | -4.7 | 5.2 | -26.0 | -9.7 | 8.4 |
| 1988 | 4.6 | -1.2 | -1.5 | 3.4 | -1.0 | 4.1 | -0.2 | -5.4 | 4.2 | 1.4 | -3.2 | 0.0 |
| 1989 | 14.4 | -2.4 | 3.6 | 2.1 | -0.2 | 1.7 | 6.8 | 4.0 | -3.7 | -6.8 | 6.3 | 6.4 |
| 1990 | -3.5 | -3.5 | -0.3 | -6.4 | 11.5 | 1.3 | -2.0 | -7.0 | -8.0 | 3.0 | 4.8 | -0.3 |
| 1991 | 1.3 | 9.7 | 3.2 | 1.2 | 0.5 | -3.4 | 7.2 | 2.2 | -0.9 | -2.1 | -5.7 | 3.0 |
| 1992 | 3.1 | -0.4 | -4.8 | 8.8 | 2.0 | -6.9 | -4.8 | -3.6 | 10.4 | 4.1 | 4.5 | 2.4 |
| 1993 | -1.4 | 2.2 | 0.4 | -2.3 | 1.0 | 2.1 | 0.9 | 5.9 | -2.0 | 4.4 | -0.1 | 7.9 |
| 1994 | 2.1 | -4.7 | -7.3 | 1.3 | -5.0 | -1.7 | 5.6 | 5.5 | -6.9 | 2.3 | -0.5 | -0.5 |
| 1995 | -2.4 | 0.6 | 4.3 | 2.5 | 3.2 | -0.1 | 4.5 | 0.4 | 0.9 | 0.6 | 3.8 | 0.7 |
| 1996 | 1.9 | -0.8 | -0.7 | 3.2 | -1.8 | -1.0 | -0.2 | 4.4 | 2.2 | 0.6 | 2.0 | 1.5 |
| 1997 | 3.8 | 0.8 | 0.1 | 2.9 | 4.2 | -0.4 | 6.6 | -1.8 | 8.9 | -7.7 | -0.2 | 6.3 |
| 1998 | 6.3 | 5.7 | 2.9 | -0.1 | -1.0 | -0.7 | 0.1 | -10.1 | -3.5 | 7.4 | 5.6 | 2.4 |
| 1999 | 0.2 | 4.7 | 1.9 | 4.1 | -5.0 | 1.5 | -1.4 | 0.2 | -3.5 | 3.7 | 5.5 | 5.0 |
| 2000 | -9.5 | -0.6 | 4.9 | -3.3 | 0.5 | -0.7 | 0.8 | 4.8 | -5.7 | 2.3 | -4.6 | 1.3 |
| 2001 | 1.2 | -6.0 | -4.8 | 5.9 | -2.9 | -2.7 | -2.0 | -3.3 | -8.3 | 2.8 | 3.3 | 0.3 |
| 2002 | -1.0 | -1.2 | 3.3 | -2.0 | -1.6 | -8.4 | -8.8 | -0.4 | -12.0 | 8.5 | 3.2 | -5.5 |
| 2003 | -9.5 | 2.5 | -1.2 | 8.7 | 3.1 | -0.4 | 3.1 | 0.1 | -1.7 | 4.8 | 1.3 | 3.1 |
| 2004 | -1.9 | 2.3 | -2.4 | 2.4 | -1.3 | 0.8 | -1.1 | 1.0 | 2.5 | 1.2 | 1.7 | 2.4 |
| 2005 | 0.8 | 2.4 | -1.5 | -1.9 | 3.4 | 3.0 | 3.3 | 0.3 | 3.4 | -2.9 | 2.0 | 3.6 |
| 2006 | 2.5 | 0.5 | 3.0 | 1.0 | -5.0 | 1.9 | 1.6 | -0.4 | 0.9 | 2.8 | -1.3 | 2.8 |
| 2007 | -0.3 | -0.5 | 2.2 | 2.2 | 2.7 | -0.2 | -3.8 | -0.9 | 2.6 | 3.9 | -4.3 | 0.4 |
| 2008 | -8.9 | 0.1 | -3.1 | 6.8 | -0.6 | -7.1 | -3.8 | 4.2 | -13.0 | -10.7 | -2.0 | 3.4 |
| 2009 | -6.4 | -7.7 | 2.5 | 8.1 | 4.1 | -3.8 | 8.5 | 6.5 | 4.6 | -1.7 | 2.9 | 4.3 |
| 2010 | -4.1 | 3.2 | 6.1 | -2.2 | -6.6 | -5.2 | 6.9 | -0.6 | 6.2 | 2.3 | -2.6 | 6.7 |
| 2011 | -0.6 | 2.2 | -1.4 | 2.7 | -1.3 | -0.7 | -2.2 | -7.2 | -4.9 | 8.1 | -0.7 | 1.2 |
| 2012 | 2.0 | 3.3 | -1.8 | -0.5 | -7.3 | 4.7 | 1.2 | 1.4 | 0.5 | 0.7 | 1.5 | 0.5 |
| 2013 | 6.4 | 1.3 | 0.8 | 0.3 | 2.4 | -5.6 | 6.5 | -2.1 | -0.3 | 4.2 | -1.2 | 1.5 |
| 2014 | -3.5 | 4.6 | -3.1 | 2.8 | 1.0 | 1.5 | -0.2 | 1.3 | -2.9 | -1.2 | 2.7 | -2.3 |
| 2015 | 2.8 | 2.9 | -2.5 | 2.8 | 0.3 | -6.6 | 2.7 | -6.7 | -3.0 | 4.9 | -0.1 | -1.8 |
| 2016 | -2.5 | 0.2 | 1.3 | 1.1 | -0.2 | 4.4 | 3.4 | 0.8 | 1.7 | 0.8 | -2.5 | 5.3 |
| 2017 | -0.6 | 2.3 | 0.8 | -1.6 | 4.4 | -2.8 | 0.8 | 0.8 | | | | |

**Observations**

1. In recent years (i.e. since 2000) the index has been weak in January and June; and strong in April, October and December.

2. In the last 20 years it can clearly be seen that the strongest month has been December (only down six times in 34 years). However, in the 1970s and 1980s, the strongest month was April (which saw positive returns every year from 1971 to 1985).

3. Looking across the table, it can be seen that the longest period of consecutive down months was April 2002–Sep 2002. While the longest periods of consecutive up months were Jul 1982–Jun 1983 and Jun 2012–May 2013 (the only times the FTSE 100 has risen 12 months without a break).

# FTSE 250 MONTH-END VALUES

The following table shows the month-end and year-end values of the FTSE 250.

NB. The FTSE 250 was launched on 12 October 1992, but the base date for the index is 31 December 1985.

| | Jan | Feb | Mar | Apr | May | Jun | Jul | Aug | Sep | Oct | Nov | Dec |
|---|---|---|---|---|---|---|---|---|---|---|---|---|
| 1986 | 1449.5 | 1575.1 | 1695.8 | 1755.2 | 1696.5 | 1771.0 | 1690.2 | 1763.1 | 1665.5 | 1751.9 | 1798.0 | 1817.9 |
| 1987 | 1990.6 | 2126.4 | 2190.2 | 2219.9 | 2357.2 | 2556.2 | 2710.1 | 2585.8 | 2753.7 | 1964.2 | 1754.0 | 1974.0 |
| 1988 | 2103.9 | 2100.1 | 2075.3 | 2156.1 | 2164.7 | 2266.2 | 2291.5 | 2147.9 | 2227.1 | 2303.1 | 2220.8 | 2176.1 |
| 1989 | 2461.7 | 2491.7 | 2545.5 | 2526.7 | 2555.5 | 2533.1 | 2701.9 | 2723.4 | 2679.3 | 2438.4 | 2528.7 | 2645.8 |
| 1990 | 2578.6 | 2451.9 | 2425.4 | 2276.2 | 2474.5 | 2524.8 | 2465.4 | 2174.9 | 1960.4 | 2052.2 | 2092.8 | 2112.9 |
| 1991 | 2082.0 | 2383.6 | 2492.9 | 2483.7 | 2441.5 | 2359.7 | 2482.7 | 2584.0 | 2608.6 | 2543.5 | 2388.6 | 2364.6 |
| 1992 | 2476.4 | 2523.5 | 2408.2 | 2712.4 | 2779.2 | 2548.7 | 2302.3 | 2192.5 | 2397.4 | 2521.6 | 2637.5 | 2862.9 |
| 1993 | 2954.8 | 3036.1 | 3107.8 | 3132.1 | 3165.4 | 3235.7 | 3306.5 | 3511.9 | 3433.2 | 3528.1 | 3484.9 | 3791.3 |
| 1994 | 4084.3 | 3960.0 | 3752.9 | 3781.1 | 3564.3 | 3414.1 | 3640.2 | 3816.6 | 3494.8 | 3516.9 | 3497.3 | 3501.8 |
| 1995 | 3370.4 | 3384.1 | 3434.7 | 3530.2 | 3653.8 | 3592.6 | 3826.0 | 3913.4 | 3948.8 | 3894.3 | 3959.1 | 4021.3 |
| 1996 | 4125.0 | 4215.0 | 4326.7 | 4551.8 | 4510.0 | 4353.2 | 4230.6 | 4416.2 | 4391.1 | 4422.5 | 4428.5 | 4490.4 |
| 1997 | 4595.4 | 4654.4 | 4576.2 | 4498.7 | 4495.8 | 4431.3 | 4492.0 | 4603.4 | 4829.9 | 4643.2 | 4656.7 | 4787.6 |
| 1998 | 4861.5 | 5201.0 | 5525.4 | 5610.8 | 5901.4 | 5503.8 | 5482.7 | 4786.2 | 4544.2 | 4811.4 | 4901.7 | 4854.7 |
| 1999 | 5024.2 | 5248.3 | 5475.2 | 5849.6 | 5639.1 | 5858.2 | 5969.5 | 6017.9 | 5687.1 | 5622.3 | 6194.8 | 6444.9 |
| 2000 | 6181.0 | 6451.2 | 6475.1 | 6194.6 | 6227.8 | 6601.0 | 6779.1 | 7057.8 | 6676.9 | 6629.3 | 6419.9 | 6547.5 |
| 2001 | 6735.9 | 6649.5 | 6094.7 | 6409.2 | 6571.1 | 6298.9 | 6082.2 | 6116.3 | 5118.6 | 5364.8 | 5849.5 | 5939.1 |
| 2002 | 5849.2 | 5834.0 | 6175.5 | 6123.7 | 6049.0 | 5496.6 | 4783.6 | 4858.8 | 4287.1 | 4417.7 | 4558.2 | 4319.3 |
| 2003 | 4016.4 | 4037.6 | 3959.8 | 4389.3 | 4815.6 | 4963.4 | 5325.6 | 5593.2 | 5457.8 | 5724.4 | 5712.6 | 5802.3 |
| 2004 | 6023.9 | 6269.9 | 6259.4 | 6210.7 | 6053.6 | 6277.9 | 6023.5 | 6087.3 | 6269.1 | 6321.8 | 6577.4 | 6936.8 |
| 2005 | 7166.2 | 7254.0 | 7130.5 | 6728.9 | 7114.3 | 7368.7 | 7605.1 | 7749.2 | 7951.1 | 7711.1 | 8327.9 | 8794.3 |
| 2006 | 9172.6 | 9448.3 | 9850.3 | 9878.7 | 9298.2 | 9422.7 | 9355.6 | 9601.2 | 9996.8 | 10372.2 | 10673.9 | 11177.8 |
| 2007 | 11100.3 | 11082.9 | 11689.3 | 11929.4 | 12111.1 | 11527.6 | 11337.5 | 11309.2 | 11037.4 | 11666.0 | 10748.8 | 10657.8 |
| 2008 | 9881.8 | 10067.9 | 10013.2 | 10122.3 | 10049.3 | 9145.8 | 8856.7 | 9381.8 | 7888.2 | 6282.6 | 6093.3 | 6360.9 |
| 2009 | 6250.8 | 6049.1 | 6373.9 | 7529.0 | 7572.0 | 7414.6 | 8000.0 | 8817.5 | 9142.3 | 8885.8 | 8918.4 | 9306.9 |
| 2010 | 9237.3 | 9344.4 | 10165.3 | 10366.0 | 9637.1 | 9366.1 | 9948.7 | 9825.1 | 10531.8 | 10843.5 | 10607.8 | 11558.8 |
| 2011 | 11471.5 | 11621.3 | 11592.0 | 12013.9 | 12060.8 | 11934.0 | 11552.1 | 10525.9 | 9819.4 | 10479.7 | 10315.3 | 10102.9 |
| 2012 | 10769.4 | 11449.5 | 11538.9 | 11417.6 | 10558.2 | 10932.1 | 11136.7 | 11410.2 | 11734.1 | 11935.0 | 12034.2 | 12375.0 |
| 2013 | 13030.5 | 13704.0 | 13923.0 | 13949.9 | 14350.9 | 13798.2 | 14872.9 | 14625.2 | 14908.2 | 15480.0 | 15466.6 | 15935.4 |
| 2014 | 15674.4 | 16726.0 | 16273.7 | 15817.2 | 16010.2 | 15723.6 | 15495.6 | 15885.7 | 15379.7 | 15501.4 | 15851.8 | 16085.4 |
| 2015 | 16305.8 | 17273.8 | 17090.6 | 17474.6 | 17468.3 | 17531.5 | 17677.4 | 17106.4 | 16683.0 | 17117.2 | 17420.7 | 17429.8 |
| 2016 | 16487.7 | 16603.1 | 16926.1 | 16801.6 | 17184.7 | 16271.1 | 17282.9 | 17732.8 | 17871.4 | 17544.2 | 17545.8 | 18077.3 |
| 2017 | 18147.8 | 18770.7 | 18971.8 | 19615.4 | 19972.2 | 19340.2 | 19781.1 | 19803.6 | | | | |

# MONTHLY PERFORMANCE OF THE FTSE 250

The table below shows the percentage performance of the FTSE 250 for every month since 1986. The months where the index fell are highlighted. By scanning the columns it is possible to get a feel for how the market moves in certain months.

| | Jan | Feb | Mar | Apr | May | Jun | Jul | Aug | Sep | Oct | Nov | Dec |
|---|---|---|---|---|---|---|---|---|---|---|---|---|
| 1986 | 2.6 | 8.7 | 7.7 | 3.5 | -3.3 | 4.4 | -4.6 | 4.3 | -5.5 | 5.2 | 2.6 | 1.1 |
| 1987 | 9.5 | 6.8 | 3.0 | 1.4 | 6.2 | 8.4 | 6.0 | -4.6 | 6.5 | -28.7 | -10.7 | 12.5 |
| 1988 | 6.6 | -0.2 | -1.2 | 3.9 | 0.4 | 4.7 | 1.1 | -6.3 | 3.7 | 3.4 | -3.6 | -2.0 |
| 1989 | 13.1 | 1.2 | 2.2 | -0.7 | 1.1 | -0.9 | 6.7 | 0.8 | -1.6 | -9.0 | 3.7 | 4.6 |
| 1990 | -2.5 | -4.9 | -1.1 | -6.2 | 8.7 | 2.0 | -2.4 | -11.8 | -9.9 | 4.7 | 2.0 | 1.0 |
| 1991 | -1.5 | 14.5 | 4.6 | -0.4 | -1.7 | -3.4 | 5.2 | 4.1 | 0.9 | -2.5 | -6.1 | -1.0 |
| 1992 | 4.7 | 1.9 | -4.6 | 12.6 | 2.5 | -8.3 | -9.7 | -4.8 | 9.3 | 5.2 | 4.6 | 8.5 |
| 1993 | 3.2 | 2.8 | 2.4 | 0.8 | 1.1 | 2.2 | 2.2 | 6.2 | -2.2 | 2.8 | -1.2 | 8.8 |
| 1994 | 7.7 | -3.0 | -5.2 | 0.8 | -5.7 | -4.2 | 6.6 | 4.8 | -8.4 | 0.6 | -0.6 | 0.1 |
| 1995 | -3.8 | 0.4 | 1.5 | 2.8 | 3.5 | -1.7 | 6.5 | 2.3 | 0.9 | -1.4 | 1.7 | 1.6 |
| 1996 | 2.6 | 2.2 | 2.7 | 5.2 | -0.9 | -3.5 | -2.8 | 4.4 | -0.6 | 0.7 | 0.1 | 1.4 |
| 1997 | 2.3 | 1.3 | -1.7 | -1.7 | -0.1 | -1.4 | 1.4 | 2.5 | 4.9 | -3.9 | 0.3 | 2.8 |
| 1998 | 1.5 | 7.0 | 6.2 | 1.5 | 5.2 | -6.7 | -0.4 | -12.7 | -5.1 | 5.9 | 1.9 | -1.0 |
| 1999 | 3.5 | 4.5 | 4.3 | 6.8 | -3.6 | 3.9 | 1.9 | 0.8 | -5.5 | -1.1 | 10.2 | 4.0 |
| 2000 | -4.1 | 4.4 | 0.4 | -4.3 | 0.5 | 6.0 | 2.7 | 4.1 | -5.4 | -0.7 | -3.2 | 2.0 |
| 2001 | 2.9 | -1.3 | -8.3 | 5.2 | 2.5 | -4.1 | -3.4 | 0.6 | -16.3 | 4.8 | 9.0 | 1.5 |
| 2002 | -1.5 | -0.3 | 5.9 | -0.8 | -1.2 | -9.1 | -13.0 | 1.6 | -11.8 | 3.0 | 3.2 | -5.2 |
| 2003 | -7.0 | 0.5 | -1.9 | 10.8 | 9.7 | 3.1 | 7.3 | 5.0 | -2.4 | 4.9 | -0.2 | 1.6 |
| 2004 | 3.8 | 4.1 | -0.2 | -0.8 | -2.5 | 3.7 | -4.1 | 1.1 | 3.0 | 0.8 | 4.0 | 5.5 |
| 2005 | 3.3 | 1.2 | -1.7 | -5.6 | 5.7 | 3.6 | 3.2 | 1.9 | 2.6 | -3.0 | 8.0 | 5.6 |
| 2006 | 4.3 | 3.0 | 4.3 | 0.3 | -5.9 | 1.3 | -0.7 | 2.6 | 4.1 | 3.8 | 2.9 | 4.7 |
| 2007 | -0.7 | -0.2 | 5.5 | 2.1 | 1.5 | -4.8 | -1.6 | -0.2 | -2.4 | 5.7 | -7.9 | -0.8 |
| 2008 | -7.3 | 1.9 | -0.5 | 1.1 | -0.7 | -9.0 | -3.2 | 5.9 | -15.9 | -20.4 | -3.0 | 4.4 |
| 2009 | -1.7 | -3.2 | 5.4 | 18.1 | 0.6 | -2.1 | 7.9 | 10.2 | 3.7 | -2.8 | 0.4 | 4.4 |
| 2010 | -0.7 | 1.2 | 8.8 | 2.0 | -7.0 | -2.8 | 6.2 | -1.2 | 7.2 | 3.0 | -2.2 | 9.0 |
| 2011 | -0.8 | 1.3 | -0.3 | 3.6 | 0.4 | -1.1 | -3.2 | -8.9 | -6.7 | 6.7 | -1.6 | -2.1 |
| 2012 | 6.6 | 6.3 | 0.8 | -1.1 | -7.5 | 3.5 | 1.9 | 2.5 | 2.8 | 1.7 | 0.8 | 2.8 |
| 2013 | 5.3 | 5.2 | 1.6 | 0.2 | 2.9 | -3.9 | 7.8 | -1.7 | 1.9 | 3.8 | -0.1 | 3.0 |
| 2014 | -1.6 | 6.7 | -2.7 | -2.8 | 1.2 | -1.8 | -1.5 | 2.5 | -3.2 | 0.8 | 2.3 | 1.5 |
| 2015 | 1.4 | 5.9 | -1.1 | 2.2 | 0.0 | 0.4 | 0.8 | -3.2 | -2.5 | 2.6 | 1.8 | 0.1 |
| 2016 | -5.4 | 0.7 | 1.9 | -0.7 | 2.3 | -5.3 | 6.2 | 2.6 | 0.8 | -1.8 | 0.0 | 3.0 |
| 2017 | 0.4 | 3.4 | 1.1 | 3.4 | 1.8 | -3.2 | 2.3 | 0.1 | | | | |

## Observations

1. Historically, the strongest months for the FTSE 250 have been February, August and December. Since 2003, the FTSE 250 has only seen negative returns in February and December in two years.
2. The poorest record for the FTSE 250 is in June and September.

# COMPARATIVE PERFORMANCE OF FTSE 100 & FTSE 250

The table below shows the monthly outperformance of the FTSE 100 index over the mid-cap FTSE 250 index. For example, in January 1986, the FTSE 100 increased 1.6%, while the FTSE 250 increased 2.6%; the outperformance of the former over the latter was therefore -1.0. The cells are highlighted if the number is negative (i.e. the FTSE 250 outperformed the FTSE 100).

| | Jan | Feb | Mar | Apr | May | Jun | Jul | Aug | Sep | Oct | Nov | Dec |
|---|---|---|---|---|---|---|---|---|---|---|---|---|
| 1986 | -1.0 | -1.1 | 0.4 | -4.0 | -0.1 | -1.5 | -1.0 | 2.3 | -0.8 | -0.3 | -2.3 | 1.5 |
| 1987 | -1.8 | 2.6 | -2.1 | 1.3 | 1.3 | -4.8 | -2.7 | -0.1 | -1.3 | 2.6 | 1.0 | -4.1 |
| 1988 | -2.0 | -1.0 | -0.3 | -0.5 | -1.4 | -0.6 | -1.3 | 0.9 | 0.5 | -2.0 | 0.3 | 2.0 |
| 1989 | 1.3 | -3.6 | 1.5 | 2.8 | -1.3 | 2.6 | 0.1 | 3.2 | -2.1 | 2.2 | 2.6 | 1.8 |
| 1990 | -1.0 | 1.4 | 0.7 | -0.3 | 2.8 | -0.8 | 0.3 | 4.8 | 1.9 | -1.7 | 2.9 | -1.2 |
| 1991 | 2.7 | -4.8 | -1.4 | 1.6 | 2.2 | 0.0 | 2.0 | -1.9 | -1.9 | 0.4 | 0.4 | 4.0 |
| 1992 | -1.6 | -2.3 | -0.2 | -3.9 | -0.4 | 1.4 | 4.8 | 1.1 | 1.0 | -1.1 | -0.1 | -6.1 |
| 1993 | -4.6 | -0.6 | -2.0 | -3.1 | -0.1 | -0.1 | -1.3 | -0.3 | 0.2 | 1.6 | 1.1 | -0.9 |
| 1994 | -5.6 | -1.6 | -2.0 | 0.5 | 0.8 | 2.5 | -1.0 | 0.6 | 1.5 | 1.7 | 0.0 | -0.6 |
| 1995 | 1.3 | 0.2 | 2.8 | -0.3 | -0.3 | 1.5 | -2.0 | -1.9 | 0.0 | 2.0 | 2.2 | -0.9 |
| 1996 | -0.7 | -3.0 | -3.4 | -2.0 | -0.9 | 2.5 | 2.6 | 0.1 | 2.8 | -0.1 | 1.8 | 0.1 |
| 1997 | 1.5 | -0.5 | 1.8 | 4.5 | 4.2 | 1.1 | 5.2 | -4.3 | 3.9 | -3.8 | -0.5 | 3.5 |
| 1998 | 4.7 | -1.3 | -3.4 | -1.6 | -6.2 | 6.1 | 0.5 | 2.6 | 1.5 | 1.5 | 3.7 | 3.4 |
| 1999 | -3.3 | 0.3 | -2.4 | -2.8 | -1.4 | -2.4 | -3.3 | -0.6 | 2.0 | 4.9 | -4.7 | 1.0 |
| 2000 | -5.5 | -4.9 | 4.6 | 1.1 | 0.0 | -6.7 | -1.9 | 0.7 | -0.3 | 3.0 | -1.4 | -0.7 |
| 2001 | -1.7 | -4.7 | 3.5 | 0.8 | -5.4 | 1.5 | 1.4 | -3.9 | 8.1 | -2.0 | -5.8 | -1.3 |
| 2002 | 0.5 | -1.0 | -2.5 | -1.2 | -0.3 | 0.7 | 4.2 | -2.0 | -0.2 | 5.5 | 0.0 | -0.3 |
| 2003 | -2.5 | 1.9 | 0.8 | -2.2 | -6.6 | -3.5 | -4.2 | -4.9 | 0.7 | -0.1 | 1.5 | 1.5 |
| 2004 | -5.7 | -1.8 | -2.2 | 3.1 | 1.2 | -3.0 | 2.9 | 0.0 | -0.5 | 0.3 | -2.3 | -3.1 |
| 2005 | -2.5 | 1.2 | 0.2 | 3.7 | -2.3 | -0.6 | 0.1 | -1.6 | 0.8 | 0.1 | -6.0 | -2.0 |
| 2006 | -1.8 | -2.5 | -1.3 | 0.7 | 0.9 | 0.6 | 2.3 | -3.0 | -3.2 | -0.9 | -4.2 | -1.9 |
| 2007 | 0.4 | -0.4 | -3.3 | 0.2 | 1.1 | 4.6 | -2.1 | -0.6 | 5.0 | -1.8 | 3.6 | 1.2 |
| 2008 | -1.7 | -1.8 | -2.6 | 5.7 | 0.2 | 1.9 | -0.6 | -1.8 | 2.9 | 9.6 | 1.0 | -1.0 |
| 2009 | -4.7 | -4.5 | -2.9 | -10.0 | 3.5 | -1.7 | 0.6 | -3.7 | 0.9 | 1.1 | 2.5 | -0.1 |
| 2010 | -3.4 | 2.0 | -2.7 | -4.2 | 0.5 | -2.4 | 0.7 | 0.6 | -1.0 | -0.7 | -0.4 | -2.2 |
| 2011 | 0.1 | 0.9 | -1.2 | -0.9 | -1.7 | 0.3 | 1.0 | 1.6 | 1.8 | 1.4 | 0.9 | 3.3 |
| 2012 | -4.6 | -3.0 | -2.5 | 0.5 | 0.3 | 1.2 | -0.7 | -1.1 | -2.3 | -1.0 | 0.6 | -2.3 |
| 2013 | 1.1 | -3.8 | -0.8 | 0.1 | -0.5 | -1.7 | -1.3 | -0.4 | -2.3 | 0.3 | -1.1 | -1.5 |
| 2014 | -1.9 | -2.1 | -0.4 | 5.6 | -0.3 | 0.3 | 1.2 | -1.2 | 0.3 | -1.9 | 0.4 | -3.8 |
| 2015 | 1.4 | -3.0 | -1.4 | 0.5 | 0.4 | -7.0 | 1.9 | -3.5 | -0.5 | 2.3 | -1.9 | -1.8 |
| 2016 | 2.9 | -0.5 | -0.7 | 1.8 | -2.5 | 9.7 | -2.8 | -1.8 | 1.0 | 2.6 | -2.5 | 2.3 |
| 2017 | -1.0 | -1.1 | -0.3 | -5.0 | 2.6 | 0.4 | -1.5 | 0.7 | | | | |

The proportion of years that the FTSE 100 has outperformed the FTSE 250 for each month since 1986 is shown in the following chart.

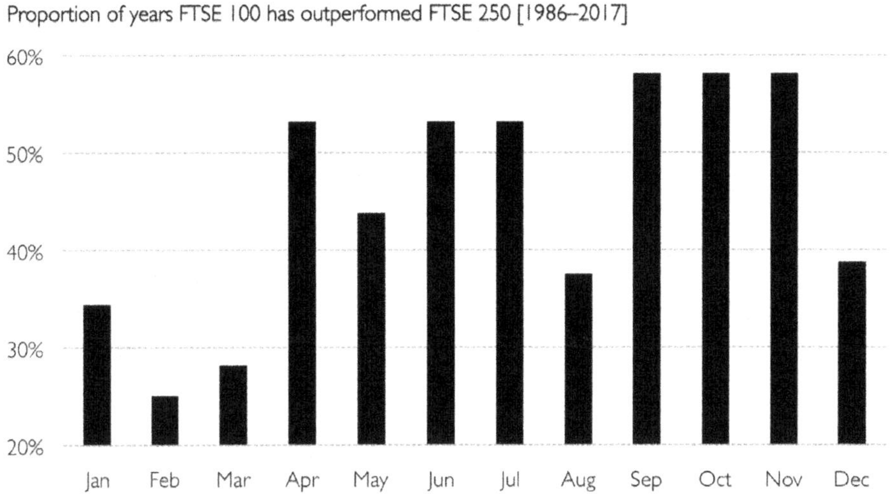


1. The FTSE 250 tends to outperform the FTSE 100 in the first three months of the year and in August and December. For example, as can be seen in the above table, the mid-cap index has outperformed the large-cap index in every March since 2006.

2. The FTSE 100 is strong relative to the FTSE 250 in September and October (and, in recent years, April – although not 2017).

3. In recent years (since 2000) the above characteristics have if anything been even stronger, suggesting a certain degree of persistency.

*See also:* The FTSE 100/250 monthly switching strategy.

# FTSE 250/FTSE 100 RATIO

The following chart shows the ratio of the FTSE 250 index divided by the FTSE 100 index since 1986. For example, on 31 Aug 2017 the close for the FTSE 250 was 19,803 and for the FTSE 100 it was 7430; dividing the former by the latter gives a ratio value of 2.7 (the last value plotted on the chart).

As can be seen, the ratio fluctuated in a sideways range from 1986 to 1999. And then the great outperformance of the FTSE 250 over the FTSE 100 began (on 18 Jan 1999 to be precise).

Over the following 17 years to today, while the FTSE 100 increased 21%, the FTSE 250 gained 304%.

The ratio mean since 1986 is 1.5 – although there is no evidence yet to suppose that this ratio will be mean-reverting.

The following chart zooms in to show the FTSE 250/100 ratio for the more recent period since 2014.

# MONTHLY SEASONALITY OF FTSE 100

A table of all the monthly returns from 1984 for the FTSE 100 index can be found elsewhere in the Statistics section.

### Mean returns

The following chart shows the average returns for each month for the index since 1980.

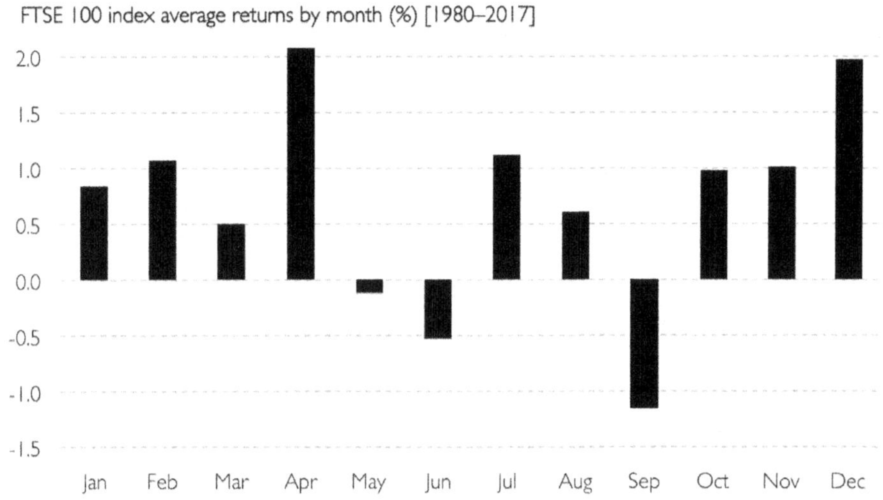


A better way of viewing the mean returns is to add error bars to the chart. So, the following chart displays the mean returns by month (as above, but this time as the short horizontal bars) and adds 1 standard deviation variation range bars. These error bars give an idea of how much the actual returns each year have varied around the mean.

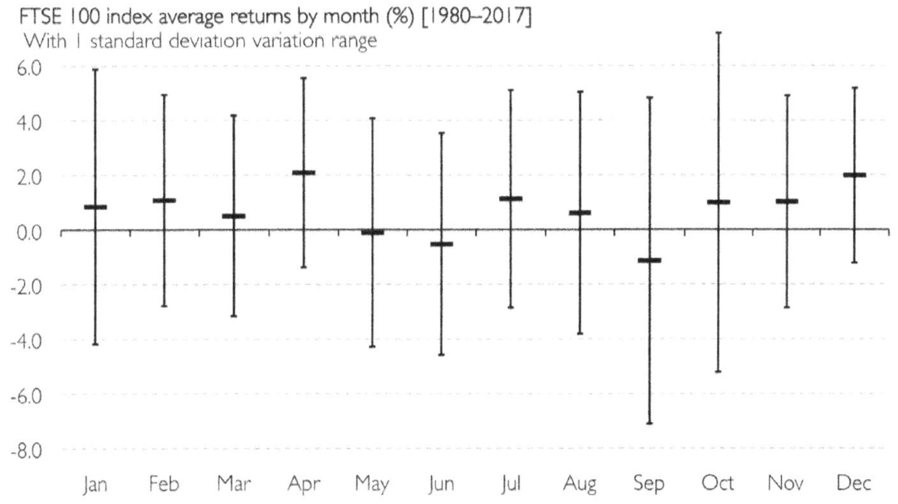

For example, from the chart we can see that although October has a positive mean, the standard variation is high, which means that the actual October returns since 1980 have varied widely around the mean, and many were actually negative.

## Positive returns

The following chart plots the proportion of years that each respective month had positive returns. For example, in the 38 years since 1980, the FTSE 100 had positive returns in January in 22 (58%) of those years (and so 58% is the value plotted for January).

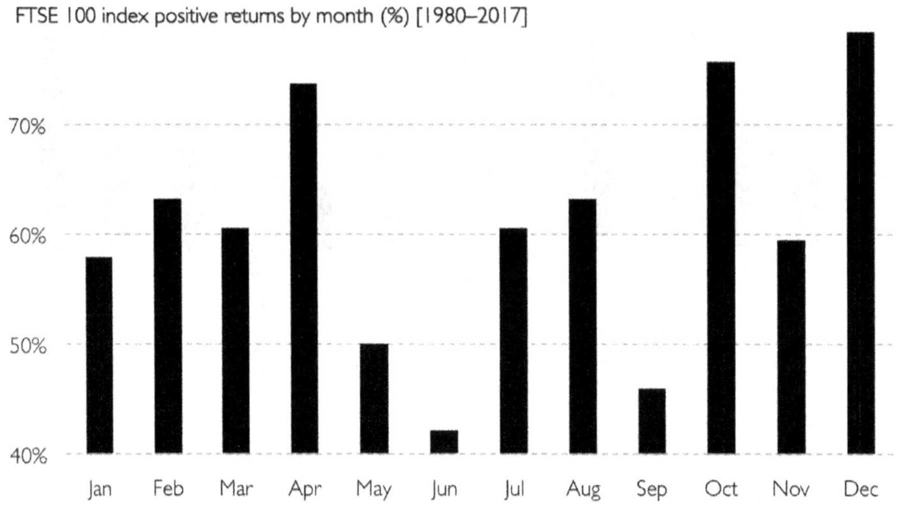


From these tables we can say that since 1980 the strong months for the FTSE 100 have been: April, October and December, and the weak months have been May, June and September.

There is some persistency in these observations as the same profile of behaviour can be seen for the recent period 2000–16 (the only difference being that January joined the list of weak months in the recent period).

## Cumulative performance by month

The following chart plots the cumulative returns of the FTSE 100 for each of the 12 months from 1980. For example, the January line plots the returns a portfolio would see if it only invested in the FTSE 100 in January each year.

FTSE 100 index cumulative returns by month [1980–2017]

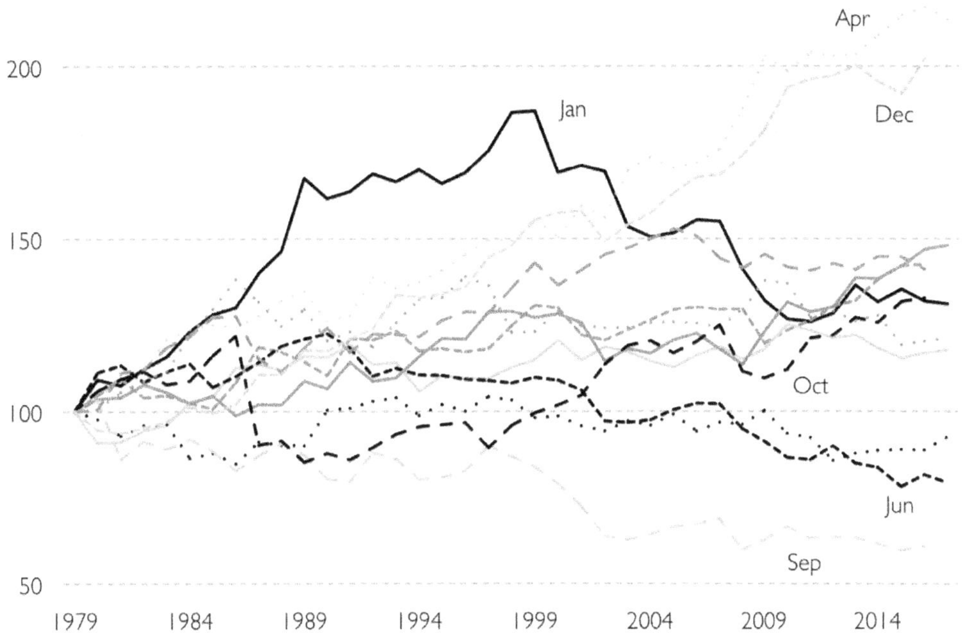


The two consistently strong months are April and December, while it can be seen that September has been consistently a poor performer since 1980. Up till year 2000 the strongest month had been January, but since then it has a suffered a steady decline in performance. Conversely, since 1989 October has been one of the stronger months.

See also: Statistics/Monthly performance of FTSE 100.

# SELL IN MAY

One of the most famous stock market adages is, "sell in May and go away, don't come back till St Leger Day". The St Leger is the last big event of the UK horse-racing calendar; it usually takes place in mid-September.

An associated anomaly (most likely originating in the US) is the Halloween Effect, which holds that stocks see the bulk of their gains in the six-month period from 31 October to 1 May.

At some point it seems the "sell in May" saying and the Halloween Effect merged to become one, such that today the sell in May adage is usually taken to mean that the summer period of (relatively) poor returns ends on 31 October. And, therefore, that the six-month period May–October is weak relative to the rest of the year (i.e. November–April).

To test this, we will define two periods of the year:

1. *winter period*: 1 November–30 April
2. *summer period*: 1 May–31 October

(We will call them "winter" and "summer" for the sake of giving them names.)

## Absolute performance

Let's look first at the historic record of market returns in the winter period.

The following chart plots the returns for the FTSE All-Share index for the period November–April for each year since 1982. For example, from 31 October 1981 to 30 April 1982, the FTSE All-Share rose 14.6%, and this is the first bar in the chart below.

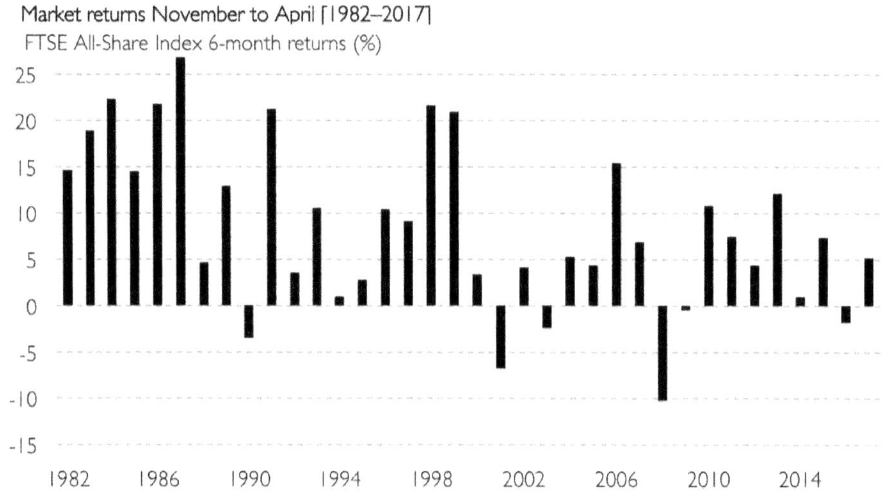


Sell in May (and the Halloween Effect) holds that the market is relatively strong November–April. The chart above would certainly appear to support this. Since 1982, the market has seen negative returns in the winter period in only six years. And the average return for the winter period since 1982 has been 8.3%.

*Now, what about the summer periods?*

The following chart plots the returns for the FTSE All-Share for the period May–October for each year since 1982. For example, from 30 April 1982 to 31 October 1982 the FTSE All-Share rose 12.7%, and this is the first bar in the chart below.

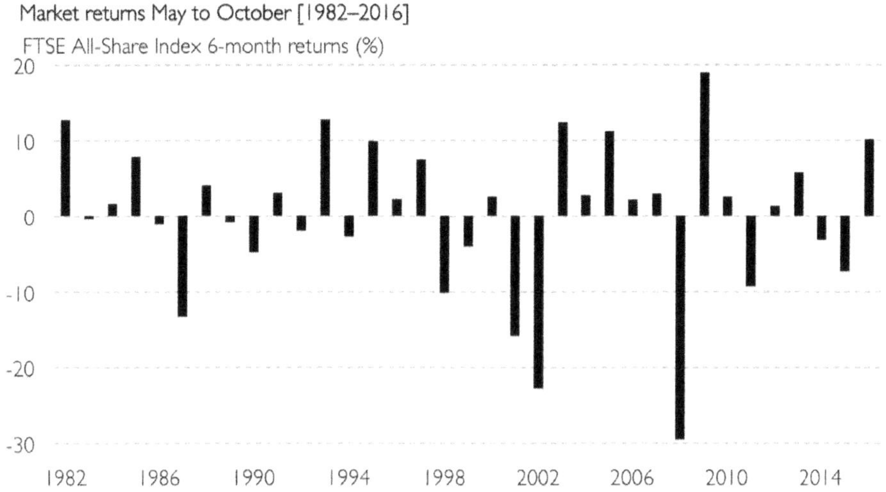


At a quick glance, the chart doesn't suggest that returns over the summer period are generally weak. In fact, in the 35 years since 1982 the market has seen positive returns in the summer period in 20 years (i.e. in significantly over half of the years). The average return since 1982 is admittedly negative (−0.1%), but that is not large, and that average return is significantly negatively affected by a few years with abnormal negative returns (i.e. 1987, 2002 and 2008 – years that might be considered outliers).

However, we are interested in relative performance here and not absolute, so let's now compare directly the performance of the winter and summer periods.

## Relative performance

The following chart compares the performance from 1982 of the FTSE All-Share for the two periods; each bar represents the outperformance of the winter period over the following summer period. For example, from 1 November 2015 to 30 April 2016 the index return was −1.8%, while during the following period 1 May 2016 to 31 October 2016 the index return was 10.1%. The outperformance of the winter over the summer period was therefore −11.9 (−1.8 − 10.1) percentage points, and that is the figure plotted on the chart for 2016 (the final bar in the chart).

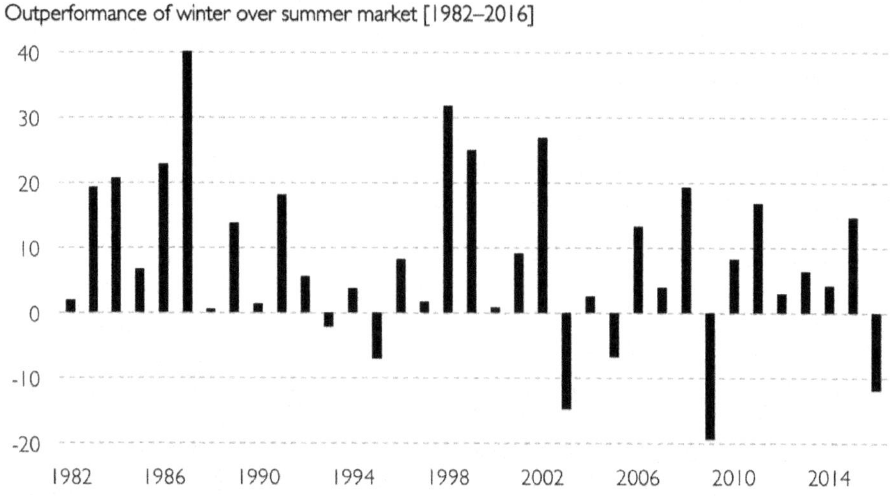


The chart clearly shows the tendency of the market to perform better in the winter period than in the corresponding summer period.

To quantify this outperformance:

- in the 35 years since 1982, the winter period has outperformed the summer period 29 times (83%)
- the average annual outperformance since 1982 has been 8.2 percentage points!

The behaviour is extraordinary and should not exist in a modern, efficient(ish) market. But exist it does.

## The average year

Another way of visualising the Sell in May effect is to look at the following chart.

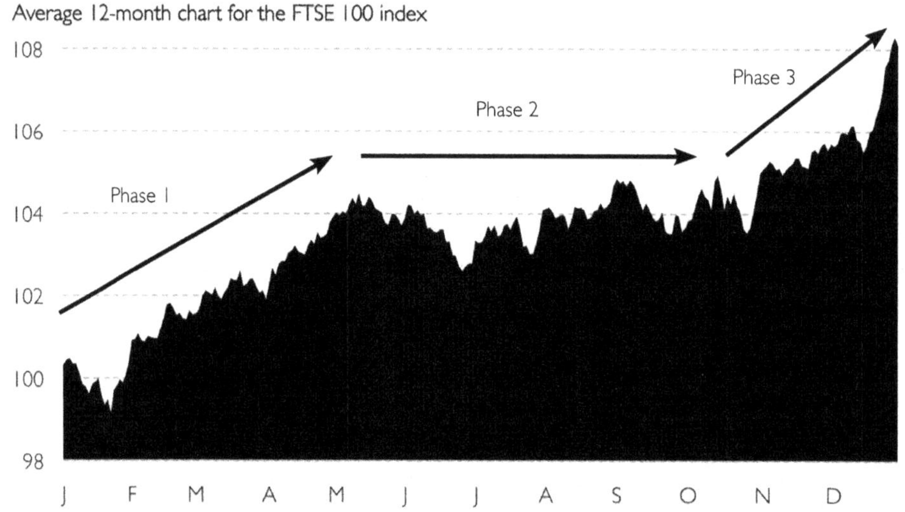

The chart is created by calculating the average daily return of the FTSE 100 for each calendar day since 1984, and then plotting these returns as a cumulative index for the year. In effect, the chart displays the average annual trend of the market.

The chart illustrates fairly clearly the different nature of the two six-month periods:

- 1 May–31 October (*summer period*): when the six-month return tends to be flat, and
- 1 November–30 April (*winter period*): when the market tends to rise.

Over the whole six-month summer period the market doesn't necessarily fall, but it does tend to be flat, and certainly the returns are less than in the winter period.

However, it can be seen in the chart that the market is absolutely weak for the two-month period May to June.

So, according to this chart (based on data since 1984), if you do sell in May, one time for coming back into the market would be the end of June, instead of September (St Leger Day) or the end of October (Halloween Effect).

### A worldwide anomaly...

It appears that the Sell in May anomaly is not unique to the UK. An academic paper[1] crunched the numbers for 108 stock markets worldwide to see how widespread the Sell in May (or Halloween) Effect might be.

The paper found evidence for the effect in 81 out 108 countries, and of it being statistically significantly in 35 countries. The strongest effects were found among Western European countries for the past 50 years. They also found that the effect had been strengthening in recent years.

The following chart from the paper shows average returns for November–April periods (back row) compared to average returns for May–October periods for developed markets.

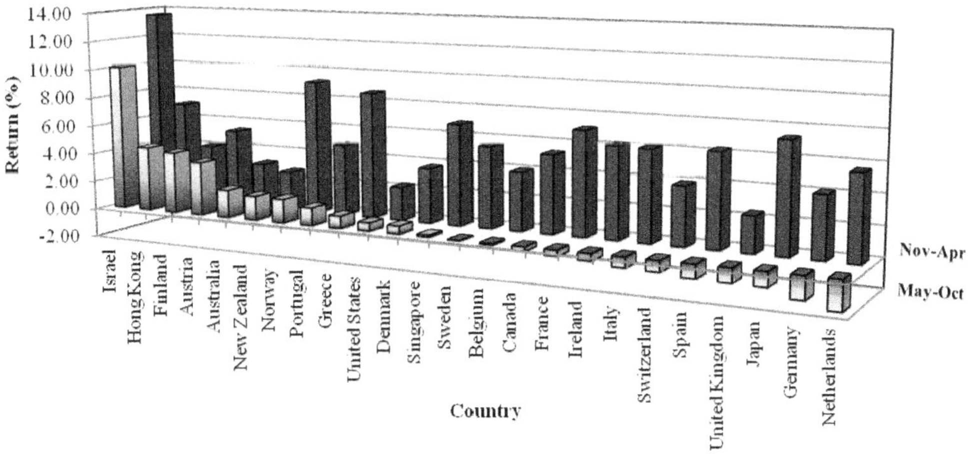


1. B. Jacobsen and Cherry Yi Zhang, 'Are Monthly Seasonals Real? A Three Century Perspective', 15 February 2012.

## ...and a persistent anomaly

Anomalies are not uncommon in financial markets, but they tend not to persist for long – as soon as they are known about they are usually arbitraged out of existence (to the extent that transaction costs allow). But this Sell in May effect is unusual – pretty much unique – due to how long it has been a feature of the market.

The following chart is similar to that above ('Outperformance of winter over summer market [1982–2016]), except it extends the time period back to 1922.

Outperformance of winter over summer portfolio [1922–2016]

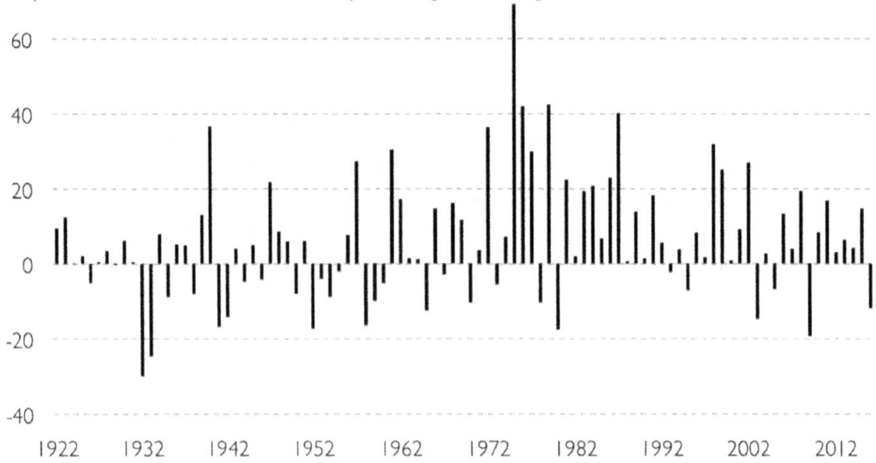


We can see from this chart that during the first half of the 20th century the market performance during the two periods was fairly equally balanced. But the behaviour changed significantly around the beginning of the 1970s.

It may be that the above study is woefully short-termist in its approach. The above cited academic paper found evidence of the Sell in May Effect starting from 1694 in the UK. The first mention of the market adage "Sell in May" the authors of the paper found was in the *Financial Times* of 10 May 1935:

> A shrewd North Country correspondent who likes a stock exchange flutter now and again writes me that he and his friends are at present drawing in their horns on the strength of the old adage "Sell in May and go away."

## Why does the Sell in May anomaly exist?

Good question! No one knows for sure.

One theory attributes the anomaly to seasonal affective disorder (SAD). This argues that as nights lengthen in the autumn investors become more risk averse, which drives prices down such that by the end of October prices are artificially depressed and ready to bounce back reverting to their 'normal' levels. The opposite happens in the spring: as days lengthen investors become less risk averse, which drives prices up, such that by the end of April prices are artificially high and ready to correct back to their normal levels.

It's an interesting hypothesis. Although if it was true, one might expect the same to apply in the antipodes (e.g. Australia) but with a timescale shifted by six-months – but this is not the case.

So, for the moment, we must observe this anomaly without fully understanding it.

# MONTHLY SEASONALITY WORLDWIDE

Elsewhere in this *Almanac*, the results are given of analysis for the monthly seasonality of the FTSE 100 index. To summarise:

- the three **strongest** months in the year were found to be: April, October, December, and
- the three **weakest** months in the year were: May, June, September.

Such seasonality behaviour is not unique to the UK. Most other stock markets around the world display similar behavior, as found in an academic paper[1] published in June 2013.

The special feature of this latest study on the topic is its scope: it analyses data from 70 of the 78 operational stock markets in the world.

The paper found that across all 70 markets, on average:

- the three **strongest** months were: January, April, December, and
- the three **weakest** months were: August, September, October.

The paper doesn't make it clear, but we assume that the averages were not market-cap weighted.

The study also split the results for developed and emerging markets (shown in the following two charts).

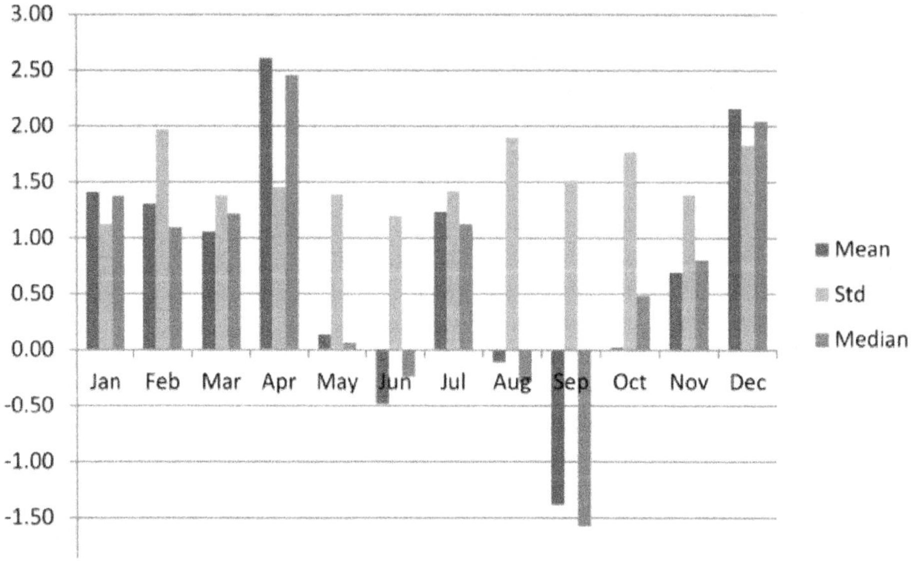


**Mean, median and standard deviation of monthly return for each month across 70 countries**

*Source: Vichet Sum*

1. V. Sum, 'Stock Market Performance: High and Low Months' (5 June 2013).

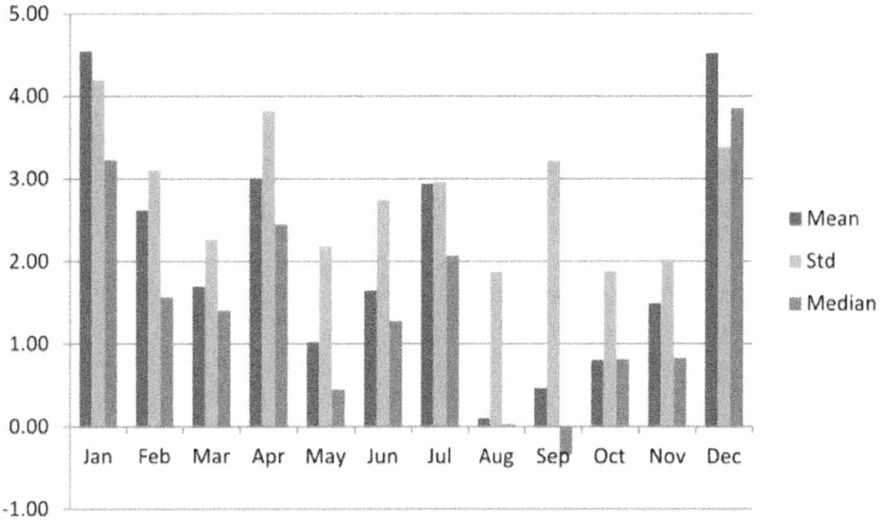


**Mean, median and standard deviation of monthly return for each month across emerging stock markets**

*Source: Vichet Sum*

The main difference between the two sets of markets is that while April was the strongest month in developed markets, it was January and December that were the strongest months for the emerging markets. In addition, the developed markets were significantly weak in June and September, which was not the case in emerging markets.

# SEASONALITY OF GBPUSD

*Does the GB pound/US dollar exchange rate exhibit a monthly seasonality in value?*

Fluctuations of the sterling currency are very important to equity investors. Over half of all aggregate revenues of FTSE 100 companies originate outside of the UK, and any overseas investors in the UK equity market, and UK investors in international markets, will be affected by the sterling exchange rate.

Of course, for a while after World War II nobody needed to worry about currency fluctuations because currencies were tied to the US dollar under the Bretton Woods system. Exchange controls were in place and some older readers may remember being restricted to taking no more than £50 out of the UK. But on 15 August 1971 President Nixon announced that the US was ending the convertibility of the US dollar to gold and this led to the end of the Bretton Woods system. Fixed-rate currencies, such as sterling, became free-floating.

## Performance since the end of Bretton Woods

Let's first take a quick look at how GBPUSD (GB pound v US dollar) has performed since currencies became free floating.

The following chart plots the GBPUSD rate since it became free-floating in 1971.

GB pound/US dollar (GBPUSD) rate [1971–2017]

In just over a decade following 1971 sterling fell against the dollar (almost reaching parity in February 1985). Afterwards it traded sideways in the approximate range 1.4–2.0 for almost 30 years. Following the EU referendum in the UK in June 2016 the rate fell out of this established range and at the time of writing is trading at 1.34.

*Now, onto the seasonality analysis.*

## Monthly seasonality

The following charts show the average monthly returns of GBPUSD since 1971. For example, on average GBPUSD has fallen 0.68% in January.

The following chart shows the proportion of years that the respective month returns were positive. For example, GBPUSD has risen in January in 44% of years since 1971.

From the charts we can observe:

- Weak months for GBPUSD have been: January, May, August and November
- Strong months for GBPUSD have been: April, July and December.

To check the persistency of these results, the following chart plots the average monthly returns of GBPUSD since 2000.

Broadly, the previous observations are still valid here. Namely, the weak months have been January, May, August and November, while the strong months have been April and July, but December has not been strong since 2000.

Given the general downward trend of GBPUSD since 1971 it is not unusual perhaps to find a number of months with high negative average monthly returns. More worthy of note, therefore, are the months where GBPUSD is actually strong (against the trend), i.e. April and July. The strength of GBPUSD in April is possibly the most significant result found here.

### However...

The following chart is similar to the first seasonality chart above: it plots the average monthly returns of GBPUSD since 1971. However, this time it also adds 1 standard deviation error bars (and the mean return is indicated with a short horizontal line instead of a vertical bar).

The error bars indicate the range of actual month returns since 1971, and how close they cluster round the calculated average return. The greater the range, the wider the dispersion of actual month returns were from the calculated average. In other words, if one believes that future price behaviour will be similar to the past, the error bars give a guide to how confident one can be that future values will be close to the average.

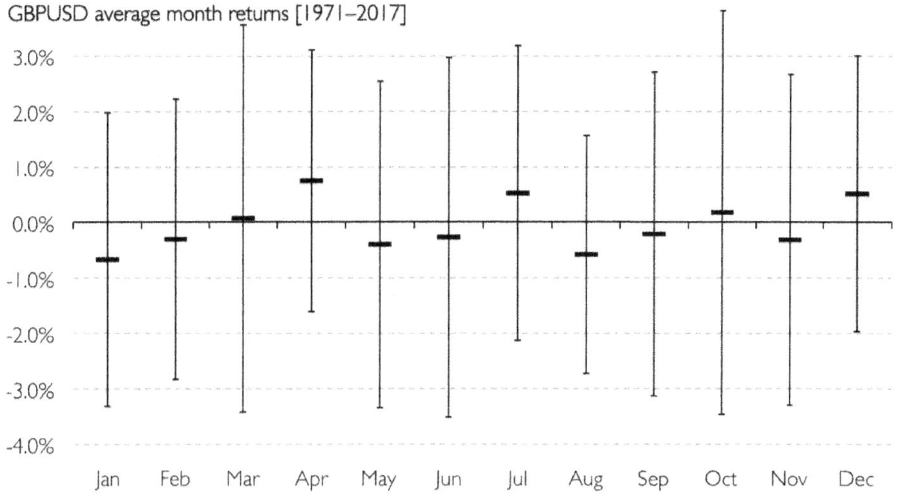


In this case, the error bars (1 standard deviation) are very large, meaning the past variation of month returns has been high. The month that has seen the greatest volatility of month returns has been March, and the month with the lowest volatility has been August.

# FTSE 100 INDEX QUARTERLY REVIEWS

To keep the FTSE 100 index in accordance with its purpose the constituents of the index are periodically reviewed. The reviews take place and are announced on the Wednesday before the first Friday of the month in March, June, September and December.

If any changes are to be made (i.e. companies ejected or introduced) these are announced sometime after the market has closed on the day of the review.

**The review dates for 2018 are: 28 February, 30 May, 5 September and 5 December.**

Changes to the index following a review are implemented on the third Friday of the month.

The accompanying table lists the companies entering and exiting the FTSE 100 in the last few years as a result of the FTSE quarterly reviews.

| Date | Company added | TIDM | Company ejected | TIDM |
|---|---|---|---|---|
| 09 Sep 09 | Segro | SGRO | Foreign & Col Inv Trust | FRCL |
| 09 Sep 09 | Whitbread | WTB | Pennon Group | PNN |
| 09 Dec 09 | Aggreko | AGK | Rentokil Initial | RTO |
| 10 Mar 10 | Investec | INVP | Resolution | RSL |
| 09 Jun 10 | African Barrick Gold | ABG | London Stock Exchange Group | LSE |
| 09 Jun 10 | Essar Energy | ESSR | Thomas Cook Group | TCG |
| 08 Sep 10 | Resolution | RSL | Cable and Wireless Worldwide | CWC |
| 08 Sep 10 | Tomkins | | Home Retail Group | HOME |
| 08 Sep 10 | Weir Group | WEIR | Segro | SGRO |
| 08 Dec 10 | IMI | IMI | Cobham | COB |
| 09 Mar 11 | Wood Group (John) | WG. | Bunzl | BNZL |
| 09 Mar 11 | ITV | ITV | Alliance Trust | ATST |
| 09 Mar 11 | Hargreaves Lansdown | HL. | African Barrick Gold | ABG |
| 25 May 11 | Glencore | GLEN | Invensys | ISYS |
| 08 Jun 11 | Tate & Lyle | TATE | TUI Travel | TT. |
| 07 Sep 11 | Ashmore Group | ASHM | Wood Group (John) | WG. |
| 07 Sep 11 | Bunzl | BNZL | 3i Group | III |
| 07 Dec 11 | CRH | CRH | Inmarsat | ISAT |
| 07 Dec 11 | Evraz | EVR | Investec | INVP |
| 07 Dec 11 | Polymetal International | POLY | Lonmin | LMI |
| 07 Mar 12 | Croda International | CRDA | Cairn Energy | CNE |
| 07 Mar 12 | Aberdeen AM | AND | Essar Energy | ESSR |
| 06 Jun 12 | Babcock International | BAB | Man Group | EMG |
| 29 Jun 12 | Pennon Group | PNN | International Power | |
| 12 Sep 12 | Melrose | MRO | ICAP | IAP |

| Date | Company added | TIDM | Company ejected | TIDM |
|---|---|---|---|---|
| 12 Sep 12 | Wood Group (John) | WG. | Ashmore Group | ASHM |
| 12 Dec 12 | TUI Travel | TT. | Pennon Group | PNN |
| 06 Mar 13 | Easyjet | EZJ | Intu Properties | INTU |
| 06 Mar 13 | London Stock Exchange | LSE | Kazakhmys | KAZ |
| 11 Sep 13 | Coca-Cola HBC AG | CCH | Wood Group (John) | WG. |
| 11 Sep 13 | Sports Direct | SPD | Eurasian Natural Resources | ENRC |
| 11 Sep 13 | Mondi | MNDI | Serco Group | SRP |
| 11 Dec 13 | Royal Mail Group | RMG | Croda International | CRDA |
| 11 Dec 13 | Ashtead Group | AHT | Vedanta Resources | VED |
| 05 Mar 14 | Barratt Developments | BDEV | Amec | AMEC |
| 05 Mar 14 | St. James's Place | STJ | Tate & Lyle | TATE |
| 04 Jun 14 | 3i Group | III | Melrose | MRO |
| 04 Jun 14 | Intu Properties | INTU | William Hill | WMH |
| 03 Sep 14 | Direct Line Insurance | DLG | Barratt Developments | BDEV |
| 03 Sep 14 | Dixons Carphone | DC. | Rexam | REX |
| 03 Dec 14 | Barratt Developments | BDEV | IMI | IMI |
| 03 Dec 14 | Taylor Wimpey | TW. | Petrofac | PFC |
| 04 Mar 15 | Hikma Pharmaceuticals | HIK | Tullow Oil | TLW |
| 03 Jun 15 | Inmarsat | ISAT | Aggreko | AGK |
| 02 Sep 15 | Berkeley Group | BKG | Weir Group | WEIR |
| 02 Dec 15 | Worldpay Group | WPG | G4S | GFS |
| 02 Dec 15 | Provident Financial | PFG | Morrison (Wm) Supermarkets | MRW |
| 02 Dec 15 | DCC | DCC | Meggitt | MGGT |
| 02 Mar 16 | Paddy Power Betfair | PPB | Smiths Group | SMIN |
| 02 Mar 16 | Mediclinic International | MDC | Hikma Pharmaceuticals | HIKN |
| 02 Mar 16 | Morrison (Wm) | MGGT | Aberdeen Asset Management | AND |
| 02 Mar 16 | Informa | INF | Sports Direct International | SPD |
| 01 Jun 16 | Hikma Pharmaceuticals | HIK | Inmarsat | ISAT |
| 31 Aug 16 | Polymetal International | POLY | Berkeley Group Holdings | BKG |
| 30 Nov 16 | ConvaTec Group | CTEC | Polymetal International | POLY |
| 30 Nov 16 | Smurfit Kappa | SKG | Travis Perkins | TPK |
| 01 Mar 17 | Scottish Mortgage IT | SMT | Capita | CPI |
| 01 Mar 17 | Rentokil Initial | RTO | Dixons Carphone | DC. |
| 31 May 17 | G4S | GFS | Hikma Pharmaceuticals | HIK |
| 31 May 17 | Segro | SGRO | Intu Properties | INTU |
| 30 Aug 17 | NMC Health | NMC | Royal Mail | RMG |
| 30 Aug 17 | Berkeley Group | BKG | Provident Financial | PFG |

# FTSE INDEX REVIEWS – ACADEMIC RESEARCH

Traders are interested in changes to equity indices due to the potential arbitrage profits; but academics have a wider interest because for them changes to indices act as something like a laboratory for testing theories of stock market efficiency and behavioural finance. Briefly, when a stock joins (or leaves) an index, nothing changes to the company itself and so (in an efficient market) there should be no change to the share price. Below is a brief overview of the major academic papers studying the effects of the FTSE quarterly reviews.

## Comovement

Kougoulis and Coakley (2004)[1] found that shares joining the FTSE 100 experienced an increase in comovement (price movement correlation with other shares); shares leaving the index experienced the opposite effect. Mase (2008)[2] supported the previous findings and in addition found that increases in comovement had become larger in recent years, and that the overall increase in comovement was due to new additions to the index rather than previous FTSE 100 constituents rejoining the index.

## Price pressures

This is a favourite of academics: if a share price moves without new information is the move temporary (price pressure hypothesis) or permanent (imperfect substitutes hypothesis)? Mazouz and Saadouni (2007)[3] found strong evidence for the price pressure hypothesis: prices increased (decreased) gradually starting before the index change announcement date of inclusion (exclusion) and then reversed completely in less than two weeks after the index change date. The existence of the temporary price changes (price pressure hypothesis) was also found by Opong and Antonios Siganos (2013)[4] and Biktimirov and Li (2014)[5]. Interestingly, Mase (2007)[6] comments that the temporary prices changes to shares joining/leaving the FTSE 100 is in contrast to the case for S&P 500 changes, where permanent price changes have been found.

## Information efficiency

Daya, Mazouz and Freeman (2012)[7] (and other papers) found that informational efficiency improved for stocks added to the FTSE 100, but did not diminish after deletion.

1. P. Kougoulis and J. Coakley, 'Comovement and Changes to the FTSE 100 Index', *EFMA 2004 Basel Meetings Paper* (2004).
2. B. Mase, 'Comovement in the FTSE 100 Index', *Applied Financial Economics Letters* 4(1) (2008).
3. K. Mazouz and B. Saadouni, 'The price effects of FTSE 100 index revision: what drives the long-term abnormal return reversal?', *Applied Financial Economics* 17(6) (2007).
4. K. Opong and A. Siganos, 'Compositional changes in the FTSE 100 index from the standpoint of an arbitrageur', *Journal of Asset Management* 14 (2013).
5. E. Biktimirov and B. Li, 'Asymmetric stock price and liquidity responses to changes in the FTSE SmallCap index', *Review of Quantitative Finance and Accounting* (2014).
6. B. Mase, 'The Impact of Changes in the FTSE 100 Index', *Financial Review* 42(3) (2007).
7. W. Daya, K. Mazouz and M. Freeman, 'Information efficiency changes following FTSE 100 index revisions', *Journal of International Financial Markets, Institutions and Money* 22(4) (2012).

## Price changes

Gregoriou and Ioannidis (2006)[1] found that price and trading volumes of newly listed firms increased. That confirms what we already knew or suspected. But, interestingly, they (and other papers here) attribute the cause to information efficiency: stocks with more available information increase investor awareness. However, Mase (2007) does say that investor awareness and monitoring due to index membership do not explain the price effects. But not mentioned here is the influence of index funds.

## Anticipatory trading

Fernandes and Mergulhao (2011)[2] found that a trading strategy based on addition/deletion probability estimates gave an average daily excess return of 11 basis points over the FTSE 100. Opong and Siganos (2013)[3] found "significant net profitability" from an investment strategy based on firms on the FTSE reserved list. And a strategy based on the FTSE 100 quarterly revisions was profitable if CFDs were used and traders could deal within the bid/ask spread.

1. A. Gregoriou and C. Ioannidis, 'Information costs and liquidity effects from changes in the FTSE 100 list', *The European Journal of Finance* 12(4) (2006).
2. M. Fernandes and J. Mergulhao, 'Anticipatory Effects in the FTSE 100 Index Revisions', *Midwest Finance Association*, Annual Meetings Paper (2011).
3. K. Opong and A. Siganos, 'Compositional changes in the FTSE 100 index from the standpoint of an arbitrageur', *Journal of Asset Management* 14 (2013).

# AN AVERAGE YEAR

*What does an average year for the FTSE 100 index look like?*

## Average month chart

Let's say we want to plot a chart of the FTSE 100 for its average day-by-day performance in January. How could we do that? One way would be to calculate the daily mean returns for each day in January over a specific period (in this case from 1984).

For example, if we take the index returns on the first trading of January for the 32 years since 1985, we can calculate the average return to be 0.30%. With this we can say that the FTSE 100 increased by an average of 0.30% on the first trading day of January over the period 1985–2017. We can repeat this process for the second trading day of January, and the third, etc., until we have a set of average returns for all the trading days of January.

With this set of returns we can plot an average daily index for the market in January (we will set the index to start at 100). For example, the average return for the market on the first trading day is 0.30%, and so the average index would close at 100.30 on the first trading day of January.

## Average year chart

By concatenating the average index data for each month, we can create an average index chart for the whole year. This is shown in the following chart.

Average 12-month chart for the FTSE 100 index

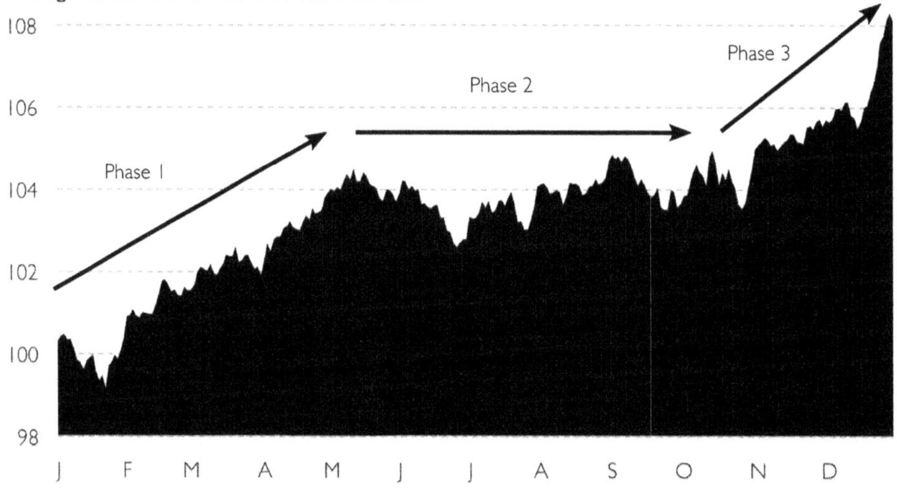


In the above chart we can see that, on average, the year appears to have three phases:

1. **Phase 1**: after a weak three weeks, the market is strong until May, then
2. **Phase 2**: from May to October the market is fairly flat, and then
3. **Phase 3**: it rises strongly in the final two months of the year.

This annual market behaviour profile concurs with what we already knew about the market, but it is illustrated simply and efficiently in this one chart.

## Annual volatility chart

Beyond simple mean returns, it is also useful to look at how volatility changes throughout the year.

The following chart shows the (five-day moving average of the) standard deviation of the daily returns throughout the year for the FTSE 100 from 1984–2017. In plain English: the chart plots the range of daily fluctuations of the FTSE 100 for each trading day throughout the year.

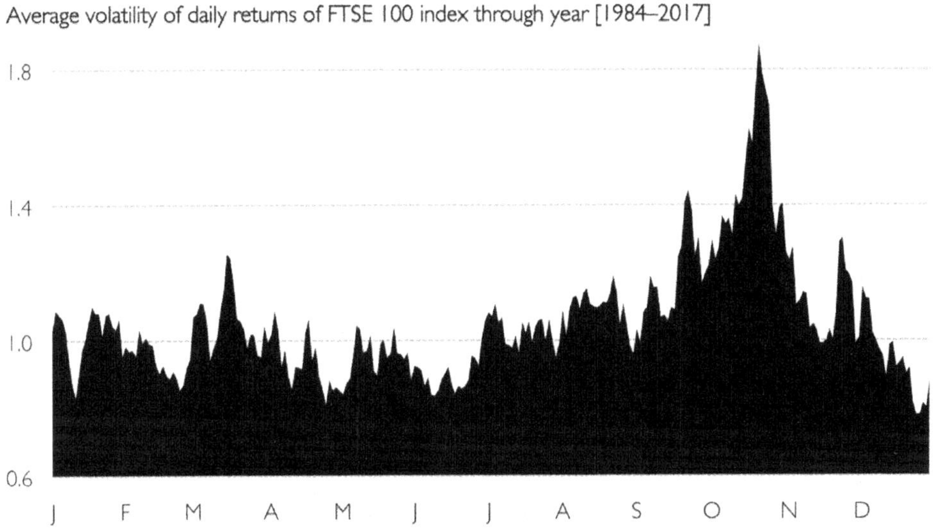


It can be seen that the volatility of daily returns fluctuates within a fairly narrow band for the first eight months of the year; it then starts to increase in September and peaks in October before trailing off for the remainder of the year. So, according to this study of daily returns throughout the year, October has been the most volatile month since 1984.

# FTSE ALL-SHARE INDEX ANNUAL RETURNS

The following chart plots the annual returns of the FTSE All-Share index since 1900. [NB. The values for 1973 and 1974 were respectively −55% and 136%, and have been truncated in the chart to make the scale more useful.]

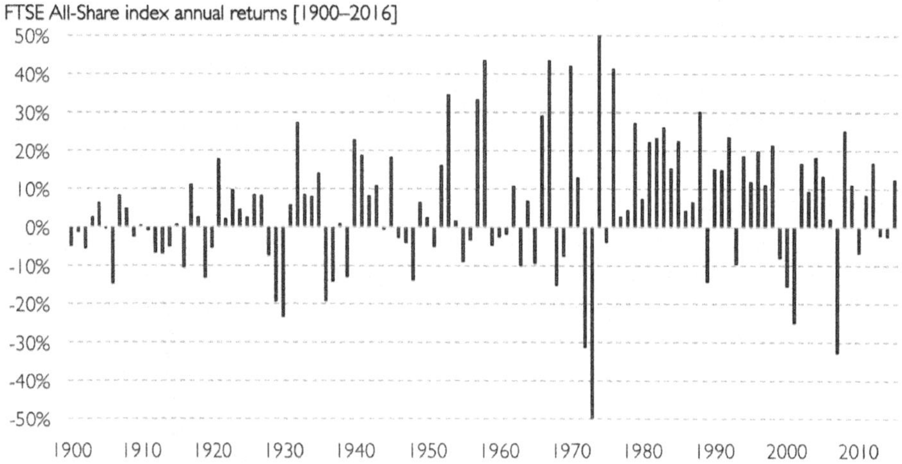


The market fell in two consecutive years in 2014 and 2015. As can be seen from the chart, this is a fairly rare occurrence. The previous time the market fell in two successive years was during the aftermath of the internet bubble, and before that in 1972–73.

The following chart plots the frequency distribution of the annual returns of the FTSE All-Share since 1900. For example, the annual return for the index has been in the range 5%–10% for 15 years since 1900.

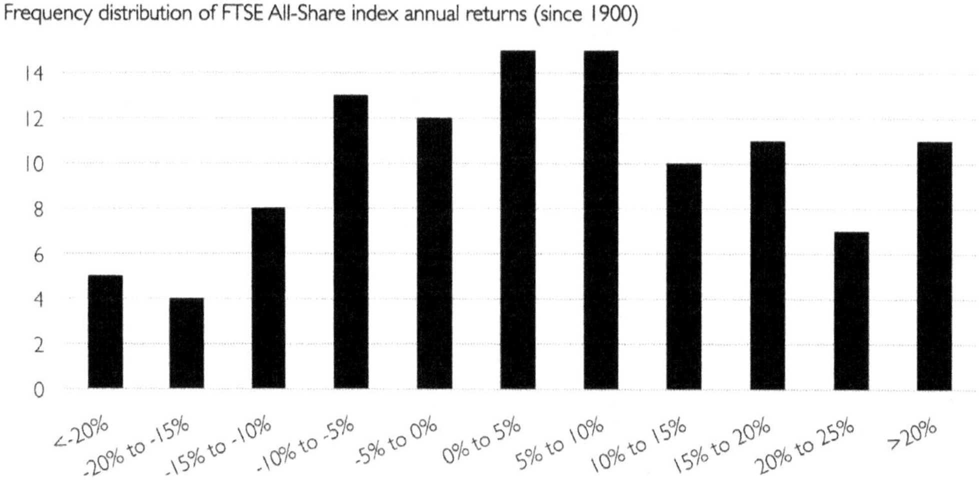


The annual returns can be seen to have roughly a normal distribution (i.e. bell-shaped curve), although with a higher frequency of both very large positive returns and very large negative returns than would be expected in a normal distribution.

# CHINESE CALENDAR AND THE STOCK MARKET

When we look at the annual performance of the stock market we naturally take our start and end points as 1 January and 31 December. For example, a long-term chart of an index will normally plot the index values on 31 December for each year.

But using different start and end points may be interesting. While the overall performance of the market will obviously not change, the path to the final point may show up differently, and thus possibly reveal a pattern of behaviour not previously noticed.

Let's take a look at a different calendar system to that in the west: the Chinese year.

The start of the Chinese year moves around (on the Western calendar) from year to year, but always falls between 21 January and 21 February. The calculation of the actual date of the Chinese New Year is sinologically complex. For example, here is one of the rules:

> Rule 5: In a leap suì, the first month that does not contain a zhongqì is the leap month, rùnyuè. The leap month takes the same number as the previous month.

That quote comes from a 52-page academic paper on 'The Mathematics of the Chinese Calendar'.[1]

However, we shall skip lightly over such details and focus on a key aspect of the Chinese calendar, which is the sexagenary cycle. This is a combination of ten heavenly stems and the 12 earthly branches. The branches are often associated with the sequence of 12 animals. (At last, the animals!)

Cutting to the chase, the Chinese calendar encompasses a 12-year cycle where each year is associated with an animal.

*Can we detect any significant behavioural patterns in the stock market correlated with the sexagenary cycle? In other words, are there monkey years in the market?*

The following chart plots the average return of the stock market[2] for each animal year since 1950. For example, Ox years started in 1961, 1973, 1985, 1997, 2009; and the average return of the market in those (Chinese) years was +14.0%.

1. Helmer Aslaksen, 'The Mathematics of the Chinese Calendar', www.math.nus.edu.sg/aslaksen (2010).
2. The S&P 500 index was used for this study; as the correlation between the US and UK markets is so high, this index is a sufficient proxy for the UK market for the purposes here.

Chinese calendar and S&P 500 [1950–2017]

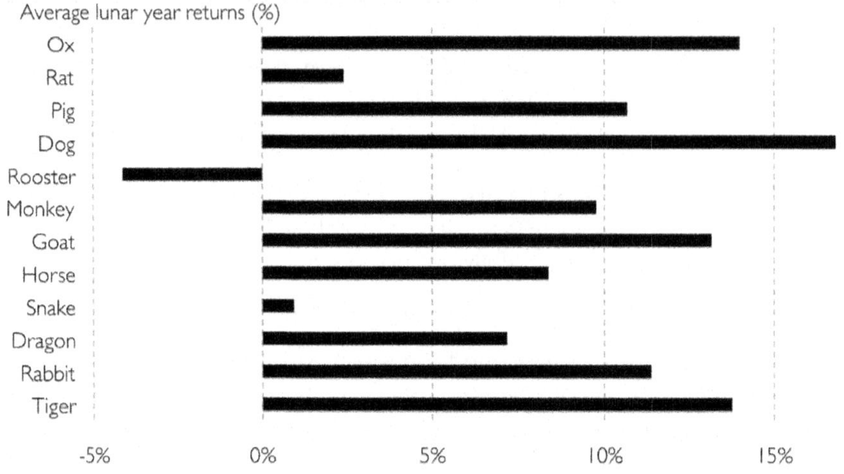


As can be seen the best performing market animals have been the goat and dog. And, coincidentally (or, is it?), the worst performing animals have been the rooster (perhaps a mistranslation for turkey?) and snake.

The Chinese year starting 16 February 2018 is the year of the dog, and in dog years the S&P 500 has had an average return of 16.8% – the best average return of all years of the Chinese zodiac!

# COMPARATIVE PERFORMANCE OF UK INDICES

The table below gives the year-end closing values for eight UK stock indices.

### Year-end closing values of UK indices

| Index | TIDM | 2007 | 2008 | 2009 | 2010 | 2011 | 2012 | 2013 | 2014 | 2015 | 2016 |
|---|---|---|---|---|---|---|---|---|---|---|---|
| FTSE 100 | UKX | 6,456.90 | 4,434.17 | 5,412.88 | 5,899.94 | 5,572.28 | 5,897.81 | 6,749.09 | 6,566.09 | 6,242.30 | 7142.83 |
| FTSE 250 | MCX | 10,657.80 | 6,360.85 | 9,306.89 | 11,558.80 | 10,102.90 | 12,375.00 | 15,935.35 | 16,085.44 | 17,429.80 | 18077.27 |
| FTSE All-Share | ASX | 3,286.67 | 2,209.29 | 2,760.80 | 3,062.85 | 2,857.88 | 3,093.41 | 3,609.63 | 3,532.74 | 3,444.26 | 3873.22 |
| FTSE Fledgling | NSX | 4,022.30 | 2,321.76 | 4,035.39 | 4,789.69 | 4,081.64 | 4,751.92 | 6,453.65 | 6,849.46 | 7,725.75 | 8904.41 |
| FTSE Small Cap | SMX | 3,420.30 | 1,854.20 | 2,780.20 | 3,228.60 | 2,748.80 | 3,419.07 | 4,431.11 | 4,365.92 | 4,634.66 | 5143.22 |
| FTSE TechMARK Focus | TIX | 1,641.10 | 1,217.00 | 1,704.80 | 2,040.00 | 2,064.10 | 2,479.80 | 3,197.32 | 3,522.00 | 4,027.41 | 4344.19 |
| FTSE4Good UK 50 | 4UK5 | 5,428.60 | 3,787.40 | 4,577.90 | 4,852.90 | 4,529.80 | 4,864.74 | 5,636.57 | 5,496.77 | 5,205.47 | 5859.22 |
| FTSE AIM | AXX | 1,049.10 | 394.32 | 653.24 | 933.63 | 693.18 | 707.21 | 850.68 | 702.00 | 738.83 | 844.41 |

The table below gives the annual returns of the eight indices. The light grey cells highlight the best performing index in each respective year; the dark grey cells the worst performing.

### Annual performance (%) of UK indices

| Index | TIDM | 2007 | 2008 | 2009 | 2010 | 2011 | 2012 | 2013 | 2014 | 2015 | 2016 |
|---|---|---|---|---|---|---|---|---|---|---|---|
| FTSE 100 | UKX | 3.8 | -31.3 | 22.1 | 9.0 | -5.6 | 5.8 | 14.4 | -2.7 | -4.9 | 14.4 |
| FTSE 250 | MCX | -4.7 | -40.3 | 46.3 | 24.2 | -12.6 | 22.5 | 28.8 | 0.9 | 8.4 | 3.7 |
| FTSE All-Share | AXX | 2.0 | -32.8 | 25.0 | 10.9 | -6.7 | 8.2 | 16.7 | -2.1 | -2.5 | 14.3 |
| FTSE Fledgling | ASX | -8.4 | -42.3 | 73.8 | 18.7 | -14.8 | 16.4 | 35.8 | 6.1 | 12.8 | 12.5 |
| FTSE Small Cap | NSX | -12.4 | -45.8 | 49.9 | 16.1 | -14.9 | 24.4 | 29.6 | -1.5 | 6.2 | 15.3 |
| FTSE TechMARK Focus | SMX | 8.5 | -25.8 | 40.1 | 19.7 | 1.2 | 20.1 | 28.9 | 10.2 | 14.4 | 11.0 |
| FTSE4Good UK 50 | TIX | 3.1 | -30.2 | 20.9 | 6.0 | -6.7 | 7.4 | 15.9 | -2.5 | -5.3 | 7.9 |
| FTSE AIM | 4UK5 | -0.5 | -62.4 | 65.7 | 42.9 | -25.8 | 2.0 | 20.3 | -17.5 | 5.2 | 12.6 |

The FTSE Fledgling and FTSE TechMARK 100 indices have been the best performing indices in the year the most number of times, while the FTSE AIM and FTSE 4Good UK 50 indices are at the bottom of the class, having been the worst performing indices in the year the most number of times.

The following chart shows the relative performance of the FTSE 100, FTSE 250, FTSE AIM and FTSE Fledgling (all indices rebased to start at 100).

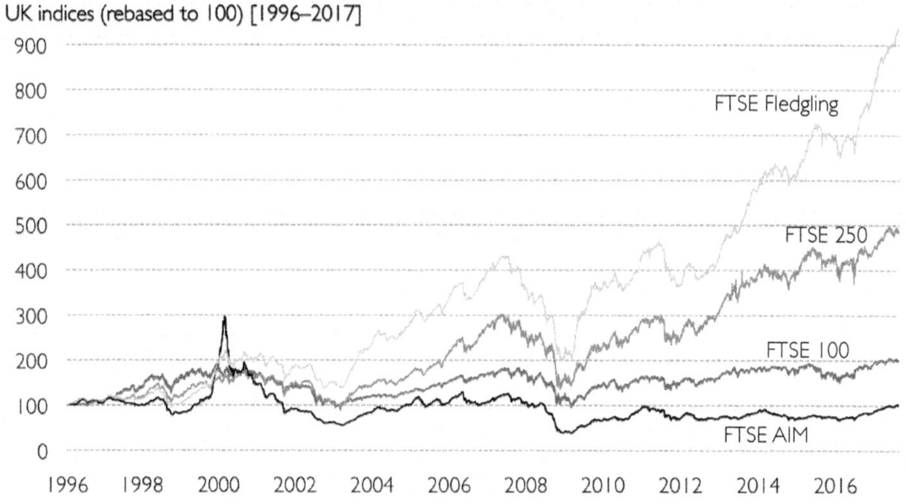
UK indices (rebased to 100) [1996–2017]
900
800
700
600
500
400
300
200
100
0
1996
1998
2000
2002
2004
2006
2008
2010
2012
2014
2016
FTSE Fledgling
FTSE 250
FTSE 100
FTSE AIM

# CORRELATION OF UK MARKETS

*How much diversification away from the FTSE 100 do the other UK equity indices offer?*

The following charts show the correlation of monthly returns between the FTSE 100 index and five UK equity indices for the period 2000–2017.

### FTSE All-Share

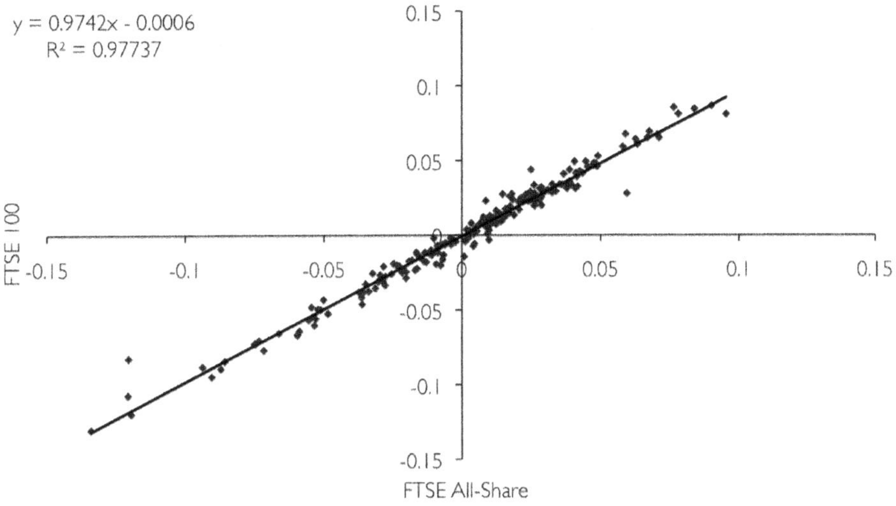


### FTSE 250

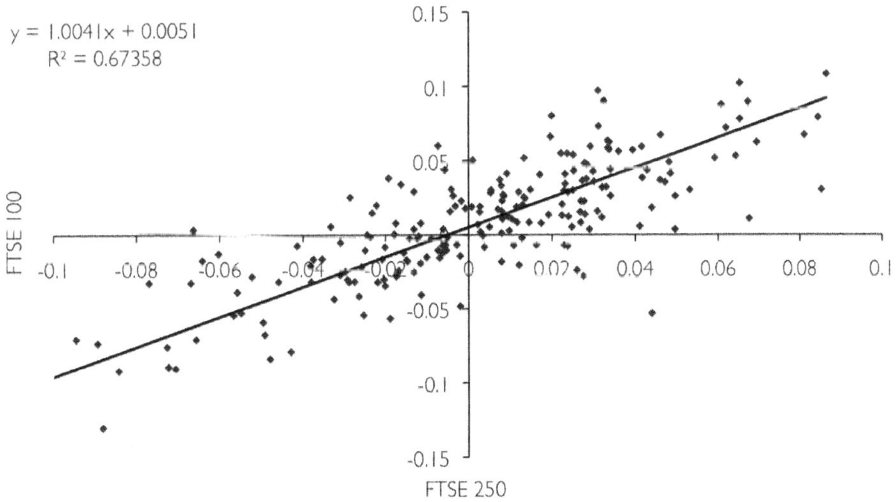

## FTSE Small Cap

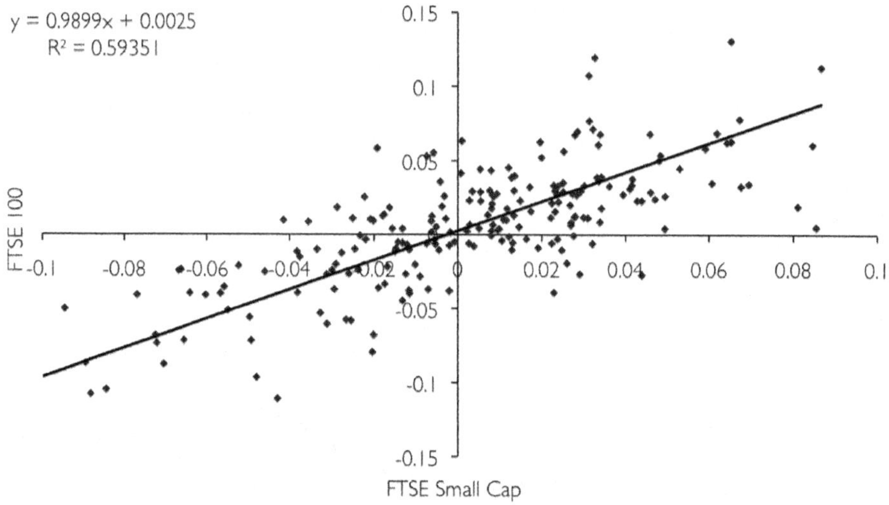


## FTSE Fledgling

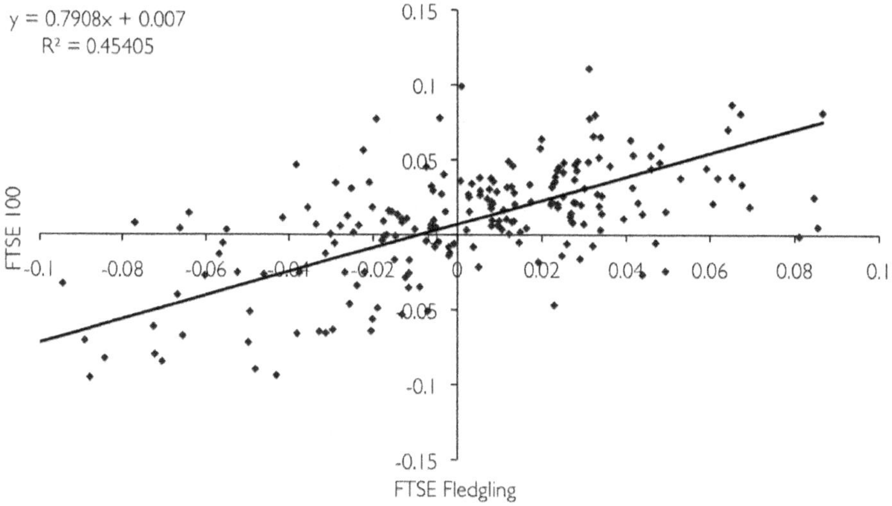

## FTSE AIM All-Share

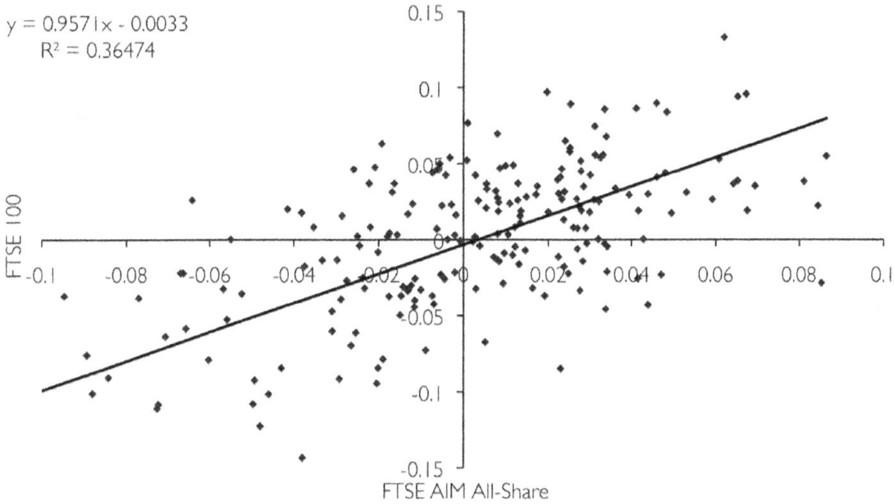


| Index | $R^2$ |
|---|---|
| FTSE All-Share | 0.98 |
| FTSE 250 | 0.67 |
| FTSE Small Cap | 0.59 |
| FTSE Fledgling | 0.45 |
| FTSE AIM All-Share | 0.36 |

The table summarises the $R^2$ values for the correlation between the FTSE 100 and the five UK equity indices. The higher the $R^2$ figure, the closer the correlation (R-Squared is a measure of correlation – visually, how close the points are to the line of best fit).

Firstly, and not surprisingly, we can observe that all the UK equity indices are correlated positively with the FTSE 100 (in other words, they all tend to rise and fall together). The FTSE All-Share has a very high correlation with the FTSE 100, which is because a very high proportion of the FTSE All Share capitalisation is composed of FTSE 100 stocks.

The FTSE 250 of mid-cap stocks has a moderately high correlation with the FTSE 100.

Correlation does begin to diminish significantly with the smaller cap indices; with the correlations of the FTSE Fledgling and FTSE AIM All-Share not particularly high. In other words, if you want to diversify the risk of the FTSE 100, these smaller indices are one place to look.

The correlation coefficients for all indices have fallen slightly in 2017 compared to the average over the period 2000–2016.

# COMPANY PROFILE OF THE FTSE 100 INDEX

| Rank 2017 | Company | TIDM | Turnover (£m) | Profit (£m) | Profit margin (%) | Capital (£m) | Weighting %) | Cumulative weighting (%) |
|---|---|---|---|---|---|---|---|---|
| 1 | Royal Dutch Shell | RDSB | 173,000 | 4,153 | 3.0 | 176,337 | 8.6 | 8.6 |
| 2 | HSBC Holdings | HSBA | 46,720 | 5,269 | | 150,749 | 7.3 | 15.9 |
| 3 | British American Tobacco | BATS | 14,750 | 6,245 | 29.6 | 110,444 | 5.4 | 21.3 |
| 4 | BP | BP. | 135,600 | -1,700 | -2.6 | 87,873 | 4.3 | 25.5 |
| 5 | GlaxoSmithKline | GSK | 27,890 | 1,939 | 25.7 | 75,360 | 3.7 | 29.2 |
| 6 | Diageo | DGE | 12,050 | 3,559 | 29.6 | 65,215 | 3.2 | 32.4 |
| 7 | Vodafone Group | VOD | 40,080 | 2,349 | 5.7 | 58,438 | 2.8 | 35.2 |
| 8 | AstraZeneca | AZN | 17,040 | 2,631 | 20.3 | 58,125 | 2.8 | 38.0 |
| 9 | Unilever | ULVR | 43,170 | 6,117 | 14.9 | 56,709 | 2.8 | 40.8 |
| 10 | Glencore | GLEN | 113,300 | -407 | 0.2 | 52,829 | 2.6 | 43.3 |
| 11 | Reckitt Benckiser Group | RB. | 9,891 | 2,394 | 24.8 | 51,669 | 2.5 | 45.8 |
| 12 | Rio Tinto | RIO | 25,020 | 4,699 | 19.9 | 51,570 | 2.5 | 48.3 |
| 13 | Prudential | PRU | 71,840 | 2,275 | | 47,137 | 2.3 | 50.6 |
| 14 | Lloyds Banking Group | LLOY | 0 | 4,238 | | 45,825 | 2.2 | 52.9 |
| 15 | Shire | SHP | 8,443 | 360 | 10.3 | 35,609 | 1.7 | 54.6 |
| 16 | National Grid | NG. | 15,040 | 2,184 | 21.4 | 33,122 | 1.6 | 56.2 |
| 17 | Barclays | BARC | 19,080 | 3,230 | | 32,724 | 1.6 | 57.8 |
| 18 | BHP Billiton | BLT | 30,200 | 8,142 | 30.7 | 31,343 | 1.5 | 59.3 |
| 19 | Imperial Brands | IMB | 27,630 | 907 | 8.1 | 30,976 | 1.5 | 60.8 |
| 20 | Royal Bank of Scotland Group | RBS | 12,240 | -4,082 | | 30,097 | 1.5 | 62.3 |
| 21 | BT Group | BT.A | 24,060 | 2,354 | 13.1 | 28,608 | 1.4 | 63.7 |
| 22 | Associated British Foods | ABF | 13,400 | 1,042 | 7.8 | 26,276 | 1.3 | 64.9 |
| 23 | Compass Group | CPG | 19,610 | 1,321 | 7.1 | 26,061 | 1.3 | 66.2 |
| 24 | Standard Chartered | STAN | 9,171 | 303 | | 25,473 | 1.2 | 67.5 |
| 25 | CRH | CRH | 22,200 | 1,426 | 7.6 | 22,867 | 1.1 | 68.6 |
| 26 | Aviva | AV. | 55,290 | 1,193 | | 20,984 | 1.0 | 69.6 |
| 27 | Anglo American | AAL | 15,840 | 1,944 | 9.5 | 19,945 | 1.0 | 70.6 |
| 28 | BAE Systems | BA. | 17,790 | 1,151 | 9.1 | 19,445 | 0.9 | 71.5 |
| 29 | RELX | REL | 6,895 | 1,473 | 24.1 | 18,004 | 0.9 | 72.4 |
| 30 | WPP Group | WPP | 14,390 | 1,891 | 15.4 | 17,971 | 0.9 | 73.2 |
| 31 | Rolls-Royce Group | RR. | 14,950 | -4,636 | 1.3 | 16,933 | 0.8 | 74.1 |
| 32 | Sky | SKY | 12,920 | 803 | 7.5 | 16,434 | 0.8 | 74.9 |
| 33 | Legal & General Group | LGEN | 77,970 | 1,582 | | 15,478 | 0.8 | 75.6 |
| 34 | Tesco | TSCO | 55,920 | 145 | 0.9 | 14,992 | 0.7 | 76.3 |
| 35 | Experian | EXPN | 3,328 | 822 | 24.6 | 14,429 | 0.7 | 77.0 |
| 36 | SSE | SSE | 29,040 | 1,777 | 6.3 | 14,349 | 0.7 | 77.7 |
| 37 | London Stock Exchange Group | LSE | 1,657 | 364 | 23.0 | 13,716 | 0.7 | 78.4 |
| 38 | Standard Life Aberdeen | SLA | 18,730 | 487 | | 13,011 | 0.6 | 79.0 |
| 39 | International Consolidated Airlines Group SA | IAG | 18,480 | 1,934 | 12.0 | 12,860 | 0.6 | 79.7 |
| 40 | Smith & Nephew | SN. | 3,459 | 787 | 20.2 | 12,155 | 0.6 | 80.3 |
| 41 | Fresnillo | FRES | 1,412 | 532 | 35.7 | 11,916 | 0.6 | 80.8 |

| Rank 2017 | Company | TIDM | Turnover (£m) | Profit (£m) | Profit margin (%) | Capital (£m) | Weighting %) | Cumulative weighting (%) |
|---|---|---|---|---|---|---|---|---|
| 42 | Ferguson | FERG | 14,430 | 727 | 5.9 | 11,757 | 0.6 | 81.4 |
| 43 | Carnival | CCL | 11,950 | 2,062 | 18.7 | 11,438 | 0.6 | 82.0 |
| 44 | Centrica | CNA | 27,100 | 2,186 | 9.3 | 11,134 | 0.5 | 82.5 |
| 45 | Antofagasta | ANTO | 2,683 | 211 | 19.4 | 10,430 | 0.5 | 83.0 |
| 46 | Mondi | MNDI | 5,456 | 690 | 15.3 | 10,313 | 0.5 | 83.5 |
| 47 | Old Mutual | OML | 14,790 | 1,216 | | 10,253 | 0.5 | 84.0 |
| 48 | Coca-Cola HBC AG | CCH | 0 | 0 | | 9,719 | 0.5 | 84.5 |
| 49 | 3i Group | III | 0 | 0 | | 9,378 | 0.5 | 84.9 |
| 50 | Schroders | SDR | 2,145 | 618 | 23.5 | 9,039 | 0.4 | 85.4 |
| 51 | Ashtead Group | AHT | 3,187 | 765 | 31.0 | 8,512 | 0.4 | 85.8 |
| 52 | Worldpay Group | WPG | 1,124 | 264 | 25.1 | 8,308 | 0.4 | 86.2 |
| 53 | Intertek Group | ITRK | 2,567 | 347 | 13.5 | 8,296 | 0.4 | 86.6 |
| 54 | Persimmon | PSN | 3,137 | 775 | 24.5 | 8,135 | 0.4 | 87.0 |
| 55 | Burberry Group | BRBY | 2,766 | 395 | 17.7 | 7,904 | 0.4 | 87.4 |
| 56 | Land Securities Group | LAND | 787 | 112 | 45.0 | 7,876 | 0.4 | 87.8 |
| 57 | TUI AG | TUI | 13,450 | 484 | 4.5 | 7,831 | 0.4 | 88.1 |
| 58 | Bunzl | BNZL | 7,429 | 363 | 5.5 | 7,744 | 0.4 | 88.5 |
| 59 | Sage Group (The) | SGE | 1,569 | 275 | 26.6 | 7,501 | 0.4 | 88.9 |
| 60 | Randgold Resources Ltd | RRS | 890 | 298 | 32.2 | 7,441 | 0.4 | 89.2 |
| 61 | InterContinental Hotels Group | IHG | 1,270 | 438 | 41.3 | 7,347 | 0.4 | 89.6 |
| 62 | Whitbread | WTB | 3,106 | 515 | 18.8 | 6,892 | 0.3 | 89.9 |
| 63 | RSA Insurance Group | RSA | 6,857 | 101 | | 6,759 | 0.3 | 90.3 |
| 64 | Hargreaves Lansdown | HL. | 386 | 266 | 67.5 | 6,650 | 0.3 | 90.6 |
| 65 | Taylor Wimpey | TW. | 3,676 | 733 | 20.7 | 6,600 | 0.3 | 90.9 |
| 66 | Kingfisher | KGF | 11,230 | 759 | 6.8 | 6,442 | 0.3 | 91.2 |
| 67 | DCC | DCC | 12,270 | 248 | 2.3 | 6,360 | 0.3 | 91.5 |
| 68 | Barratt Developments | BDEV | 4,235 | 682 | 15.8 | 6,319 | 0.3 | 91.8 |
| 69 | ITV | ITV | 3,064 | 553 | 20.2 | 6,308 | 0.3 | 92.1 |
| 70 | British Land Co | BLND | 589 | 195 | 35.3 | 6,194 | 0.3 | 92.4 |
| 71 | United Utilities Group | UU. | 1,704 | 442 | 36.6 | 6,181 | 0.3 | 92.7 |
| 72 | Smiths Group | SMIN | 2,949 | 346 | 15.4 | 6,164 | 0.3 | 93.0 |
| 73 | St James's Place | STJ | 11,350 | 141 | | 6,118 | 0.3 | 93.3 |
| 74 | Next | NXT | 4,097 | 790 | 19.9 | 6,079 | 0.3 | 93.6 |
| 75 | Scottish Mortgage Investment Trust | SMT | 0 | 0 | | 6,073 | 0.3 | 93.9 |
| 76 | Paddy Power Betfair | PPB | 1,501 | 12 | 6.0 | 5,813 | 0.3 | 94.2 |
| 77 | Morrison (Wm) Supermarkets | MRW | 16,320 | 325 | 2.4 | 5,777 | 0.3 | 94.5 |
| 78 | Informa | INF | 1,346 | 178 | 20.2 | 5,669 | 0.3 | 94.8 |
| 79 | Smurfit Kappa Group | SKG | 6,682 | 536 | 10.3 | 5,632 | 0.3 | 95.0 |
| 80 | Mediclinic International | MDC | 2,749 | 307 | 13.0 | 5,622 | 0.3 | 95.3 |
| 81 | Rentokil Initial | RTO | 2,168 | 209 | 11.0 | 5,586 | 0.3 | 95.6 |
| 82 | GKN | GKN | 8,822 | 292 | 2.9 | 5,544 | 0.3 | 95.9 |
| 83 | Admiral Group | ADM | 0 | 278 | | 5,492 | 0.3 | 96.1 |
| 84 | ConvaTec Group | CTEC | 1,251 | -93 | 10.7 | 5,456 | 0.3 | 96.4 |
| 85 | Johnson Matthey | JMAT | 12,030 | 462 | 4.1 | 5,386 | 0.3 | 96.6 |
| 86 | Segro | SGRO | 284 | 426 | 146.0 | 5,372 | 0.3 | 96.9 |

| Rank 2017 | Company | TIDM | Turnover (£m) | Profit (£m) | Profit margin (%) | Capital (£m) | Weighting %) | Cumulative weighting (%) |
|---|---|---|---|---|---|---|---|---|
| 87 | Severn Trent | SVT | 1,819 | 336 | 29.6 | 5,325 | 0.3 | 97.2 |
| 88 | Direct Line Insurance Group | DLG | 3,188 | 353 | | 5,220 | 0.3 | 97.4 |
| 89 | Marks & Spencer Group | MKS | 10,620 | 176 | 5.3 | 5,204 | 0.3 | 97.7 |
| 90 | Micro Focus International | MCRO | 1,070 | 152 | 23.9 | 5,203 | 0.3 | 97.9 |
| 91 | Sainsbury (J) | SBRY | 26,220 | 503 | 2.4 | 5,168 | 0.3 | 98.2 |
| 92 | Croda International | CRDA | 1,244 | 276 | 24.4 | 5,038 | 0.2 | 98.4 |
| 93 | Pearson | PSON | 4,552 | -2,557 | 6.2 | 4,960 | 0.2 | 98.7 |
| 94 | easyJet | EZJ | 4,669 | 495 | 10.7 | 4,727 | 0.2 | 98.9 |
| 95 | Merlin Entertainments | MERL | 1,457 | 277 | 21.9 | 4,674 | 0.2 | 99.1 |
| 96 | G4S | GFS | 7,590 | 296 | 5.6 | 4,447 | 0.2 | 99.3 |
| 97 | Hammerson | HMSO | 251 | 323 | 61.5 | 4,402 | 0.2 | 99.5 |
| 98 | Babcock International Group | BAB | 4,547 | 362 | 7.7 | 4,100 | 0.2 | 99.7 |
| 99 | Royal Mail Group | RMG | 9,776 | 335 | 3.6 | 3,924 | 0.2 | 99.9 |
| 100 | Provident Financial | PFG | 1,183 | 344 | 36.0 | 1,293 | 0.1 | 100.0 |

## Notes to the table

1. The *Weighting* column expresses a company's market capitalisation as a percentage of the total capitalisation of all companies in the FTSE 100 index. The table is ranked (in descending order) by this column.
2. Figures accurate as of September 2017.

## Observations

1. The five largest companies in the FTSE 100 account for 29.2% of the total market capitalisation. In 2004 the top five companies accounted for 36% of the FTSE 100. By 2015 it had fallen to 23.7%, but it has bounced back in the last couple of years.
2. The 13 largest companies in the index account for just over half of total index capitalisation (2004: 10).
3. The 21 smallest companies in the index account for only 5% of total capitalisation. In other words, the individual movements of these 25 companies have very little impact on the level of the index.
4. The aggregate capitalisation of all 100 companies in the index is £2,059bn (2015: £1,764bn, 2012: £1,640bn, 2006: £1,397bn). When the index started in 1984 the aggregate capitalisation was £100bn.

# DIVERSIFICATION WITH ETFS

The following chart shows the 40 ETFs with the highest trading volumes on the LSE and their correlations with the FTSE 100 index. The ETFs are ranked by the correlation value; the ETFs at the top of the chart have the closest correlation with the FTSE 100.

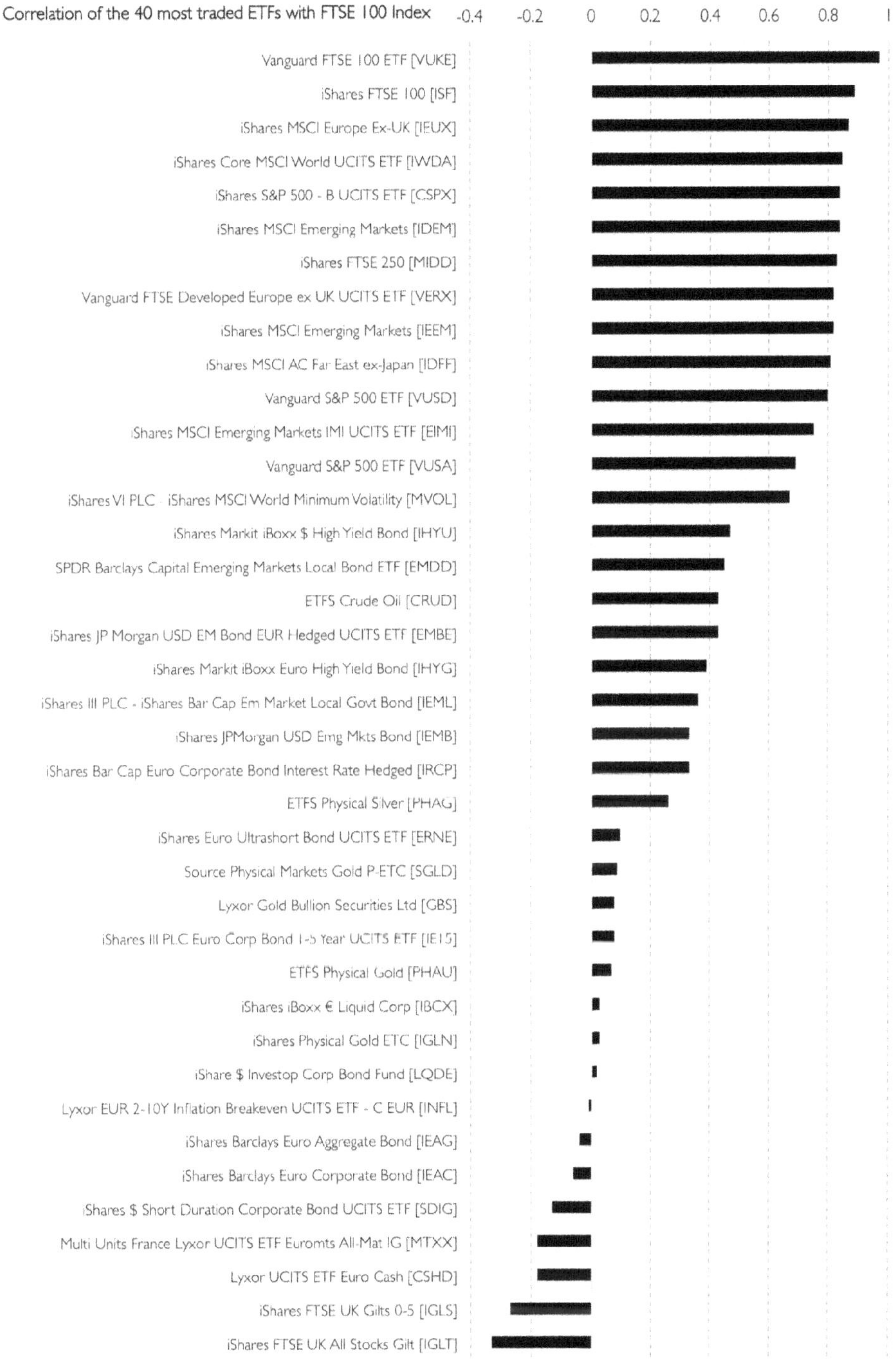

*An attractive feature of ETFs is that they can offer cheap and easy diversification. But how effective really is that diversification? A few notes follow on the diversification properties of the most traded ETFs on the LSE with reference to the chart on the facing page.*

As might be expected, the FTSE 100 tracker ETFs are at the top of the above ranking – led by the **Vanguard ETF [VUKE]**.

Rather surprisingly, very close behind the **iShares FTSE 100 [ISF]** we have **iShares MSCI Europe Ex-UK [IEUX]**, **iShares Core MSCI World [IWDA]**, and **iShares S&P 500 [IDUS]**. Perhaps most surprising is the high position of **iShares MSCI Emerging Markets [IDEM].**

In summary, don't expect much diversification (away from the FTSE 100) by investing in any of the above ETFs.

The gold ETFs (**Source Physical Markets Gold P-ETC [SGLD]**, **Lyxor Gold Bullion Securities Ltd [GBS]** and **ETFS Physical Gold [PHAU]**) are ranked near the bottom. But note that while their correlations are low, they are not negative.

For maximum diversification away from the FTSE 100 an investor needs to look at the bottom of the list, to those ETFs with an actual negative correlation with the FTSE 100 Index, such as the **iShares FTSE UK All Stocks Gilt [IGLT]**.

# SECTORS

# SECTOR QUARTERLY PERFORMANCE

The following four tables show the performance of FTSE 350 sectors in the four quarters of the year for the past ten years.

Notes:

1. The tables are ranked by the *Avg* column – the average performance for each sector over the ten years.

2. For each year the top five performing sectors are highlighted in light grey, the bottom five in dark grey.

The general clustering of light grey highlights at the top of the table, and dark grey at the bottom, suggests that certain sectors consistently perform well (or badly) in certain quarters. This effect is the strongest in the first quarter and weakest in the third.

| Quarter | Strong | Weak |
|---|---|---|
| 1 | Chemicals<br>Industrial Engineering<br>Household Goods | Oil & Gas Producers<br>Banks<br>Fixed Line Telecoms |
| 2 | Personal Goods<br>Pharm & Biotech<br>Software & Comp Srvs | Construction & Materials<br>Food & Drug Retailers<br>Mining |
| 3 | Banks<br>Nonlife Insurance<br>Life Insurance | Oil & Gas Producers<br>Industrial Transportation<br>Fixed Line Telecoms |
| 4 | Chemicals<br>Food Producers<br>Oil & Gas Producers | Industrial Transportation<br>Real Estate Inv Trusts<br>Oil Equip, Services & Dist |

The table on the right gives a subjective listing of the three strongest and three weakest sectors in each quarter (sectors with just one or two constituents are not included here).

## First quarter

| Sector | Avg | 2008 | 2009 | 2010 | 2011 | 2012 | 2013 | 2014 | 2015 | 2016 | 2017 |
|---|---|---|---|---|---|---|---|---|---|---|---|
| Industrial Metals | 15.2 | 21.0 | 80.7 | 39.5 | 0.1 | 5.1 | -18.5 | -24.7 | 21.5 | 22.9 | 4.85 |
| Forestry & Paper | 12.9 | -1.6 | -27.4 | 38.5 | 16.7 | 29.6 | 33.5 | 0.3 | 23.6 | 0.2 | 15.67 |
| Industrial Engineering | 8.6 | 3.2 | 10.2 | 21.0 | 1.6 | 7.8 | 17.3 | 2.5 | 3.3 | 10.3 | 8.92 |
| Oil Equip; Srvs & Dist | 8.4 | -0.3 | 19.6 | 11.1 | 2.5 | 20.1 | 3.1 | 11.1 | 11.6 | 7.0 | -1.76 |
| Household Goods | 6.5 | -4.4 | 3.6 | 5.6 | -5.0 | 14.2 | 23.9 | 4.1 | 10.8 | 1.6 | 10.08 |
| Personal Goods | 5.8 | -18.6 | 6.7 | 11.7 | 1.8 | 21.2 | 8.3 | -6.2 | 7.0 | 7.9 | 17.88 |
| Chemicals | 5.7 | 7.4 | -3.0 | 14.0 | -4.1 | 25.5 | 6.7 | 2.2 | 2.7 | 1.9 | 3.96 |
| Software & Comp Srvs | 5.2 | -11.7 | 10.8 | 15.8 | 0.9 | 14.5 | 11.5 | 2.2 | 4.0 | 2.6 | 1.11 |
| Electronic & Elect Equip | 4.5 | -2.0 | -20.8 | 12.3 | 3.8 | 25.6 | 12.3 | -6.1 | 5.3 | 2.2 | 12.46 |
| Industrial Transportation | 4.5 | -12.6 | 3.2 | 19.7 | 3.0 | 15.8 | 7.5 | 1.7 | -0.3 | 6.8 | 0.04 |
| Construction & Materials | 4.4 | -2.7 | -2.3 | 10.8 | 5.8 | 1.5 | 11 | 7.4 | 12.7 | -1.2 | 0.52 |
| Real Estate Inv & Srvs | 4.0 | | | -0.6 | 2.8 | 5.9 | 11.9 | 7.8 | 11.5 | -12.4 | 5.35 |
| Support Services | 4.0 | -4.8 | -6.9 | 8.7 | 1.5 | 14.7 | 15.8 | 1.8 | 5.2 | -2.3 | 6.3 |
| General Industrials | 3.8 | -4.7 | -20.6 | 12.6 | 5.9 | 21.1 | 9.6 | -8.8 | 11.6 | 5.4 | 5.67 |
| Mining | 3.7 | -0.9 | 13.4 | 11.5 | -4.2 | 2.7 | -10.1 | 1.4 | -4.2 | 22.5 | 5.15 |
| Aerospace & Defense | 3.0 | -9.4 | -12.2 | 10.1 | 0.1 | 9.9 | 22.5 | -9.3 | 7.6 | 3.8 | 6.64 |
| Media | 3.0 | -13.5 | -4.2 | 11.3 | 3.8 | 9.4 | 13.7 | -5.9 | 13.8 | 1.4 | -0.13 |
| Health Care Equip & Srvs | 2.8 | 6.9 | -2.3 | 2.1 | 3.1 | 1.2 | 9.9 | 7.1 | 0.8 | -2.2 | 1.12 |
| Tobacco | 2.7 | -7.9 | -12.1 | 9.3 | 0.5 | 3.4 | 8.5 | 3.2 | 1.1 | 8.2 | 13.11 |
| Automobiles & Parts | 2.7 | 7.9 | -29.6 | 17.9 | -9.6 | 12.6 | 15.6 | 4.6 | 4.2 | -6.4 | 9.53 |
| Financial Services | 2.6 | -15.6 | -2.9 | -1.2 | -4.0 | 17.5 | 18.2 | 2.2 | 11.4 | -4.9 | 5.51 |
| Equity Inv Instruments | 2.3 | -5.8 | -2.4 | 6.7 | -0.1 | 7.7 | 9.6 | 0.3 | 4.3 | -2.8 | 5.03 |
| General Retailers | 2.0 | -19.1 | 20.6 | -3.8 | -9.0 | 19.9 | 7.3 | 11.2 | 3.3 | -7.9 | -2.87 |
| Nonlife Insurance | 2.0 | -10.4 | -8.2 | 7.5 | 2.3 | 7.7 | 6.3 | 1.2 | 7.7 | 2.0 | 3.47 |

| Sector | Avg | 2008 | 2009 | 2010 | 2011 | 2012 | 2013 | 2014 | 2015 | 2016 | 2017 |
|---|---|---|---|---|---|---|---|---|---|---|---|
| Travel & Leisure | 1.8 | -16.5 | -6.5 | 17.8 | -8.3 | 8.5 | 14.4 | 0.5 | 9.0 | -5.2 | 4.13 |
| Beverages | 1.3 | -9.2 | -15.5 | 3.9 | -1.2 | 8.6 | 18.4 | -5.7 | 2.5 | 2.7 | 8.91 |
| Life Insurance | -0.5 | -10.7 | -28.5 | -4.6 | 9.5 | 15.3 | 11.3 | -1.9 | 12.6 | -10.4 | 2.8 |
| Mobile Telecom | -0.8 | -19.6 | -11.2 | 5.9 | 5.9 | -3.4 | 20.8 | -10.3 | -0.1 | -1.0 | 4.67 |
| Real Estate Inv Trusts | -1.0 | 1.8 | -31.5 | -2.1 | 4.8 | 9.6 | 0.5 | 5.3 | 8.7 | -7.0 | 0.22 |
| Gas; Water & Multiutilities | -1.1 | -13.6 | -18.6 | 1.0 | 1.5 | 5.1 | 8.6 | 3.0 | -5.4 | 3.4 | 4.16 |
| Food & Drug Retailers | -1.2 | -19.3 | -7.2 | 2.3 | -7.6 | -12.5 | 12.5 | -11.0 | 16.1 | 17.7 | -3.14 |
| Pharm & Biotech | -1.3 | -15.3 | -14.3 | -0.7 | -1.7 | -5.5 | 14 | 2.5 | 9.1 | -7.0 | 6.07 |
| Food Producers | -1.5 | -9.7 | -15.6 | 2.6 | -3.3 | -2.0 | 17.5 | 3.4 | -6.9 | 0.2 | -1.26 |
| Oil & Gas Producers | -1.7 | -14.4 | -7.2 | 2.6 | 5.7 | -2.7 | 4.3 | -2.6 | -3.1 | 8.1 | -8.16 |
| Electricity | -2.2 | -7.0 | -10.5 | -3.3 | 2.1 | 2.5 | 5.7 | 5.0 | -9.1 | -1.5 | -5.75 |
| Fixed Line Telecoms | -3.0 | -19.9 | -32.5 | -4.6 | -0.5 | 17.1 | 19.7 | 0.2 | 8.8 | -5.8 | -12.25 |
| Banks | -3.5 | -10.1 | -27.4 | 6.7 | -2.3 | 17.0 | 7.5 | -8.8 | -1.7 | -18.5 | 2.11 |

## Second quarter

| Sector | Avg | 2008 | 2009 | 2010 | 2011 | 2012 | 2013 | 2014 | 2015 | 2016 | 2017 |
|---|---|---|---|---|---|---|---|---|---|---|---|
| Personal Goods | 7.2 | -1.1 | 35.2 | 7.0 | 17.1 | -11.5 | 0.8 | 0.9 | -3.4 | 22.6 | 3.94 |
| Pharm & Biotech | 7.0 | 6.0 | 2.3 | -2.8 | 10.4 | 2.2 | 2.5 | 9.8 | -11.8 | 52.4 | -1.4 |
| Software & Comp Srvs | 4.6 | 7.1 | 20.8 | -8.2 | 5.1 | -0.5 | 4.4 | -4.0 | 12.9 | 1.5 | 6.63 |
| Electronic & Elect Equip | 4.1 | 9.1 | 23.6 | 12.1 | 13.7 | -4.6 | -14.3 | -8.4 | 0.5 | 4.1 | 4.79 |
| Automobiles & Parts | 3.7 | -26.7 | 81.7 | -15.7 | 15.4 | -12.4 | 13.9 | -7.0 | -6.7 | 4.4 | -10.27 |
| Electricity | 3.1 | 6.8 | 2.8 | -0.7 | 12.3 | 4.4 | 1.5 | 2.5 | 1.9 | 0.7 | -1.42 |
| Beverages | 2.7 | -5.2 | 13.9 | -3.1 | 5.2 | 5.7 | -8.9 | 4.4 | -2.9 | 17.7 | 0.24 |
| Fixed Line Telecoms | 2.0 | -6.5 | 16.9 | 2.8 | 5.4 | -2.9 | 8.7 | 0.1 | 4.0 | -1.1 | -7.18 |
| Equity Inv Instruments | 1.4 | -2.7 | 10.7 | -6.3 | 1.7 | -4.7 | -2.3 | 1.0 | -1.3 | 14.0 | 3.41 |
| Industrial Engineering | 1.1 | 14.7 | 4.8 | -1.2 | 8.7 | -11.4 | -5.4 | -2.7 | -6.0 | 9.7 | -0.25 |
| Real Estate Inv & Srvs | 0.9 | | | -14.5 | 8.6 | 1.2 | 11.8 | -9.3 | 5.3 | 0.1 | 4.4 |
| General Retailers | 0.7 | -15.9 | 14.5 | -10.3 | 9.8 | -5.8 | 9.2 | -7.6 | 3.1 | 14.1 | -3.6 |
| Travel & Leisure | 0.6 | -7.6 | 6.3 | -11.7 | 3.1 | 1.3 | 3.3 | -1.0 | -4.9 | 11.5 | 5.42 |
| Support Services | 0.3 | -9.4 | 11.0 | -5.0 | 3.1 | -4.8 | -2.9 | -5.1 | 3.6 | 9.3 | 2.81 |
| Nonlife Insurance | 0.2 | -7.8 | -3.3 | 0.4 | 5.8 | 3.8 | 1.7 | 4.1 | -0.7 | -8.9 | 7.26 |
| General Industrials | 0.2 | -1.8 | 13.1 | -6.6 | 0.9 | -6.2 | 1.0 | 0.4 | 1.9 | -4.7 | 4.24 |
| Financial Services | -0.4 | -3.6 | 21.7 | -8.1 | -1.5 | -8.7 | -0.1 | 0.8 | -1.6 | -9.1 | 6.31 |
| Tobacco | -0.4 | -7.8 | 2.8 | -6.1 | 8.7 | 1.1 | -3.6 | 5.4 | -0.4 | -0.4 | -3.87 |
| Life Insurance | -0.4 | -18.5 | 31.8 | -13.1 | 0.9 | -6.5 | 0.6 | 4.2 | -8.5 | 1.4 | 3.39 |
| Food Producers | -0.4 | -13.1 | 7.2 | -6.2 | 5.0 | 2.7 | -4.7 | 4.5 | 0.1 | -5.1 | 5.25 |
| Banks | -0.5 | -21.2 | 34.9 | -11.9 | -4.7 | -7.6 | -2.2 | -3.2 | 2.2 | 5.2 | 3.68 |
| Chemicals | -0.7 | -6.5 | 7.6 | -4.6 | 9.4 | -3.4 | -3.0 | -8.1 | -5.1 | 6.4 | 0.55 |
| Mobile Telecom | -0.9 | -0.7 | -4.0 | -8.3 | -6.4 | 4.2 | 0.5 | -10.8 | 3.9 | 8.9 | 3.72 |
| Health Care Equip & Srvs | -0.9 | -22.0 | 6.8 | -2.6 | -4.3 | 0.9 | -2.6 | 12.3 | -6.4 | -2.4 | 11.03 |
| Oil & Gas Producers | -1.0 | 16.4 | 1.4 | -25.9 | -3.2 | -5.0 | -2.2 | 9.1 | -4.3 | 7.4 | -4.1 |
| Oil Equip; Srvs & Dist | -1.3 | 21.0 | 21.8 | -3.8 | -1.3 | -17.8 | -10.7 | -0.2 | -2.4 | 5.6 | -25.29 |
| Real Estate Inv Trusts | -1.3 | -21.7 | 15.9 | -13.9 | 9.0 | 3.1 | 3.8 | 3.0 | -4.0 | -9.1 | 0.72 |
| Gas; Water & Multiutilities | -1.4 | -2.1 | 2.4 | -5.4 | 2.7 | 5.4 | -2.2 | 1.4 | -2.6 | -6.6 | -7.42 |
| Household Goods | -1.7 | -24.9 | 5.3 | -15.3 | 7.1 | -3.8 | 1.7 | 0.4 | 5.4 | 2.6 | 4.58 |
| Forestry & Paper | -1.7 | -29.1 | 39.9 | -17.2 | 3.5 | -7.5 | -8.5 | 1.2 | 5.6 | -9.4 | 4.51 |
| Industrial Transportation | -2.1 | -19.0 | 14.6 | -7.0 | 3.8 | -6.8 | 5.5 | -9.3 | 8.6 | -12.3 | 1.07 |
| Aerospace & Defense | -2.3 | -9.6 | 8.2 | -9.5 | 1.7 | 0.4 | 0.6 | 2.1 | -10.1 | -13.1 | 6.33 |
| Media | -3.2 | -14.5 | 1.0 | -5.8 | 3.1 | -3.2 | 0.2 | 0.5 | -4.0 | -7.4 | -1.96 |
| Mining | -4.2 | 16.9 | 17.2 | -21.6 | -2.0 | -13.2 | -18.3 | -0.8 | -7.8 | -6.8 | -5.73 |
| Industrial Metals | -5.1 | -2.9 | 79.2 | -25.0 | -8.1 | -29.4 | -48.9 | 4.5 | -34.4 | 9.8 | 4.59 |
| Food & Drug Retailers | -5.1 | -3.4 | 2.9 | -10.7 | 4.5 | -6.3 | -8.9 | -6.5 | -5.1 | -12.6 | -4.69 |
| Construction & Materials | -6.0 | -16.5 | 0.0 | -17.8 | -9.8 | -1.7 | -5.1 | -11.3 | 2.8 | 0.9 | -2.03 |

## Third quarter

| Sector | Avg | 2007 | 2008 | 2009 | 2010 | 2011 | 2012 | 2013 | 2014 | 2015 | 2016 |
|---|---|---|---|---|---|---|---|---|---|---|---|
| Life Insurance | 5.9 | -2.2 | -3.5 | 35.8 | 26.2 | -21.4 | 10.7 | 8.9 | 1.7 | -7.9 | 10.5 |
| Software & Comp Srvs | 5.7 | 3.6 | -5.4 | 23.8 | 14.0 | -7.1 | 9.3 | 3.0 | -2.2 | -2.9 | 20.9 |
| Forestry & Paper | 5.7 | -45.0 | -13.0 | 49.2 | 33.9 | -23.7 | 15.6 | 27.5 | -4.8 | 0.9 | 16.3 |
| Automobiles & Parts | 5.3 | -11.1 | -12.2 | 35.9 | 45.7 | -24.1 | 18.9 | 13.5 | -12.1 | -19.9 | 18.8 |
| Nonlife Insurance | 5.3 | 3.8 | 18.3 | 16.5 | 8.5 | -16.1 | 5.7 | -1.1 | -1.8 | 11.9 | 7.1 |
| Industrial Engineering | 4.6 | -1.7 | -20.5 | 47.6 | 25.1 | -20.4 | 11.5 | 13.7 | -5.6 | -18.0 | 14.1 |
| Household Goods | 3.8 | -6.9 | 6.7 | 14.3 | 11.1 | -6.4 | 8.2 | -2.2 | 3.4 | 5.8 | 4.2 |
| Banks | 3.5 | -8.5 | -1.4 | 39.2 | 10.7 | -24.1 | 7.8 | 2.7 | 4.5 | -13.3 | 17.6 |
| Real Estate Inv Trusts | 3.3 | -9.4 | 4.4 | 27.8 | 13.2 | -21.9 | 3.7 | 4.3 | 1.2 | 5.5 | 4.5 |
| Beverages | 3.3 | 4.1 | -1.0 | 15.2 | 5.4 | -5.3 | 6.2 | 2.9 | -2.3 | 2.7 | 5.0 |
| Tobacco | 3.2 | 0.9 | 1.5 | 16.4 | 8.0 | 1.3 | -3.2 | -1.9 | 0.4 | 8.1 | 0.7 |
| Personal Goods | 3.2 | -3.4 | -7.9 | 20.3 | 35.8 | -16.4 | -21.2 | 21.5 | 2.8 | -3.7 | 4.2 |
| Media | 3.1 | -5.2 | -8.2 | 24.7 | 9.2 | -16.1 | 7.5 | 11.3 | 2.4 | -0.9 | 6.8 |
| General Industrials | 3.0 | -3.8 | -6.1 | 24.8 | 20.0 | -21.2 | 5.7 | 8.2 | -4.8 | -6.1 | 13.7 |
| Gas; Water & Multiutilities | 2.9 | 1.6 | 3.8 | 6.7 | 9.1 | -0.3 | 1.9 | 0.7 | 1.6 | 4.2 | -0.4 |
| Food Producers | 2.5 | -11.3 | -0.1 | 30.2 | 2.4 | 0.0 | 4.2 | -5.7 | -9.0 | 12.4 | 2.3 |
| Mobile Telecom | 2.5 | 5.3 | -17.4 | 18.9 | 12.0 | 0.2 | -1.4 | 14.7 | 4.2 | -8.3 | -3.1 |
| Pharm & Biotech | 2.5 | -3.4 | 10.4 | 11.9 | 6.2 | -2.7 | 0.2 | -0.6 | -0.7 | -2.4 | 6.1 |
| Oil Equip; Srvs & Dist | 2.4 | 7.1 | -26.9 | 24.5 | 26.1 | -22.3 | 14.5 | 8.7 | -7.7 | -13.6 | 13.6 |
| Chemicals | 2.4 | 2.1 | -21.4 | 23.0 | 25.4 | -20.3 | 9.8 | 6.6 | -6.1 | -8.6 | 13.2 |
| Health Care Equip & Srvs | 2.1 | -5.8 | 5.6 | 24.6 | -7.3 | -12.0 | 6.6 | 4.3 | 0.1 | 7.2 | -2.8 |
| General Retailers | 1.6 | -10.7 | -12.1 | 16.2 | 10.8 | -10.8 | 5.1 | 14.6 | -2.2 | -2.7 | 7.4 |
| Equity Inv Instruments | 1.4 | 2.5 | -14.4 | 16.5 | 8.5 | -13.6 | 3.8 | 3.6 | 2.1 | -5.9 | 10.7 |
| Travel & Leisure | 1.3 | -9.2 | -11.2 | 22.1 | 8.5 | -16.8 | 5.6 | 3.9 | -0.6 | 1.0 | 9.6 |
| Aerospace & Defense | 1.3 | 8.2 | -5.8 | 15.6 | 6.7 | -12.4 | 3.5 | 6.2 | -3.1 | -8.6 | 2.3 |
| Food & Drug Retailers | 1.0 | 1.9 | 4.0 | 12.3 | 12.7 | -7.2 | 7.6 | 9.1 | -27.7 | -9.9 | 6.8 |
| Financial Services | 0.5 | -4.0 | -21.9 | 21.6 | 12.4 | -21.8 | 7.2 | 8.8 | -5.3 | -5.1 | 13.2 |
| Support Services | 0.5 | -10.9 | -10.5 | 19.4 | 8.8 | -13.7 | 9.0 | 6.8 | -1.8 | -8.3 | 5.9 |
| Real Estate Inv & Srvs | 0.5 | | | | 7.9 | -18.8 | 6.7 | 6.0 | -3.0 | 0.0 | 4.4 |
| Construction & Materials | 0.4 | -0.6 | -24.2 | 10.9 | 13.1 | -15.7 | -1.3 | 12.7 | -6.4 | -2.1 | 17.8 |
| Electronic & Elect Equip | 0.3 | -8.8 | -18.1 | 24.4 | 22.0 | -26.9 | 7.1 | 11.5 | -8.6 | -7.9 | 8.3 |
| Electricity | 0.3 | 1.4 | -1.0 | 7.7 | 8.3 | -6.7 | -1.2 | -0.4 | -1.0 | -4.9 | 0.4 |
| Fixed Line Telecoms | -0.7 | -7.0 | -14.1 | 21.5 | 2.9 | -14.6 | 8.5 | 10.0 | -1.8 | -7.5 | -5.0 |
| Mining | -1.4 | 12.8 | -44.1 | 26.5 | 19.1 | -30.9 | 3.2 | 14.4 | -3.6 | -31.7 | 20.1 |
| Industrial Transportation | -3.0 | -9.9 | -19.1 | 26.9 | 7.1 | -19.3 | -1.3 | 8.3 | -12.1 | -14.1 | 3.0 |
| Oil & Gas Producers | -3.2 | -2.5 | -21.9 | 13.0 | 19.2 | -12.2 | 0.1 | -1.8 | -7.2 | -15.8 | -2.4 |
| Industrial Metals | -9.9 | -65.5 | -60.8 | 10.9 | 30.6 | -44.7 | -7.5 | 32.7 | 29.2 | -40.8 | 17.4 |

## Fourth quarter

| Sector | Avg | 2007 | 2008 | 2009 | 2010 | 2011 | 2012 | 2013 | 2014 | 2015 | 2016 |
|---|---|---|---|---|---|---|---|---|---|---|---|
| Food Producers | 7.2 | 14.9 | 2.2 | 6.1 | 7.9 | 6.2 | 7.8 | 7.6 | 14.1 | 3.8 | 0.92 |
| Chemicals | 6.4 | 9.2 | -21.3 | 12.0 | 16.3 | 10.3 | 1.8 | 10.2 | 18.2 | 6.9 | 0.1 |
| Oil & Gas Producers | 6.1 | 10.1 | 8.1 | 6.5 | 11.0 | 16.6 | -4.6 | 7.9 | -12.2 | 1.6 | 16.11 |
| Beverages | 4.9 | 3.4 | 3.8 | 16.3 | 9.0 | 11.0 | 3.3 | 0.7 | 0.7 | 6.5 | -5.34 |
| Real Estate Inv & Srvs | 4.7 | | | | 6.8 | 8.8 | 7.8 | 6.6 | 4.6 | -2.2 | 0.63 |
| Health Care Equip & Srvs | 4.2 | 3.2 | -27.6 | 13.1 | 16.7 | 6.7 | 0.8 | 12.0 | 15.6 | 6.4 | -4.6 |
| Mobile Telecom | 4.2 | 6.7 | 12.8 | 3.3 | 5.4 | 9.3 | -11.8 | 9.6 | 9.2 | 6.7 | -9.04 |
| Construction & Materials | 4.0 | -12.6 | 4.3 | -8.4 | 16.3 | 8.0 | 1.9 | 4.0 | 7.5 | 10.6 | 8.82 |
| Media | 3.7 | -4.7 | -2.9 | 6.4 | 6.2 | 9.3 | 4.7 | 6.3 | 4.7 | 4.9 | 2.55 |
| Travel & Leisure | 3.7 | -7.6 | -13.6 | 0.9 | 10.0 | 6.9 | 7.9 | 12.4 | 11.1 | 7.3 | 2.13 |
| Tobacco | 3.3 | 15.4 | -0.9 | 4.5 | 3.7 | 12.0 | -0.4 | -0.3 | 2.2 | 4.0 | -7.61 |

| Sector | Avg | 2007 | 2008 | 2009 | 2010 | 2011 | 2012 | 2013 | 2014 | 2015 | 2016 |
|---|---|---|---|---|---|---|---|---|---|---|---|
| Life Insurance | 3.2 | -4.8 | -19.2 | -1.1 | -2.5 | 9.7 | 11.3 | 11.6 | 4.9 | 9.2 | 12.6 |
| Electronic & Elect Equip | 3.2 | -15.7 | -21.6 | 1.1 | 18.0 | 8.2 | 10.5 | 13.1 | 13.0 | 7.7 | -2.6 |
| Fixed Line Telecoms | 2.9 | -9.2 | -13.7 | 2.5 | 18.7 | 5.9 | 0.9 | 13.0 | 5.3 | 11.2 | -5.8 |
| Mining | 2.6 | 2.7 | -31.5 | 24.1 | 22.8 | 8.5 | 8.8 | -0.5 | -10.2 | -14.7 | 16.4 |
| Aerospace & Defense | 2.6 | 4.4 | -6.2 | 5.4 | 1.3 | 13.3 | 2.3 | 5.2 | -1.7 | -1.4 | 3.8 |
| Support Services | 2.3 | -6.3 | -5.7 | 4.3 | 6.5 | 8.0 | 1.1 | 5.4 | 4.2 | 5.7 | -0.2 |
| Financial Services | 2.1 | 0.3 | -29.9 | -2.7 | 19.0 | -3.2 | 7.4 | 10.8 | 11.9 | 6.6 | 0.6 |
| Industrial Metals | 2.0 | 10.0 | -65.0 | 13.5 | 26.3 | -9.6 | 2.8 | -6.9 | 6.3 | 0.5 | 41.8 |
| Household Goods | 1.9 | -7.9 | -6.8 | 5.0 | 1.6 | -0.5 | 11 | 9.6 | 6.4 | 4.2 | -3.2 |
| Personal Goods | 1.9 | -1.8 | -23.0 | 18.7 | 8.6 | -1.3 | 22.3 | -4.9 | 2.3 | 5.3 | -7.1 |
| Pharm & Biotech | 1.7 | -4.7 | 8.9 | 6.2 | -3.6 | 8.4 | -3.9 | 7.4 | -2.6 | 8.0 | -7.3 |
| General Industrials | 1.6 | -13.2 | -20.4 | 10.0 | 9.0 | 4.1 | 7.4 | 11.7 | -3.2 | 5.7 | 5.1 |
| Equity Inv Instruments | 1.4 | -1.7 | -18.6 | 4.3 | 9.3 | 1.5 | 3.3 | 3.4 | 3.5 | 6.3 | 3.1 |
| Automobiles & Parts | 1.0 | -20.3 | -50.4 | 2.9 | 31.2 | 4.0 | 6.5 | 9.2 | 7.8 | 15.1 | 3.6 |
| Nonlife Insurance | 0.8 | -4.8 | 3.5 | -5.0 | 0.4 | -3.4 | 4.8 | 4.2 | 2.2 | 6.1 | 0.3 |
| Food & Drug Retailers | 0.8 | 2.7 | -4.3 | 4.9 | -1.1 | 7.5 | -0.3 | -4.8 | 6.9 | -11.0 | 7.6 |
| Gas; Water & Multiutilities | 0.7 | 4.3 | -6.4 | 11.8 | 3.5 | -1.1 | 0.3 | 1.0 | 2.0 | 0.9 | -9.4 |
| General Retailers | 0.5 | -12.1 | -12.9 | 9.2 | 2.0 | -1.0 | 11.5 | -1.3 | 11.9 | -2.6 | 0.3 |
| Software & Comp Srvs | 0.4 | -9.5 | -17.5 | -1.1 | 2.0 | 3.6 | 3.3 | 4.8 | 11.1 | 16.1 | -8.5 |
| Electricity | 0.3 | 4.6 | -14.8 | -0.1 | 9.6 | 1.4 | 2.6 | -3.1 | -0.1 | 2.0 | 0.8 |
| Industrial Engineering | 0.3 | -18.8 | -26.8 | 7.3 | 19.2 | 17.5 | 7.8 | 0.9 | -9.6 | 1.7 | 3.7 |
| Industrial Transportation | -0.9 | -5.3 | -32.2 | 1.5 | 5.3 | 1.7 | 6.4 | 6.3 | 7.7 | -1.3 | 1.1 |
| Forestry & Paper | -1.6 | -8.6 | -21.0 | 8.4 | -0.2 | -3.9 | 6.3 | 0.3 | 3.9 | -3.5 | 2.7 |
| Real Estate Inv Trusts | -1.8 | -12.8 | -33.6 | 4.7 | 7.6 | -2.1 | 7.2 | 5.8 | 9.5 | -3.2 | -0.7 |
| Banks | -3.3 | -10.3 | -38.2 | -9.2 | -4.0 | -0.3 | 15.4 | -0.2 | -1.9 | 0.2 | 15.9 |
| Oil Equip; Srvs & Dist | -4.4 | 14.5 | -38.3 | 3.6 | 15.9 | 14.0 | -6.1 | -6.4 | -27.3 | -16.0 | 2.6 |

Note to the tables: In January 2017, the 'Technology Hardware & Equipment' sector was removed by the FTSE. This may have impacted some of the four quarterly tables in this article.

# SECTOR ANNUAL PERFORMANCE

The table below shows the year-on-year percentage returns of the FTSE 350 sectors for the past ten years. The three best [worst] performing sectors in each year are highlighted in light grey [dark grey]. The table is ranked by the final column – the average annual return for the sector for the period 2007–2016.

## Sector performance 2007–2016 (percentage change YoY)

| EPIC | Sector | 2007 | 2008 | 2009 | 2010 | 2011 | 2012 | 2013 | 2014 | 2015 | 2016 | Avg |
|---|---|---|---|---|---|---|---|---|---|---|---|---|
| NMX1750 | Industrial Metals | -56.6 | -83.9 | 307.3 | 72.4 | -54.0 | -29.4 | -48.6 | 8.0 | -52.6 | 211.6 | 27.4 |
| NMX3760 | Personal Goods | 2.2 | -42.9 | 105.8 | 76.1 | -1.6 | 3.4 | 26.2 | -0.5 | 4.9 | 13.6 | 18.7 |
| NMX2750 | Industrial Engineering | -7.2 | -31.1 | 83.1 | 78.2 | 3.2 | 14.7 | 27.5 | -14.9 | -19.1 | 43.2 | 17.8 |
| NMX1350 | Chemicals | 41.3 | -37.8 | 43.8 | 58.5 | -7.8 | 35.5 | 21.5 | 4.2 | -4.8 | 14.2 | 16.9 |
| NMX3350 | Automobiles & Parts | 1.4 | -65.6 | 78.7 | 89.9 | -17.6 | 25.0 | 63.2 | -7.8 | -10.4 | 7.6 | 16.4 |
| NMX9530 | Software & Computer Services | -7.5 | -26.2 | 63.9 | 23.7 | 2.1 | 28.8 | 25.6 | 6.6 | 32.4 | 14.5 | 16.4 |
| NMX1730 | Forestry & Paper | -49.7 | -52.1 | 64.4 | 53.3 | -11.4 | 47.1 | 56.2 | 0.4 | 27.1 | 24.9 | 16.0 |
| NMX2730 | Electronic & Electrical Equip | -5.5 | -31.4 | 23.0 | 81.2 | -6.6 | 41.8 | 21.3 | -11.1 | 4.9 | 15.8 | 13.3 |
| NMX1770 | Mining | 50.4 | -55.7 | 108.5 | 27.8 | -29.7 | 0.2 | -16.3 | -13.0 | -48.6 | 101.5 | 12.5 |
| NMX4530 | Health Care Equip & Services | 18.6 | -36.3 | 47.0 | 7.5 | -7.2 | 9.7 | 25.0 | 39.3 | 7.6 | 1.1 | 11.2 |
| NMX3780 | Tobacco | 34.0 | -14.6 | 9.9 | 15.0 | 23.9 | 0.8 | 2.3 | 11.7 | 13.3 | 14.7 | 11.1 |
| NMX3530 | Beverages | 14.4 | -11.6 | 28.9 | 15.6 | 9.3 | 25.8 | 11.7 | -3.1 | 8.9 | 8.5 | 10.8 |
| NMX0570 | Oil Equip, Services & Dist | 38.1 | -45.7 | 87.8 | 56.3 | -10.4 | 6.2 | -6.3 | -25.7 | -20.9 | 25.5 | 10.5 |
| NMX3720 | Household Goods | -15.0 | -28.6 | 30.9 | 1.0 | -5.2 | 31.9 | 35.1 | 14.9 | 28.8 | -2.8 | 9.1 |
| NMX2720 | General Industrials | -13.1 | -30.0 | 23.2 | 37.6 | -12.3 | 28.9 | 33.9 | -15.7 | 12.9 | 25.6 | 9.1 |
| NMX5550 | Media | 0.2 | -34.1 | 28.3 | 21.5 | -1.9 | 19.2 | 34.9 | 1.4 | 13.5 | 5.8 | 8.9 |
| NMX8630 | Real Estate Inv & Services | | | | -2.0 | -1.3 | 23.4 | 41.4 | -0.8 | 14.8 | -19.6 | 8.0 |
| NMX8530 | Nonlife Insurance | -6.2 | 1.2 | -1.7 | 17.6 | -12.3 | 23.8 | 11.4 | 5.7 | 27.1 | 11.9 | 7.8 |
| NMX3570 | Food Producers | 12.9 | -19.9 | 25.1 | 6.3 | 7.8 | 13.2 | 13.7 | 12.1 | 8.8 | -9.3 | 7.1 |
| NMX2790 | Support Services | -9.7 | -27.2 | 28.7 | 19.7 | -2.4 | 20.2 | 26.6 | -1.1 | 5.7 | 3.4 | 6.4 |
| NMX8770 | Financial Services | 2.0 | -55.4 | 39.7 | 21.5 | -28.5 | 23.5 | 42.3 | 9.1 | 10.8 | -1.6 | 6.3 |
| NMX2710 | Aerospace & Defense | 20.4 | -27.6 | 15.8 | 7.7 | 1.1 | 16.9 | 37.6 | -11.8 | -12.9 | 11.9 | 5.9 |
| NMX8980 | Equity Investment Instruments | 6.5 | -36.1 | 31.3 | 18.5 | -10.9 | 10.1 | 14.6 | 7.0 | 3.0 | 13.8 | 5.8 |
| NMX6570 | Mobile Telecommunications | 32.9 | -25.7 | 4.6 | 14.7 | 8.6 | -12.5 | 52.7 | -8.9 | 1.7 | -11.5 | 5.7 |
| NMX5750 | Travel & Leisure | -15.9 | -40.8 | 22.5 | 24.2 | -15.9 | 25.2 | 38.1 | 9.9 | 12.4 | -3.5 | 5.6 |
| NMX8570 | Life Insurance | -10.1 | -43.3 | 26.5 | 2.0 | -4.6 | 32.8 | 36.0 | 9.1 | 3.7 | 1.1 | 5.3 |
| NMX5370 | General Retailers | -25.9 | -47.8 | 75.2 | -2.5 | -11.7 | 32.4 | 32.6 | 12.4 | 0.9 | -13.8 | 5.2 |
| NMX2350 | Construction & Materials | 4.5 | -35.7 | -0.7 | 19.6 | -13.1 | 0.3 | 23.4 | -4.1 | 25.4 | 31.8 | 5.1 |
| NMX4570 | Pharmaceuticals & Biotech | -9.5 | 8.0 | 4.2 | -1.2 | 14.5 | -7.0 | 24.8 | 8.7 | 1.4 | 4.4 | 4.8 |
| NMX6530 | Fixed Line Telecommunications | -5.4 | -44.5 | -1.7 | 19.8 | -5.2 | 24.4 | 61.8 | 3.6 | 16.4 | -21.5 | 4.8 |
| NMX0530 | Oil & Gas Producers | 19.3 | -16.0 | 13.3 | 0.5 | 4.8 | -11.8 | 8.1 | -13.4 | -20.6 | 50.1 | 3.4 |
| NMX7570 | Gas, Water & Multiutilities | 7.3 | -17.8 | -0.6 | 7.9 | 2.8 | 13.2 | 8.0 | 8.2 | -3.2 | 1.9 | 2.8 |
| NMX7530 | Electricity | 6.5 | -16.2 | -1.0 | 14.0 | 8.5 | 8.4 | 3.6 | 6.4 | -10.2 | 4.9 | 2.5 |
| NMX2770 | Industrial Transportation | -20.8 | -61.2 | 52.3 | 25.7 | -12.2 | 13.4 | 30.7 | -12.6 | -8.1 | 17.4 | 2.5 |
| NMX5330 | Food & Drug Retailers | 20.2 | -22.5 | 12.5 | 1.8 | -3.6 | -12.0 | 6.5 | -35.6 | -11.7 | 23.2 | -2.1 |
| NMX8670 | Real Estate Investment Trusts | -36.5 | -44.7 | 6.2 | 2.7 | -12.6 | 25.7 | 15.1 | 20.2 | 6.6 | -10.6 | -2.8 |
| NMX8350 | Banks | -21.3 | -56.8 | 23.8 | -0.1 | -29.6 | 34.5 | 7.8 | -9.5 | -12.7 | 8.4 | -5.6 |

### Note

Since 2007, the sector with the highest average annual return has been Industrial Metals, due to the sector's extraordinary strength in years 2009 and 2016; but note that the sector was also among the three worst sectors in six years over the period.

# SECTOR PROFILES OF THE FTSE 100 & FTSE 250 INDICES

The chart below shows the FTSE 350 sector weightings in the FTSE 100 and FTSE 250 indices. The chart is ranked by the size of capitalisation of the sectors in the FTSE 100. For example, the Banks sector has a weighting of 13.8% in the FTSE 100 (2.2% in the FTSE 250), and the General Retailers has a weighting of 0.9% in the FTSE 100 (6.5% in the FTSE 250).

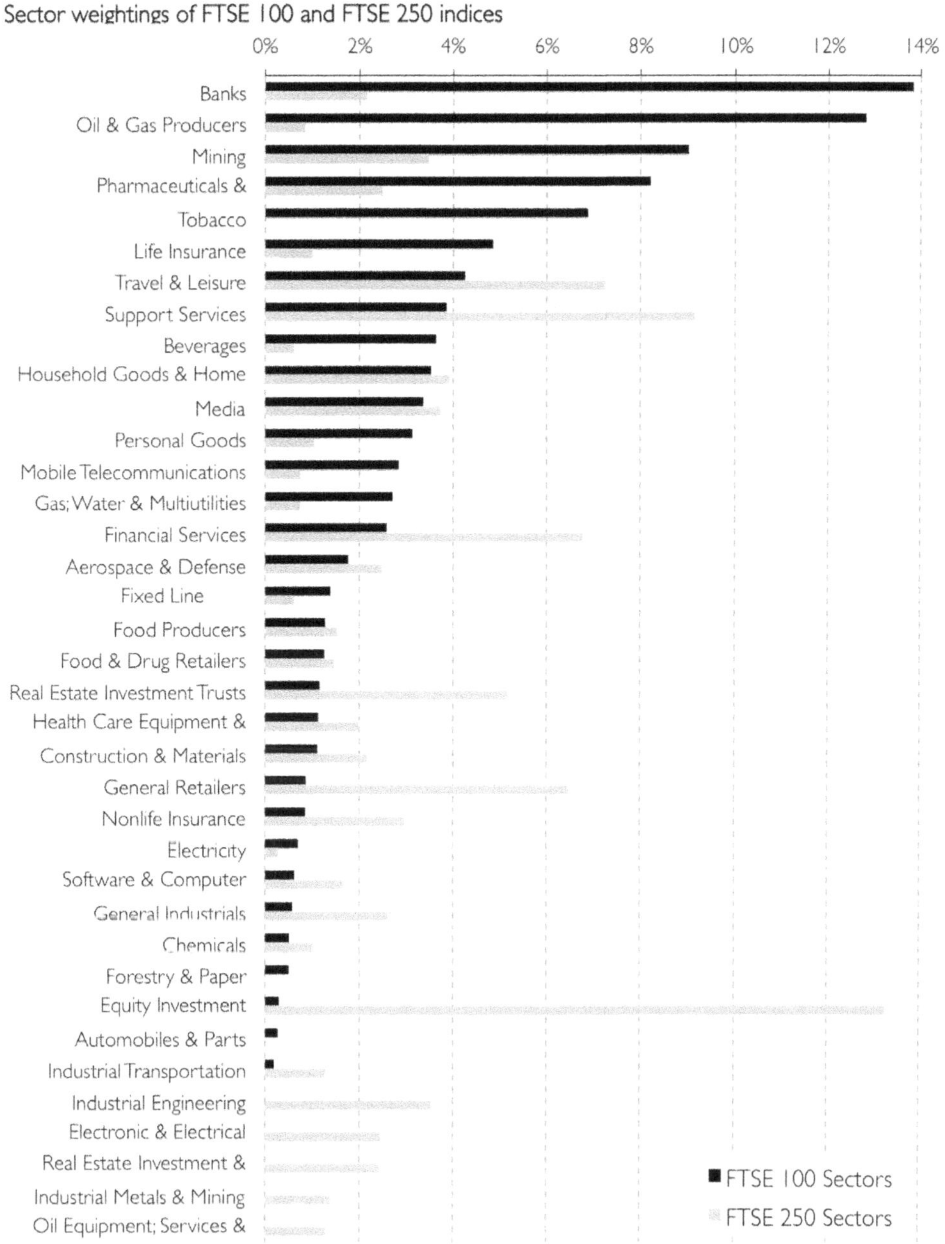


*Note*: Figures as of September 2017

## Observations

1. The top four FTSE 350 sectors (Oil & Gas Producers, Banks, Pharmaceuticals and Beverages) together account for 44% of the total market capitalisation of the FTSE 100. (In 2006, the top four sectors accounted for 55% of the index capitalisation.)

2. Last year, Oil & Gas Producers was the largest sector in the FTSE 100, and Banks was second; this year they have switched positions. Mining stocks have been very strong recently; the sector was ranked sixth by size last year and has today moved up to third. The sector that has fallen the most in the sector ranking in the FTSE 100 has been Beverages (fourth in 2016 and has today slipped to ninth).

3. In 1935 the FT30 was dominated by engineering and machinery companies. Today, the sector isn't represented at all in the FTSE 100.

4. The FTSE 100 is still dominated by the old industries of oil, banks, mining, beverages and tobacco, while the FTSE 250 has, proportionately a greater representation of service (support, financial and computer) companies.

# COMPANIES

# COMPANY RANKINGS

On the following pages are tables with companies ranked according to various criteria. The tables are grouped into the following categories:

1. FTSE 350
2. AIM
3. Investment Trusts

## Table index

A summary of the tables is given below.

1. 10 largest companies by **market capitalisation** [FTSE 350]
2. 10 companies with largest average **daily trade value** [FTSE 350]
3. 5-year **share performance** [FTSE 350]
4. 10-year **share performance** [FTSE 350]
5. 10 companies with highest **turnover** [FTSE 350]
6. 10 companies with greatest **turnover growth** in 5 the last years [FTSE 350]
7. 10 companies with highest **ROCE** [FTSE 350]
8. 10 companies with highest **profits** [FTSE 350]
9. 10 companies with greatest **profit growth** in the last 5 years [FTSE 350]
10. 10 companies with highest **operating margins** [FTSE 350]
11. 10 companies with highest **EPS growth** in the last 5 years [FTSE 350]
12. 10 companies with highest **dividend growth** in the last 5 years [FTSE 350]
13. 10 companies paying the most **tax** in last year [FTSE 350]
14. 10 companies with largest **market capitalisation** [AIM]
15. 10 companies with largest average **daily trade value** [AIM]
16. 5-year **share performance** [AIM]
17. 10 companies with largest **turnover** [AIM]
18. 10 companies with largest **profits** [AIM]
19. 10 companies with highest **ROCE** [AIM]
20. 10 largest investment trusts by **capitalisation [ITs]**
21. 10 **best performing** investment trusts in the last 5 years **[ITs]**
22. 10 investment trusts with highest average **daily trading value [ITs]**

*Note*: All figures accurate as of September 2017.

# FTSE 350

## Size, volume and performance

Table 1: 10 largest companies by market capitalisation [FTSE 350]

| Rank | Company | TIDM | Capital (£m) |
|---|---|---|---|
| 1 | Royal Dutch Shell | RDSB | 176,337 |
| 2 | HSBC Holdings | HSBA | 150,749 |
| 3 | British American Tobacco | BATS | 110,444 |
| 4 | BP | BP. | 87,873 |
| 5 | GlaxoSmithKline | GSK | 75,360 |
| 6 | Diageo | DGE | 65,215 |
| 7 | Vodafone Group | VOD | 58,438 |
| 8 | AstraZeneca | AZN | 58,125 |
| 9 | Unilever | ULVR | 56,709 |
| 10 | Glencore | GLEN | 52,829 |

Table 2: 10 companies with largest average daily trade value [FTSE 350]

| Rank | Company | TIDM | Average daily trade value (£m) |
|---|---|---|---|
| 1 | British American Tobacco | BATS | 201 |
| 2 | HSBC Holdings | HSBA | 178 |
| 3 | BP | BP. | 155 |
| 4 | Rio Tinto | RIO | 154 |
| 5 | Glencore | GLEN | 150 |
| 6 | GlaxoSmithKline | GSK | 141 |
| 7 | Vodafone Group | VOD | 131 |
| 8 | Lloyds Banking Group | LLOY | 129 |
| 9 | AstraZeneca | AZN | 127 |
| 10 | BHP Billiton | BLT | 123 |

Table 3: 5-year share performance [FTSE 350]

| Rank | Company | TIDM | 5-yr change (%) |
|---|---|---|---|
| 1 | NMC Health | NMC | 1,283 |
| 2 | Paysafe Group | PAYS | 1,222 |
| 3 | JD Sports Fashion | JD. | 899 |
| 4 | Thomas Cook Group | TCG | 801 |
| 5 | Ashtead Group | AHT | 502 |
| 6 | Marshalls | MSLH | 417 |
| 7 | Ocado Group | OCDO | 404 |
| 8 | GVC Holdings | GVC | 379 |
| 9 | 3i Group | III | 369 |
| 10 | Smurfit Kappa Group | SKG | 356 |

Table 4: 10-year share performance [FTSE 350]

| Rank | Company | TIDM | 10-yr change (%) |
|---|---|---|---|
| 1 | JD Sports Fashion | JD. | 1,582 |
| 2 | Ashtead Group | AHT | 1,227 |
| 3 | Paysafe Group | PAYS | 1,087 |
| 4 | Booker Group | BOK | 770 |
| 5 | Melrose Industries | MRO | 745 |
| 6 | Micro Focus International | MCRO | 667 |
| 7 | BTG | BTG | 660 |
| 8 | Rightmove | RMV | 607 |
| 9 | Hargreaves Lansdown | HL. | 577 |
| 10 | Randgold Resources Ltd | RRS | 564 |

## Turnover

Table 5: 10 companies with highest turnover [FTSE 350]

| Rank | Company | TIDM | Turnover (£m) |
|---|---|---|---|
| 1 | Royal Dutch Shell | RDSB | 173,000 |
| 2 | BP | BP. | 135,600 |
| 3 | Glencore | GLEN | 113,300 |
| 4 | Legal & General Group | LGEN | 77,970 |
| 5 | Prudential | PRU | 71,840 |
| 6 | Tesco | TSCO | 55,920 |
| 7 | Aviva | AV. | 55,290 |
| 8 | HSBC Holdings | HSBA | 46,720 |
| 9 | Unilever | ULVR | 43,170 |
| 10 | Vodafone Group | VOD | 40,080 |

Table 6: 10 companies with greatest turnover growth in the last 5 years [FTSE 350]

| Rank | Company | TIDM | Turnover 5-yr growth (%) |
|---|---|---|---|
| 1 | Dixons Carphone | DC. | 9,999 |
| 2 | GVC Holdings | GVC | 1,652 |
| 3 | ZPG | ZPG | 1,331 |
| 4 | Just Eat | JE. | 1,013 |
| 5 | John Laing Infrastructure Fund Ltd | JLIF | 862 |
| 6 | Paysafe Group | PAYS | 836 |
| 7 | NewRiver REIT | NRR | 651 |
| 8 | RSA Insurance Group | RSA | 517 |
| 9 | Legal & General Group | LGEN | 326 |
| 10 | Micro Focus International | MCRO | 292 |

Table 7: 10 companies with highest ROCE [FTSE 350]

| Rank | Company | TIDM | ROCE (%) |
|---|---|---|---|
| 1 | Rightmove | RMV | 2,140 |
| 2 | Indivior | INDV | 115 |
| 3 | Restaurant Group (The) | RTN | 95 |
| 4 | Hargreaves Lansdown | HL. | 93 |
| 5 | FDM Group Holdings | FDM | 69 |
| 6 | PayPoint | PAY | 67 |
| 7 | WH Smith | SMWH | 64 |
| 8 | Auto Trader Group | AUTO | 59 |
| 9 | Domino's Pizza UK & IRL | DOM | 58 |
| 10 | Dunelm Group | DNLM | 54 |

## Profits

Table 8: 10 companies with highest profits [FTSE 350]

| Rank | Company | TIDM | Profit (£m) |
|---|---|---|---|
| 1 | BHP Billiton | BLT | 8,142 |
| 2 | British American Tobacco | BATS | 6,245 |
| 3 | Unilever | ULVR | 6,117 |
| 4 | HSBC Holdings | HSBA | 5,269 |
| 5 | Rio Tinto | RIO | 4,699 |
| 6 | Lloyds Banking Group | LLOY | 4,238 |
| 7 | Royal Dutch Shell | RDSB | 4,153 |
| 8 | Diageo | DGE | 3,559 |
| 9 | Barclays | BARC | 3,230 |
| 10 | AstraZeneca | AZN | 2,631 |

Table 9: 10 companies with greatest profit growth in the last 5 years [FTSE 350]

| Rank | Company | TIDM | 5-yr profit growth (%) |
|---|---|---|---|
| 1 | Just Group | JUST | 7,852 |
| 2 | UNITE Group | UTG | 4,185 |
| 3 | Hiscox Ltd | HSX | 1,953 |
| 4 | Hansteen Holdings | HSTN | 1,249 |
| 5 | International Public Partnership Ltd | INPP | 1,231 |
| 6 | Grafton Group | GFTU | 1,183 |
| 7 | Londonmetric Property | LMP | 1,157 |
| 8 | DS Smith | SMDS | 1,117 |
| 9 | Safestore Holdings | SAFE | 1,010 |
| 10 | Redrow | RDW | 888 |

Table 10: 10 companies with highest operating margins [FTSE 350]

| Rank | Company | TIDM | Operating margin (%) |
|---|---|---|---|
| 1 | Shaftesbury | SHB | 168 |
| 2 | Assura | AGR | 165 |
| 3 | Daejan Holdings | DJAN | 150 |
| 4 | Segro | SGRO | 146 |
| 5 | Tritax Big Box REIT | BBOX | 144 |
| 6 | CLS Holdings | CLI | 115 |
| 7 | Londonmetric Property | LMP | 108 |
| 8 | Hansteen Holdings | HSTN | 101 |
| 9 | Big Yellow Group | BYG | 101 |
| 10 | Workspace Group | WKP | 97 |

Table 11: 10 companies with highest EPS growth in the last 5 years [FTSE 350]

| Rank | Company | TIDM | EPS 5-yr growth % |
|---|---|---|---|
| 1 | Just Group | JUST | 9,999 |
| 2 | Jimmy Choo | CHOO | 7,300 |
| 3 | Coats Group | COA | 3,678 |
| 4 | UNITE Group | UTG | 2,218 |
| 5 | Hiscox Ltd | HSX | 2,146 |
| 6 | Barratt Developments | BDEV | 1,322 |
| 7 | Hansteen Holdings | HSTN | 1,214 |
| 8 | Redrow | RDW | 823 |
| 9 | Taylor Wimpey | TW. | 732 |
| 10 | Ashtead Group | AHT | 710 |

## Dividends

Table 12: 10 companies with highest dividend growth in the last 5 years [FTSE 350]

| Rank | Company | TIDM | 5-yr div growth (%) |
|---|---|---|---|
| 1 | Howden Joinery Group | HWDN | 2040 |
| 2 | Persimmon | PSN | 1250 |
| 3 | UNITE Group | UTG | 929 |
| 4 | Bovis Homes Group | BVS | 800 |
| 5 | Bellway | BWY | 764 |
| 6 | Assura | AGR | 707 |
| 7 | Ashtead Group | AHT | 686 |
| 8 | Taylor Wimpey | TW. | 642 |
| 9 | Northgate | NTG | 477 |
| 10 | Smurfit Kappa Group | SKG | 465 |

## Tax

Table 13: 10 companies paying the most tax in the last year

| Rank | Company | TIDM | Tax paid (£m) |
|---|---|---|---:|
| 1 | Vodafone Group | VOD | 4,010 |
| 2 | BHP Billiton | BLT | 3,360 |
| 3 | HSBC Holdings | HSBA | 2,720 |
| 4 | Lloyds Banking Group | LLOY | 1,720 |
| 5 | Unilever | ULVR | 1,570 |
| 6 | British American Tobacco | BATS | 1,410 |
| 7 | Royal Bank of Scotland Group | RBS | 1,170 |
| 8 | Rio Tinto | RIO | 1,160 |
| 9 | Barclays | BARC | 993 |
| 10 | GlaxoSmithKline | GSK | 877 |

## AIM

Table 14: 10 companies with largest market capitalisation [AIM]

| Rank | Name | TIDM | Capital (£m) |
|---|---|---|---:|
| 1 | ASOS | ASC | 4,740 |
| 2 | Fevertree Drinks | FEVR | 2,864 |
| 3 | boohoo.com | BOO | 2,643 |
| 4 | Burford Capital Ltd | BUR | 2,395 |
| 5 | Hutchison China Meditech Ltd | HCM | 2,332 |
| 6 | Abcam | ABC | 2,197 |
| 7 | Phoenix Global Resources | PGR | 1,427 |
| 8 | Clinigen Group | CLIN | 1,313 |
| 9 | Breedon Group | BREE | 1,291 |
| 10 | Purplebricks Group | PURP | 1,289 |

Table 15: 10 companies with largest average daily trade value [AIM]

| Rank | Name | TIDM | Average daily trade value (£m) |
|---|---|---|---:|
| 1 | ASOS | ASC | 28.0 |
| 2 | boohoo.com | BOO | 18.7 |
| 3 | Fevertree Drinks | FEVR | 12.2 |
| 4 | IQE | IQE | 6.5 |
| 5 | Burford Capital Ltd | BUR | 5.5 |
| 6 | Abcam | ABC | 5.4 |
| 7 | UK Oil & Gas Investments | UKOG | 4.9 |
| 8 | Plus500 Ltd | PLUS | 4.8 |
| 9 | Sound Energy | SOU | 4.6 |
| 10 | Hurricane Energy | HUR | 4.3 |

### Table 16: 5-year share performance [AIM]

| Rank | Name | TIDM | 5-yr share price (%) |
|---|---|---|---|
| 1 | UK Oil & Gas Investments | UKOG | 2,015 |
| 2 | Redde | REDD | 1,980 |
| 3 | Best of the Best | BOTB | 1,618 |
| 4 | Victoria | VCP | 1,225 |
| 5 | Sigma Capital Group | SGM | 1,033 |
| 6 | Somero Enterprises Inc | SOM | 1,004 |
| 7 | Burford Capital Ltd | BUR | 965 |
| 8 | CVS Group | CVSG | 955 |
| 9 | Sound Energy | SOU | 953 |
| 10 | Cropper (James) | CRPR | 907 |

### Table 17: 10 companies with largest turnover [AIM]

| Rank | Name | TIDM | Turnover (£m) |
|---|---|---|---|
| 1 | Datatec Ltd | DTC | 4,612 |
| 2 | Vertu Motors | VTU | 2,823 |
| 3 | Total Produce | TOT | 2,543 |
| 4 | Impellam Group | IPEL | 2,140 |
| 5 | Marshall Motor Holdings | MMH | 1,899 |
| 6 | Dart Group | DTG | 1,729 |
| 7 | Conviviality Retail | CVR | 1,560 |
| 8 | Origin Enterprises | OGN | 1,521 |
| 9 | ASOS | ASC | 1,445 |
| 10 | Applegreen | APGN | 965 |

### Table 18: 10 companies with largest profits [AIM]

| Rank | Name | TIDM | Profit (£m) |
|---|---|---|---|
| 1 | Plus500 Ltd | PLUS | 113 |
| 2 | Secure Income REIT | SIR | 94 |
| 3 | Dart Group | DTG | 90 |
| 4 | Burford Capital Ltd | BUR | 77 |
| 5 | Rockhopper Exploration | RKH | 73 |
| 6 | Origin Enterprises | OGN | 66 |
| 7 | Summit Germany Ltd | SMTG | 64 |
| 8 | Abbey | ABBY | 63 |
| 9 | EPE Special Opportunities | ESO | 61 |
| 10 | Highland Gold Mining Ltd | HGM | 49 |

Table 19: 10 companies with highest ROCE [AIM]

| Rank | Name | TIDM | ROCE |
|---|---|---|---|
| 1 | Pathfinder Minerals | PFP | 6,130 |
| 2 | Andalas Energy and Power | ADL | 5,970 |
| 3 | Infinity Energy SA | INFT | 2,350 |
| 4 | Jangada Mines | JAN | 640 |
| 5 | Hague and London Oil | HNL | 503 |
| 6 | Frontera Resources Corporation | FRR | 387 |
| 7 | Imaginatik | IMTK | 366 |
| 8 | STM Group | STM | 319 |
| 9 | BOS Global Holdings NL | BOS | 267 |
| 10 | System1 Group | SYS1 | 210 |

## Investment Trusts

Table 20: 10 largest investment trusts by capitalisation

| Rank | Investment Trust | TIDM | Capital (£m) |
|---|---|---|---|
| 1 | 3i Group | III | 9,378 |
| 2 | Land Securities Group | LAND | 7,876 |
| 3 | British Land Co | BLND | 6,194 |
| 4 | Scottish Mortgage Investment Trust | SMT | 6,073 |
| 5 | Segro | SGRO | 5,372 |
| 6 | Hammerson | HMSO | 4,402 |
| 7 | Foreign & Colonial Investment Trust | FRCL | 3,355 |
| 8 | Intu Properties | INTU | 3,338 |
| 9 | Derwent London | DLN | 3,084 |
| 10 | RIT Capital Partners | RCP | 2,998 |

### Table 21: 10 best performing investment trusts in the last 5 years

| Rank | Investment Trust | TIDM | 5-yr price change (%) |
|---|---|---|---|
| 1 | Downing Two VCT D | DP3E | 9,910 |
| 2 | Hazel Renewable Energy VCT 1 | HR1A | 4,950 |
| 3 | Hazel Renewable Energy VCT 2 | HR2A | 4,950 |
| 4 | Downing Structured Opps VCT 1 | DO1C | 4,910 |
| 5 | Downing Two VCT E | DP2E | 4,910 |
| 6 | Premier Veterinary Group | PVG | 3,739 |
| 7 | Burford Capital Ltd | BUR | 965 |
| 8 | JPMorgan Fleming Japanese Smaller Cos Inv Tr | JPSS | 519 |
| 9 | EPE Special Opportunities | ESO | 462 |
| 10 | 3i Group | III | 369 |

### Table 22: 10 investment trusts with highest average daily trading value

| Rank | Investment Trust | TIDM | Average daily trade value( £m) |
|---|---|---|---|
| 1 | British Land Co | BLND | 27.20 |
| 2 | Land Securities Group | LAND | 23.64 |
| 3 | Hammerson | HMSO | 17.72 |
| 4 | 3i Group | III | 16.88 |
| 5 | Segro | SGRO | 11.25 |
| 6 | Intu Properties | INTU | 9.80 |
| 7 | Scottish Mortgage Investment Trust | SMT | 9.45 |
| 8 | Derwent London | DLN | 9.24 |
| 9 | Great Portland Estates | GPOR | 7.94 |
| 10 | Alliance Trust | ATST | 6.34 |

# ANNOUNCEMENT DATES OF COMPANY RESULTS

Companies listed on the London Stock Exchange are required to release certain information to the public. Some of these statements are one-offs and unpredictable, such as news of takeovers or board changes, while others follow a more regular timetable. For investors, two important announcements each year are:

1. **Interim results** (known as *interims*): usually reported about eight months into a company's financial year, they relate to the unaudited headline figures for the first half of the company's year.

2. **Preliminary results** (known as *prelims*): unaudited figures published prior to the full annual report at the end of the company's financial year. (Note that although these are termed "preliminary", these are very much the real final results.)

These announcements are watched very carefully and have the potential to significantly move the share price of a company.

## FTSE 100

The following chart plots the frequency distribution of the dates of these announcements for FTSE 100 companies.

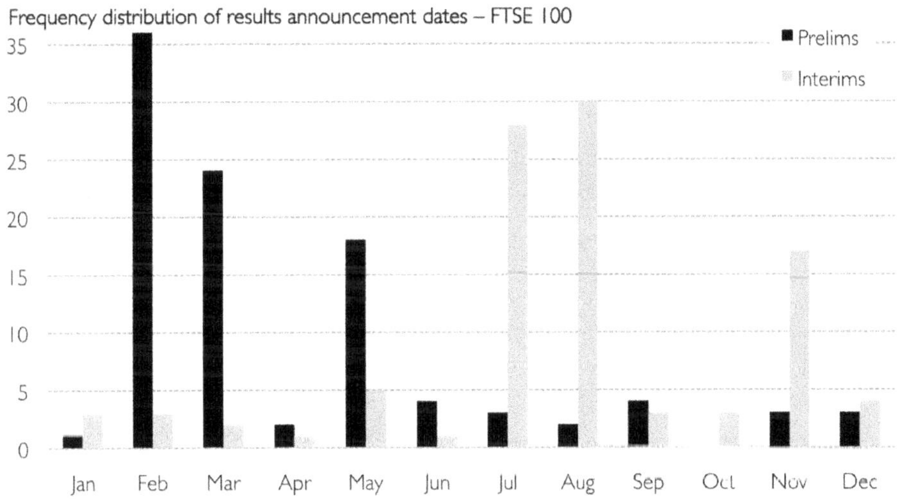


As can be seen, the majority of interim results are announced in July and August, while preliminary results are clustered in February and March (60 companies announce their prelims in this two-month period).

## FTSE 250

The following chart is similar to that above, except this time the companies are in the FTSE 250.

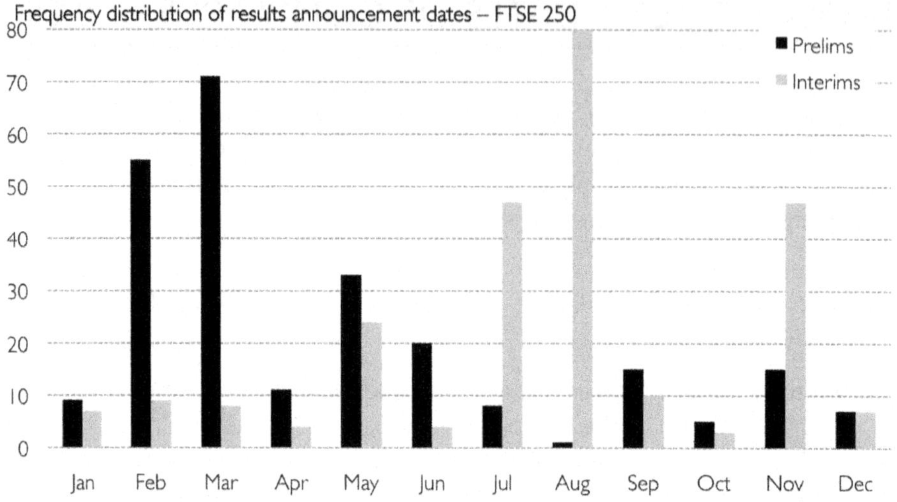


For the FTSE 250 companies, the announcements are a little more evenly distributed throughout the year, but the main months are the same as those for the FTSE 100: July/August are the busiest months (with November) for interims, and February/March are the busiest for the prelims.

# TEN BAGGERS

The term *ten bagger* was coined by Peter Lynch, the legendary manager of the Fidelity Magellan fund, in his book *One Up on Wall Street*. The term ten-bagger comes from baseball, but Lynch used it to describe stocks that rise ten times in value.

The table below shows the UK stocks that rose ten times or more in the ten years to September 2017.

### UK ten baggers over ten years to September 2017

| Company | TIDM | Price increase (%) | Mkt cap (£m) | Sector | Index |
|---|---|---|---|---|---|
| ASOS | ASC | 4,776 | 4,740 | General Retailers | AIM UK 50 |
| Accesso Technology Group | ACSO | 4,746 | 415 | Software & Computer Services | AIM 100 |
| Hutchison China Meditech Ltd | HCM | 2,101 | 2,332 | Pharmaceuticals & Biotechnology | AIM 100 |
| Judges Scientific | JDG | 1,983 | 115 | Electronic & Electrical Equipment | AIM All-Share |
| Abcam | ABC | 1,616 | 2,197 | Pharmaceuticals & Biotechnology | AIM UK 50 |
| JD Sports Fashion | JD. | 1,582 | 3,199 | General Retailers | FTSE Mid 250 |
| Scapa Group | SCPA | 1,429 | 693 | Chemicals | AIM UK 50 |
| Advanced Medical Solutions Group | AMS | 1,313 | 689 | Health Care Equipment & Services | AIM UK 50 |
| GB Group | GBG | 1,310 | 586 | Software & Computer Services | AIM UK 50 |
| Ashtead Group | AHT | 1,227 | 8,512 | Support Services | FTSE 100 |
| Paysafe Group | PAYS | 1,087 | 2,835 | Support Services | FTSE Mid 250 |

### Observations

1. The table above does not include those companies that rose ten times in the interim, only to see their share prices fall back again. For example, companies such as Ashtead, Aveva, Babcock Intl, Domino's Pizza, Dragon Oil, Goodwin, and Randgold Resources, have all been ten baggers at some point.

2. Jim Slater's comment that "elephants don't gallop" would seem to hold true. Many of the above ten baggers were very small companies ten years ago.

3. It can be seen that the ten baggers come from quite a wide range of sectors. In other words, it's not necessary to look for ten baggers in just a few glamour sectors.

As Peter Lynch says:

> The very best way to make money in a market is in a small growth company that has been profitable for a couple of years and simply goes on growing.

# THE DIVIDEND PAYMENT CALENDAR

It is easy to forget about the importance of dividends. After all, the prospect of a share price rising (or falling) by 50% seems a lot more exciting than a company paying a 3p dividend. But Jeremy Siegel (author of the famous book ***Stocks for the Long Run***) calculated that for US stocks roughly three-quarters of the real return from the stock market came from dividends, with only one-quarter from capital gains. The case for UK stocks would not be very different.

Dividends are also important for what they say about the fundamentals of a company. Making capital gains on a company that has paper profits may be nice, but profits that produce real cash dividends can be a lot more reassuring.

Of course, dividends can be especially important for some investors, such as retirees, who look to the regular dividend cheque as a vital source of income. The aggregate dividend yield on the FTSE 100 companies is currently around 4%, which is attractive, particularly when the base rate is 0.25%.

However, for income investors, it is not only the size of the dividend cheque that can matter, but also its timing.

The following chart plots the frequency distribution of dividend payment dates by month for the FTSE 100 companies. For example, in January eight companies pay a final dividend and 28 companies pay an interim dividend.

Frequency distribution of dividend payment dates [FTSE 100]

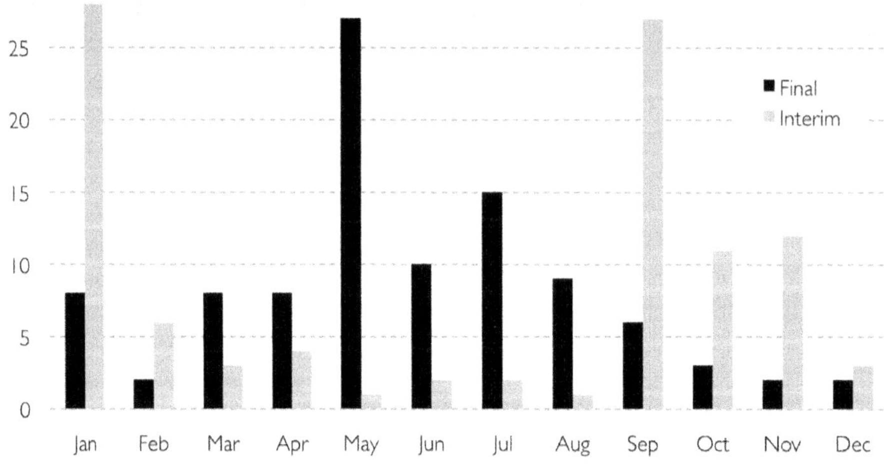


As can be seen, although dividend payments occur in all months of the year, the months with most dividend payments are January, May and September.

However, not all dividends are equal, some companies pay a higher dividend (measured by the dividend yield) than others. So, this has been accounted for in the following chart, which plots aggregate dividends for all FTSE 100 companies in each month.

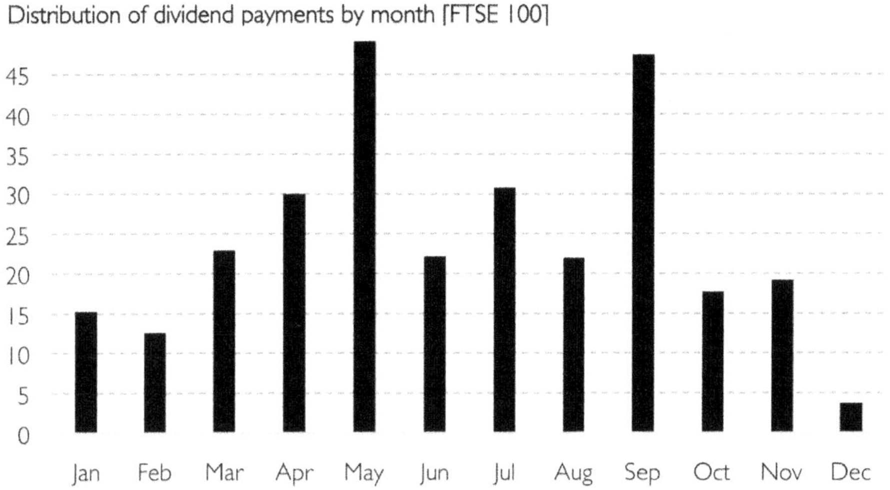


As can be seen, the best months for receiving FTSE 100 dividends are May and September. In this chart (compared to the first one above), January falls back because while number-wise many companies pay dividends in January they are largely interim dividends which tend to be for smaller amounts than final dividends.

## Dividend cover

Dividend cover is the ratio of a company's earnings over the dividend paid to shareholders. The ratio measures the ease with which a company can pay its dividend from net income. For an investor, if the dividend cover is low they may be concerned about the company's ability to pay future dividends or its ability to increase those payments.

The following chart plots the dividend cover of the 89 FTSE 100 companies last year that made a profit and paid a dividend. The chart is ordered along the X-axis by dividend cover.

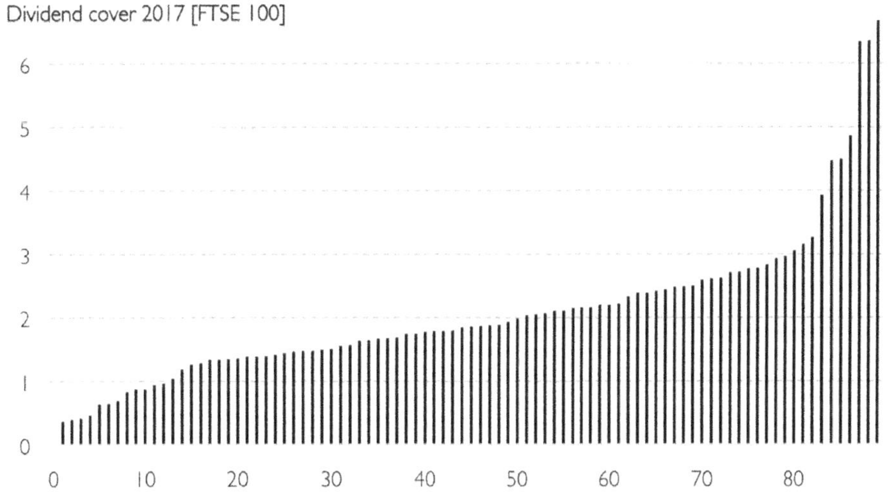

The company with the lowest dividend cover was Scottish Mortgage Investment Trust, with cover of 0.36, while the highest was Shire with 6.7.

The median cover was 1.9 (i.e. the cover of the 45th company in the ranking), while the mean (average) cover was 2.1.

# LONG TERM

# CORRELATION BETWEEN UK AND US MARKETS

*Here we look at how close the movements of the US and UK markets are on a monthly basis and how this has changed over time.*

The following charts plot the correlation of monthly returns of the FTSE All-Share and S&P 500 indices for each decade since the 1970s.

**1970s**

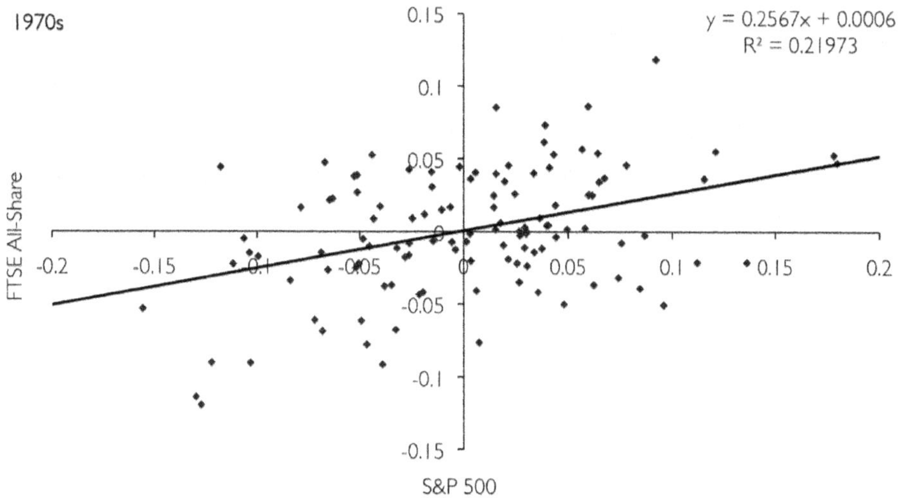


**1980s**

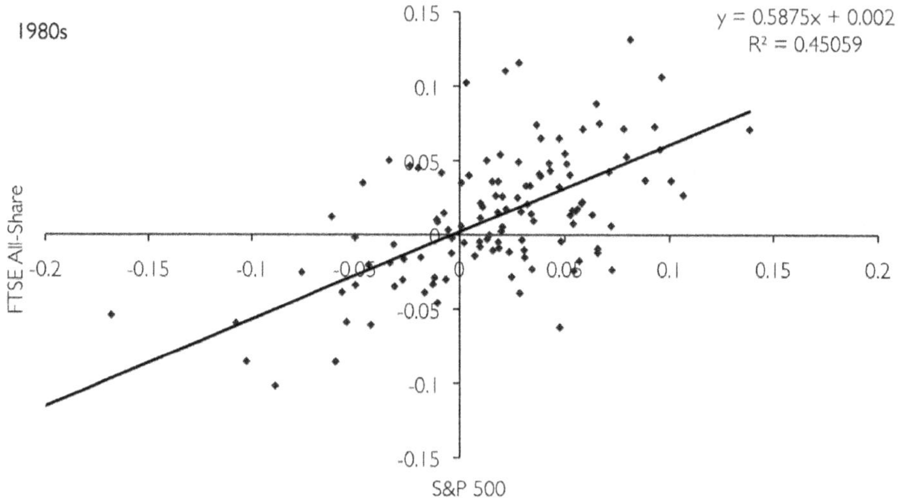

## 1990s

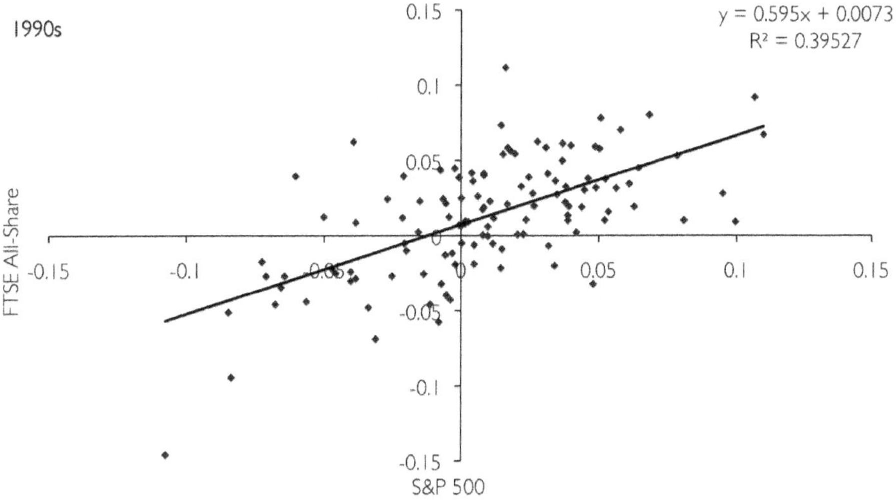
1990s
y = 0.595x + 0.0073
R² = 0.39527
0.15
0.1
0.05
0
-0.05
-0.1
-0.15
-0.15
-0.1
-0.05
0.05
0.1
0.15
FTSE All-Share
S&P 500

## 2000s

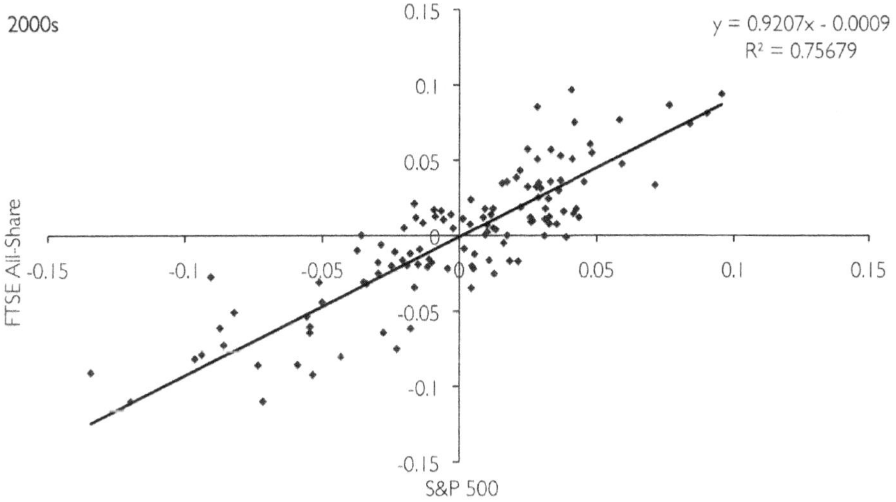
2000s
y = 0.9207x - 0.0009
R² = 0.75679
0.15
0.1
0.05
0
-0.05
-0.1
-0.15
-0.15
-0.1
-0.05
0.05
0.1
0.15
FTSE All-Share
S&P 500

## 2010s

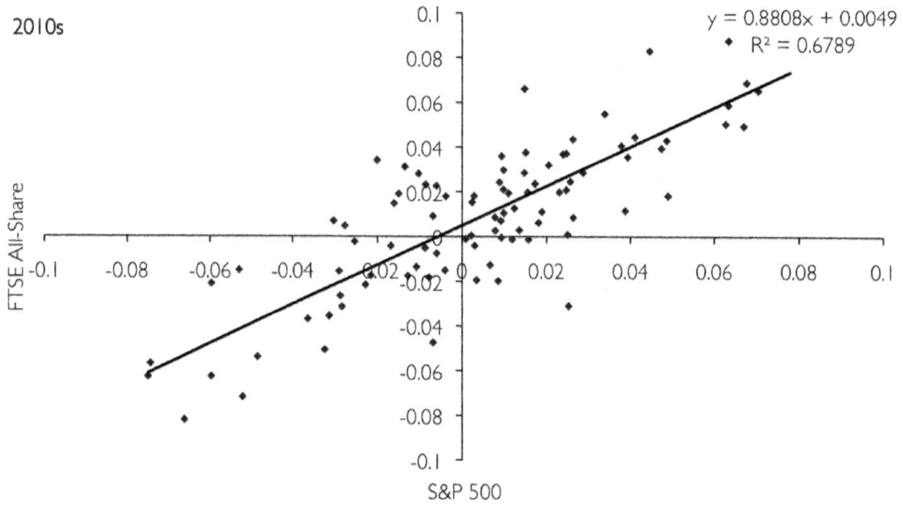


There is obviously a trend of increasing correlation throughout the decades. In the 1970s there was negligible correlation (measured by the $R^2$ value in the charts) between the UK and US markets on a monthly basis. The US equity market might rise one month and the UK would respond by rising or falling – there was little connection. The evidence for correlation between the two markets was very weak.

But in the 1980s the monthly correlation of the two markets jumped and became statistically significant. There could be many reasons for this increase in correlation, but one contributing factor was undoubtedly the increasing presence of computers in trading rooms. And, of course, the October crash in 1987 would have alerted many for the first time to the scale of the inter-connectedness of worldwide markets.

Correlation rose somewhat again in the 1990s, but then increased hugely in the 2000s. This can be clearly seen in the last two charts, where the points are closely aligned along the line of best fit.

The correlation of monthly returns for the two markets has been drifting lower since 2010. Last year the $R^2$ was 0.73 (for the period 2010–2016), and this year it has decreased again to 0.68, though this is still a very high correlation.

# CORRELATION BETWEEN UK AND WORLD MARKETS

*This is an update of the analysis of the correlation of the UK equity market with six other markets worldwide.*

The charts in this article show the correlation of monthly returns between the FTSE All-Share index and six international indices for the period 2000–2017.

## DAX

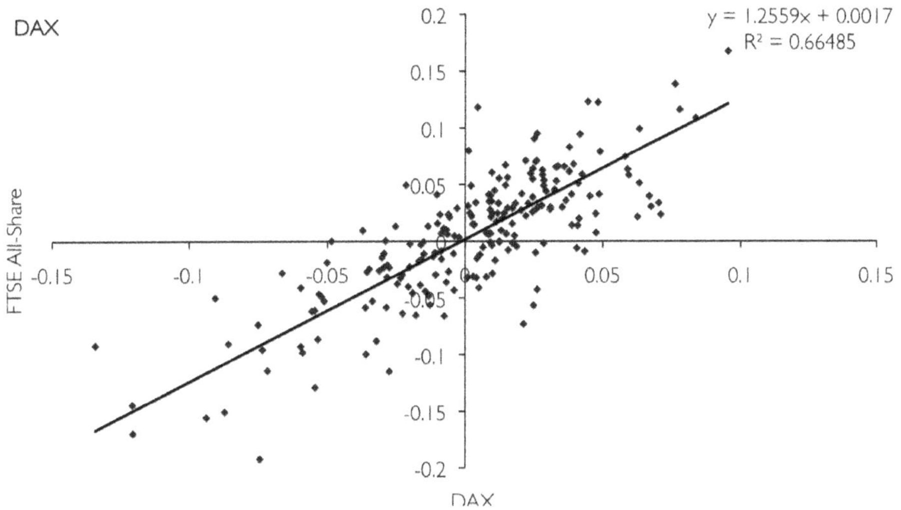


## CAC 40

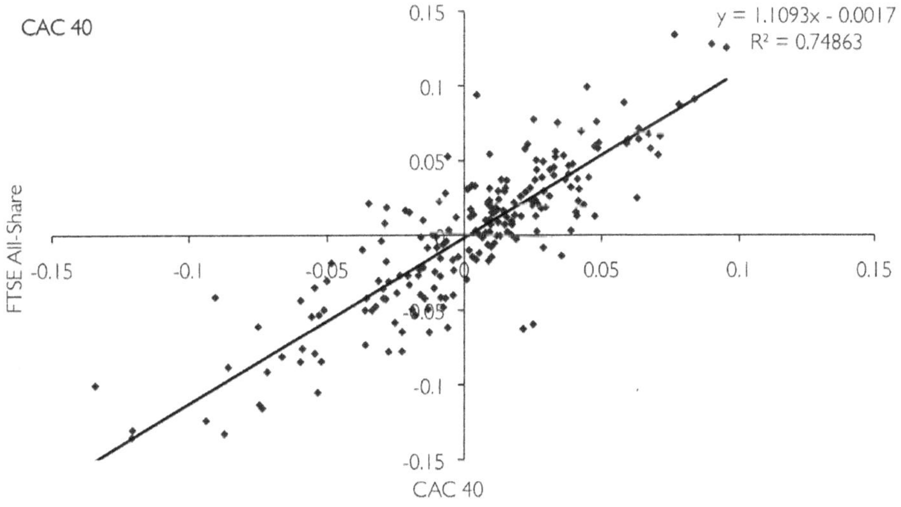

## Nikkei 225

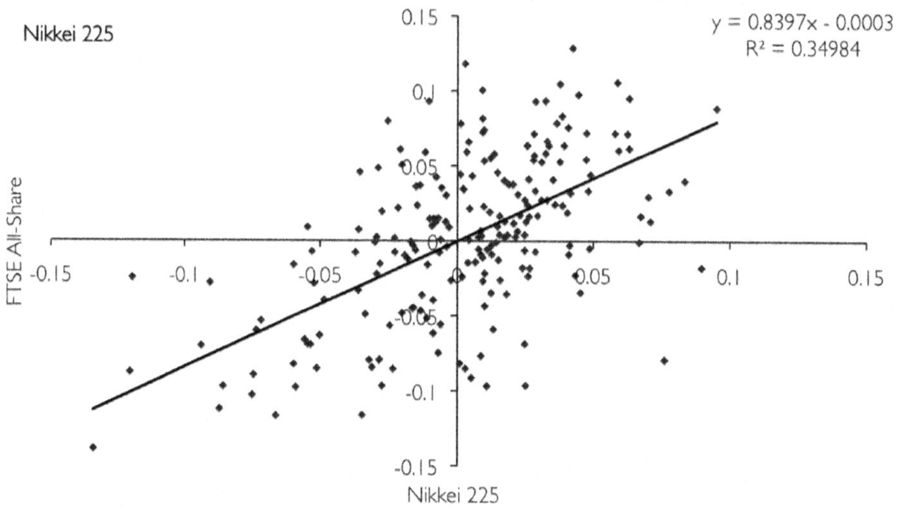


## Hang Seng

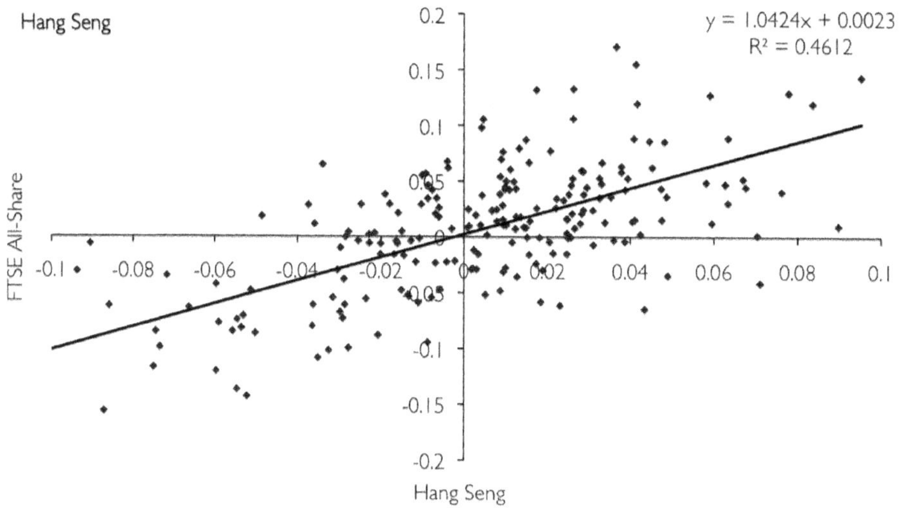

## All Ordinaries

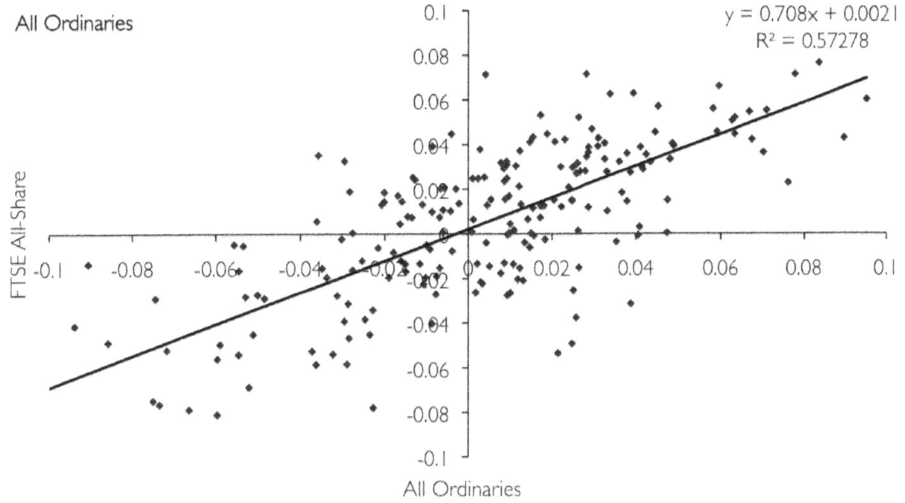


## Bovespa

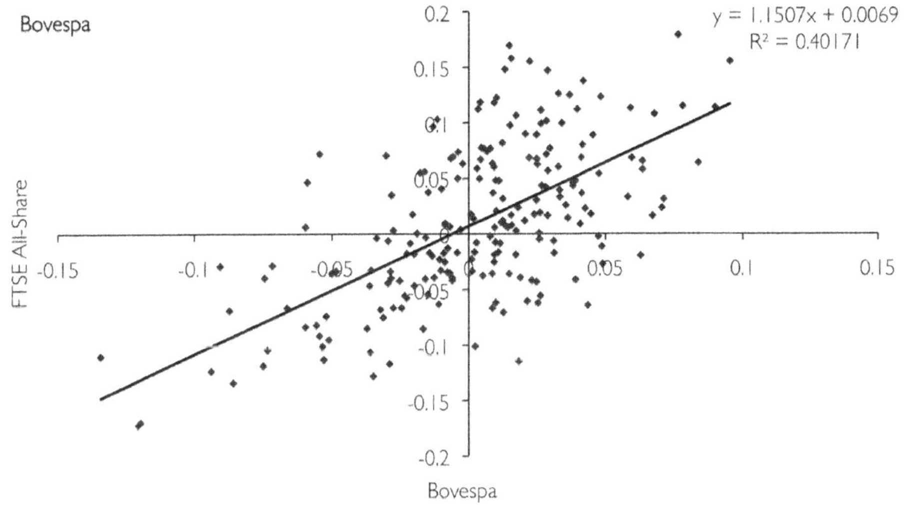


## Analysis

| Index | $R^2$ (2017) | $R^2$ (2016) | $R^2$ (2015) | $R^2$ (2014) | $R^2$ (2013) |
|---|---|---|---|---|---|
| CAC 40 | 0.75 | 0.76 | 0.77 | 0.78 | 0.79 |
| DAX | 0.66 | 0.67 | 0.67 | 0.69 | 0.70 |
| All Ordinaries | 0.57 | 0.59 | 0.60 | 0.61 | 0.62 |
| Hang Seng | 0.46 | 0.48 | 0.47 | 0.48 | 0.49 |
| Bovespa | 0.40 | 0.42 | 0.43 | 0.45 | 0.47 |
| Nikkei 225 | 0.35 | 0.36 | 0.36 | 0.37 | 0.39 |

The first observation is that all the markets are positively correlated with the UK market.

*The next question is how closely correlated are they?*

The table summarises the $R^2$ values for the correlation between the FTSE All-Share and the six international indices (values are also given for previous years). The higher the $R^2$ figure, the closer the correlation (R-squared is a measure of correlation – in effect, how close the points are to the line of best fit).

By visual inspection it can be seen that in the charts of the CAC 40 and DAX the points are more closely distributed around the line of best fit. This is confirmed in the table where it can be seen these two markets have the highest $R^2$ values (the CAC 40 value of 0.75 is now higher than that of 0.68 for the S&P 500). Among the sample, the index with the lowest correlation with the UK market is the Nikkei.

The practical impact of this is that if a UK investor is looking to internationally diversify a portfolio they would do better by investing in markets at the bottom of the table (low $R^2$) than at the top.

And the good news for investors looking for diversification is that the correlation between the UK market and all the international markets in this study has been falling steadily every year since 2013.

# THE LONG-TERM FORMULA

*What can the very long term tell us about the trend of the UK market?*

## 1946–2017

The chart below plots the FTSE All-Share index from 1946 to the present day.

1. The Y-scale is logarithmic, which presents percentage (rather than absolute) changes better over long periods, and so is more suitable for long-term charts.
2. The straight line is a line of best fit calculated by regression analysis.

## Observations

1. The $R^2$ for the line of best fit is 0.96, which is impressively high for such a simple model (i.e. the line of best fit fairly accurately approximates the real data points).
2. The FTSE All-Share fluctuated closely around the trend line (line of best fit) from 1946 to 1973; it then traded consistently below the trend line until 1983, when it crossed over to trade above the trend line until 2001. From 2001 the index was close to the trend, but then in 2008 fell significantly below it and has yet to revert to the long-term trend line.

## Forecasts

The equation of the line of best fit in the chart above (with a little more precision) is:

$$y = 0.872684e^{0.000206x}$$

This equation allows us to make forecasts for the FTSE All-Share. It is, in effect, the Holy Grail, the key to the stock market – as simple as that!

For example, at the time of writing the FTSE All-Share is at 4075.5, while the above equation forecasts a value today (according to the long-term trend line) of 6110. This suggests the index is currently underpriced relative to the long-term trend line. But as can be seen in the above chart the index can spend long periods trading above or below the long-term trend line.

Now, if we think that the trend of the market in the last 70 years will broadly continue, then we can use the equation to forecast the level of the FTSE All-Share in the future. And this is what has been done in the following table. Equivalent forecasts for the FTSE 100 have also been given.

| Date | FTAS Forecast | FTSE 100 Forecast | Premium over current (%) |
|---|---|---|---|
| Dec 2018 | 6,749 | 12,318 | 66 |
| Dec 2020 | 7,846 | 14,320 | 93 |
| Dec 2030 | 16,647 | 30,384 | 308 |
| Dec 2040 | 35,329 | 64,482 | 767 |

The equation says that the trend line value for FTSE 100 at the end 2018 will be 12,318 (66% above its current level in September 2017, the time of writing).

By the end of 2020, the forecast is for a FTSE 100 level of **14,320** (+93%), and by the end of 2040 the equation forecasts a FTSE 100 trend value of **64,482** (+767%).

*So, that's easy.*

Well, except this…

## 1920–2017

We will now look at a trend line calculated from data for 1920 to 2017.

First, here is the chart from 1920 with its trend line.

In this case, the $R^2$ is 0.93, slightly lower than that calculated above for the data from 1946, but still impressively high.

Again, we can use the equation of the trend line to forecast trend values for future dates.

| Date | FTAS Forecast | FTSE 100 Forecast | Premium over current (%) |
|---|---:|---:|---:|
| Dec 2018 | 4,428 | 8,081 | 9 |
| Dec 2020 | 5,004 | 9,134 | 23 |
| Dec 2030 | 9,227 | 16,840 | 126 |
| Dec 2040 | 17,014 | 31,053 | 317 |

Whereas the data from 1946 forecast a FTSE 100 level of **12,318** at end of 2018, the 1920 data forecasts a level of **8081** (9% above the current level).

As can be seen above, the trend-line equation is very sensitive to the sample data (i.e. in this case, the choice of start date).

*So, which trend do you think the market will follow from here, that from 1920, or that from 1946?*

# THE MARKET'S DECENNIAL CYCLE

The following table shows the annual performance of the FTSE All-Share index since 1801. The table is arranged to compare the performance of the market for the same year in each decade. For example, in the third year of the 1801–1810 decade (1803), the market fell 21.9%, while in the third year of the 1811–1820 decade (1813), the market fell 0.2%. Years are highlighted in which the market fell.

| Decades | 1st | 2nd | 3rd | 4th | 5th | 6th | 7th | 8th | 9th | 10th |
|---|---|---|---|---|---|---|---|---|---|---|
| 1801-1810 | 11.0 | 1.4 | -21.9 | 10.3 | 8.5 | 0.7 | 3.5 | 4.7 | 10.4 | -9.2 |
| 1811-1820 | -14.6 | -7.5 | -0.2 | 2.4 | -6.2 | -12.2 | 32.6 | 5.5 | -8.3 | 3.2 |
| 1821-1830 | 4.5 | 9.4 | 9.2 | 90.7 | -22.7 | -20.1 | 4.6 | -14.5 | 3.3 | -14.8 |
| 1831-1840 | -15.7 | 2.2 | 16.5 | -9.3 | 5.0 | 5.2 | -8.5 | -3.6 | -12.7 | 3.1 |
| 1841-1850 | -9.7 | 7.1 | 12.3 | 16.5 | -2.1 | -1.8 | -13.9 | -13.5 | -7.3 | 14.4 |
| 1851-1860 | -0.2 | 9.6 | -6.8 | -3.2 | -3.4 | 5.4 | -5.9 | 6.5 | -2.0 | 11.1 |
| 1861-1870 | 3.1 | 16.6 | 12.8 | 5.0 | 1.4 | -22.4 | -2.2 | 6.8 | 7.4 | 8.6 |
| 1871-1880 | 18.9 | 4.0 | 3.6 | -5.2 | -7.9 | -2.4 | -9.6 | -11.0 | 12.1 | 4.9 |
| 1881-1890 | -0.6 | -6.3 | -5.0 | -2.1 | 0.2 | 0.6 | -3.6 | 5.8 | 13.1 | -6.2 |
| 1891-1900 | 0.7 | -0.1 | 1.6 | 6.0 | 11.2 | 22.0 | 5.2 | 0.3 | -2.0 | -0.9 |
| 1901-1910 | -4.9 | -1.3 | -5.6 | 2.5 | 6.2 | -0.4 | -14.7 | 8.1 | 4.8 | -2.5 |
| 1911-1920 | 0.3 | -0.9 | -6.7 | -6.9 | -5.1 | 0.5 | -10.5 | 11.0 | 2.4 | -13.3 |
| 1921-1930 | -5.4 | 17.6 | 2.0 | 9.5 | 4.4 | 2.4 | 8.3 | 8.1 | -7.4 | -19.4 |
| 1931-1940 | -23.5 | 5.6 | 27.2 | 8.3 | 7.8 | 13.9 | -19.3 | -14.3 | 0.8 | -13.0 |
| 1941-1950 | 22.6 | 18.6 | 8.1 | 10.7 | -0.6 | 18.1 | -2.7 | -4.0 | -13.9 | 6.4 |
| 1951-1960 | 2.4 | -5.1 | 16.0 | 34.5 | 1.6 | -9.0 | -3.3 | 33.2 | 43.4 | -4.7 |
| 1961-1970 | -2.5 | -1.8 | 10.6 | -10.0 | 6.7 | -9.3 | 29.0 | 43.4 | -15.2 | -7.5 |
| 1971-1980 | 41.9 | 12.8 | -31.4 | -55.3 | 136.3 | -3.9 | 41.2 | 2.7 | 4.3 | 27.1 |
| 1981-1990 | 7.2 | 22.1 | 23.1 | 26.0 | 15.2 | 22.3 | 4.2 | 6.5 | 30.0 | -14.3 |
| 1991-2000 | 15.1 | 14.8 | 23.3 | -9.6 | 18.5 | 11.7 | 19.7 | 10.9 | 21.2 | -8.0 |
| 2001-2010 | -15.4 | -25.0 | 16.6 | 9.2 | 18.1 | 13.2 | 2.0 | -32.8 | 25.0 | 10.9 |
| 2011-2020 | -6.7 | 8.2 | 16.7 | -2.1 | -2.4 | 12.3 | | | | |

## Analysis

| Since 1810 | | | | | | | | | | |
|---|---|---|---|---|---|---|---|---|---|---|
| Positive: | 50% | 64% | 68% | 59% | 64% | 59% | 48% | 67% | 62% | 43% |
| Average(%): | 1.3 | 4.6 | 5.5 | 5.8 | 8.7 | 2.1 | 2.7 | 2.9 | 5.2 | -1.2 |
| **Since 1921** | | | | | | | | | | |
| Positive: | 50% | 70% | 90% | 60% | 80% | 70% | 67% | 67% | 67% | 33% |
| Average(%): | 3.6 | 6.8 | 11.2 | 2.1 | 20.6 | 7.2 | 8.8 | 6.0 | 9.8 | -2.5 |
| **Since 1951** | | | | | | | | | | |
| Positive: | 57% | 57% | 86% | 43% | 86% | 57% | 83% | 83% | 83% | 33% |
| Average(%): | 6.0 | 3.7 | 10.7 | -1.0 | 27.7 | 5.3 | 15.5 | 10.6 | 18.1 | 0.6 |

## Observations

1. Since 1801, the strongest years have been the 2nd, 3rd, and 5th years in the decades. The market has risen with an average annual return over 4%. But the single year champion has got to be the 5th year in each decade, which has risen an average of 8.7%.

2. The stand-out weakest year in the decade since 1801 has been the 10th – this is the only year to have risen less than ten times in the 21 decades, and also the only year to have a negative average return (−1.2%).

3. Generally, performance in the more recent decades has not changed too much from the long-term picture. In the six decades since 1951, the strong years are still the 3rd, and 5th years, although now also joined by the 7th and 9th years. And the 10th year continues to be weakest, with positive returns only twice in the past six decades.

## 2018

The following chart plots the annual returns for the FTSE All-Share for all the 8th years of the decade since 1801.

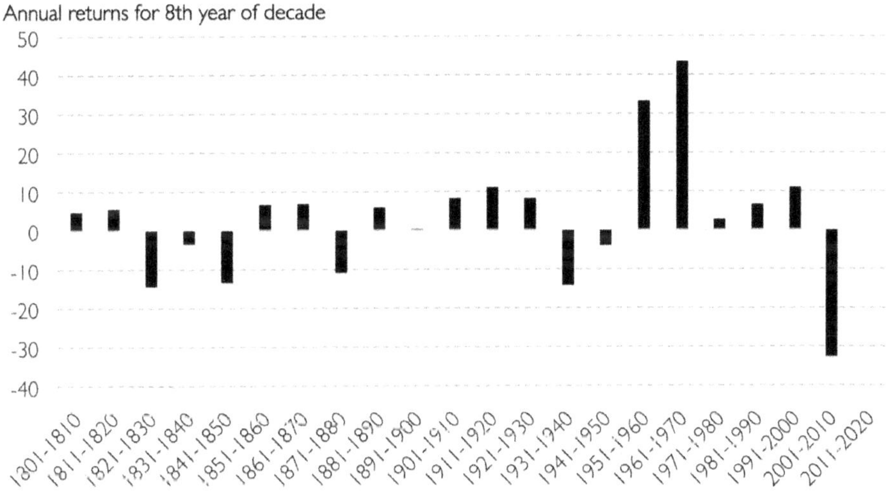


From 1958 the market had been on quite a roll in the 8th year of the decades. But then along came 2008, which wasn't so good!

# BUY AND HOLD

*An update on whether buy and hold still works.*

The last decade or so has not been the best for buy-and-hold investors. At the time of writing (September 2017) the FTSE 100 index is just 7% above its level nearly 17 years ago.

*The question must be asked: is buy and hold dead?*

Such thinking inspired Richard Bernstein to write a paper[1] in July 2012 called, appropriately, 'Is buy and hold dead?' In the paper, which advocates longer-term investing, Bernstein says:

> There are sound economic reasons why extending one's time horizon can benefit investment returns. Changes within the economy tend to be very gradual, and significant adjustments rarely happen within a short period of time. Certainly, there is plenty of daily news, but how much of that news is actually important and worth acting on? The data suggest very little of that information is meaningful and valuable. Most of it is simply noise.

He also writes:

> Investment returns can be significantly hurt by strategies based on short-term, noise-driven strategies. The data clearly and consistently showed that extending one's investment time horizon was a simple method for improving investment returns.

In the paper he presents a chart showing the probability of sustaining a loss over different time horizons for an investment in the S&P 500 index.

The chart on this page does the same for the FTSE All-Share index. The analysis was carried out on daily data for the FTSE All-Share from 1970–2017.

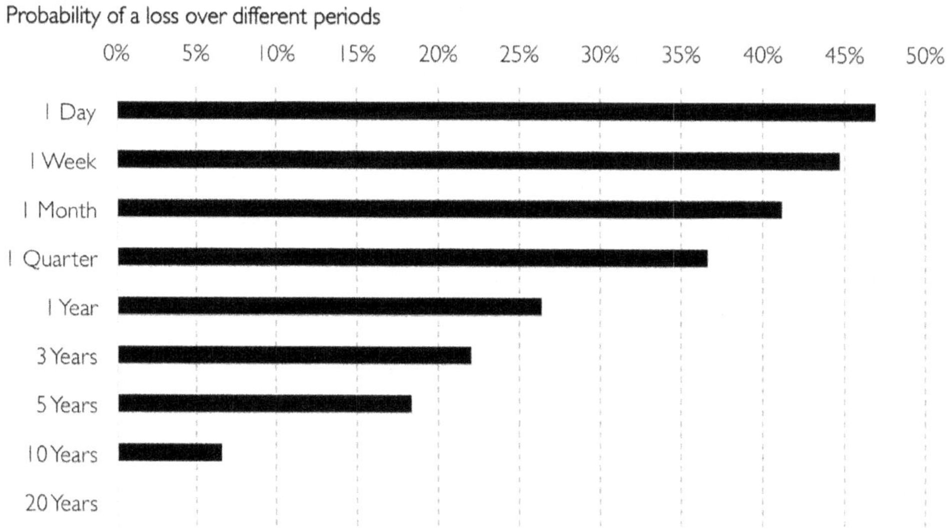


1. www.rbadvisors.com.

The analysis found that if an investment was made in the index on any day since 1970, the chance of the index being lower one week later (i.e. five trading days later) was 45%. Similarly, since 1970, investing on any day would see a 41% chance the market would be lower a month later.

As can be seen in the chart, the longer the time horizon of an investment, the lower the chance of loss. Conversely, the shorter the time horizon, the closer the probability of loss tends to 50/50 (i.e. the closer it becomes to a simple coin toss). By the time one gets to a holding period of ten years, the chance of loss is down to 7%; and it is zero at a holding period of 20 years (based on the historic data since 1970).

Finally, Bernstein's paper makes the useful point that while longer time horizons tend to progressively improve investment returns in many financial assets (e.g. shares), this is not necessarily the case for real assets such as gold and other commodities.

# ULTIMATE DEATH CROSS

*An update on the* Almanac's *study of the Ultimate Death Cross.*

A previous edition of the *Almanac* showed a chart with the FTSE All-Share index poised to make an *ultimate death cross* (when the 50-month moving average moves down through the 200-month moving average). Readers were left hanging with the comment:

> If the 50-month average *does* fall below the 200-month average, will that signal a lost decade(s) for the UK market as in Japan?

*So, what happened?*

The chart below updates the action.

UK stock market with 50/200 month moving averages [1945–2017]

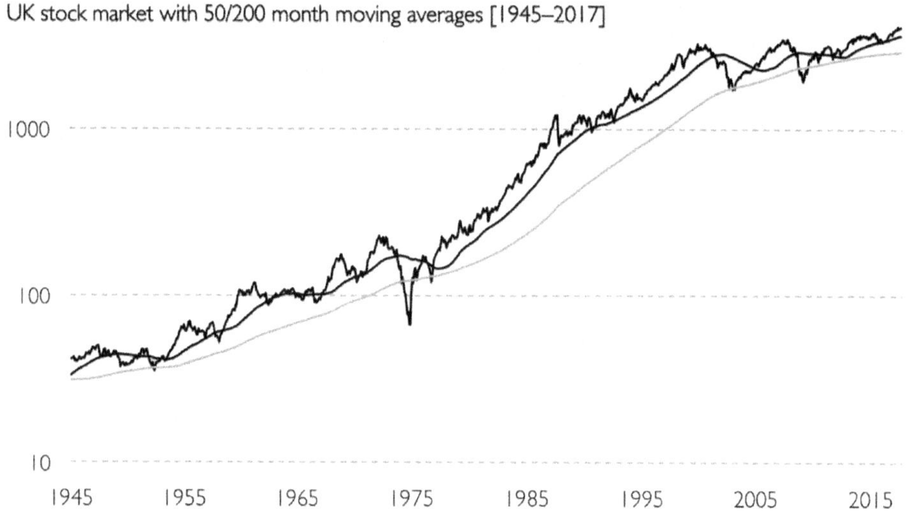


As can be (just) seen, the 50M MAV narrowly avoided crossing the 200M MAV. We were saved. And, in fact, the narrow avoidance of an ultimate death cross in the past has been a strong buy signal for an ensuing massive bull market.

## 1845–1945

The last time the FTSE All-Share made an ultimate death cross was 1945. So, this signal is fairly rare. But this has not always been the case.

The following chart plots the FTSE All-Share with 50-month and 200-month moving averages for the period 1845–1945.

UK stock market with 50/200 month moving averages [1845–1945]

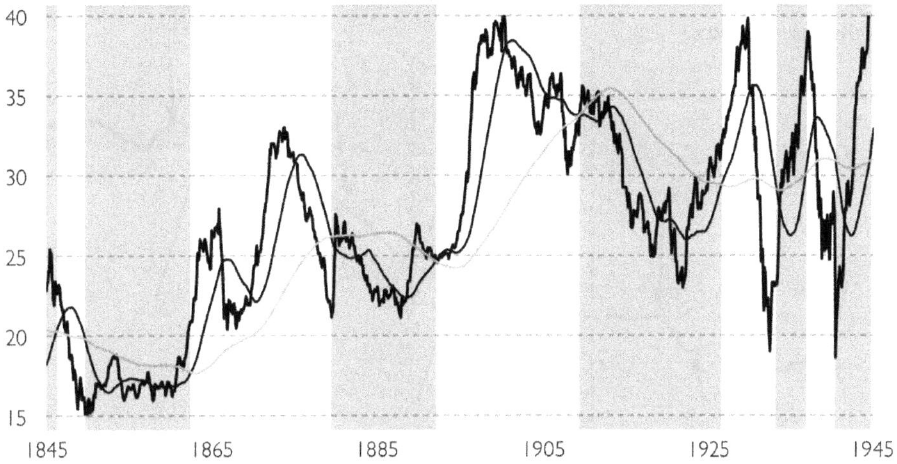


As can be seen for the 100 years prior to 1945, ultimate death crosses were not uncommon. In fact, the 50-month MAV was below the 200-month MAV (shaded in the chart) for 51 of the 100 years.

# POLITICS AND FINANCIAL MARKETS

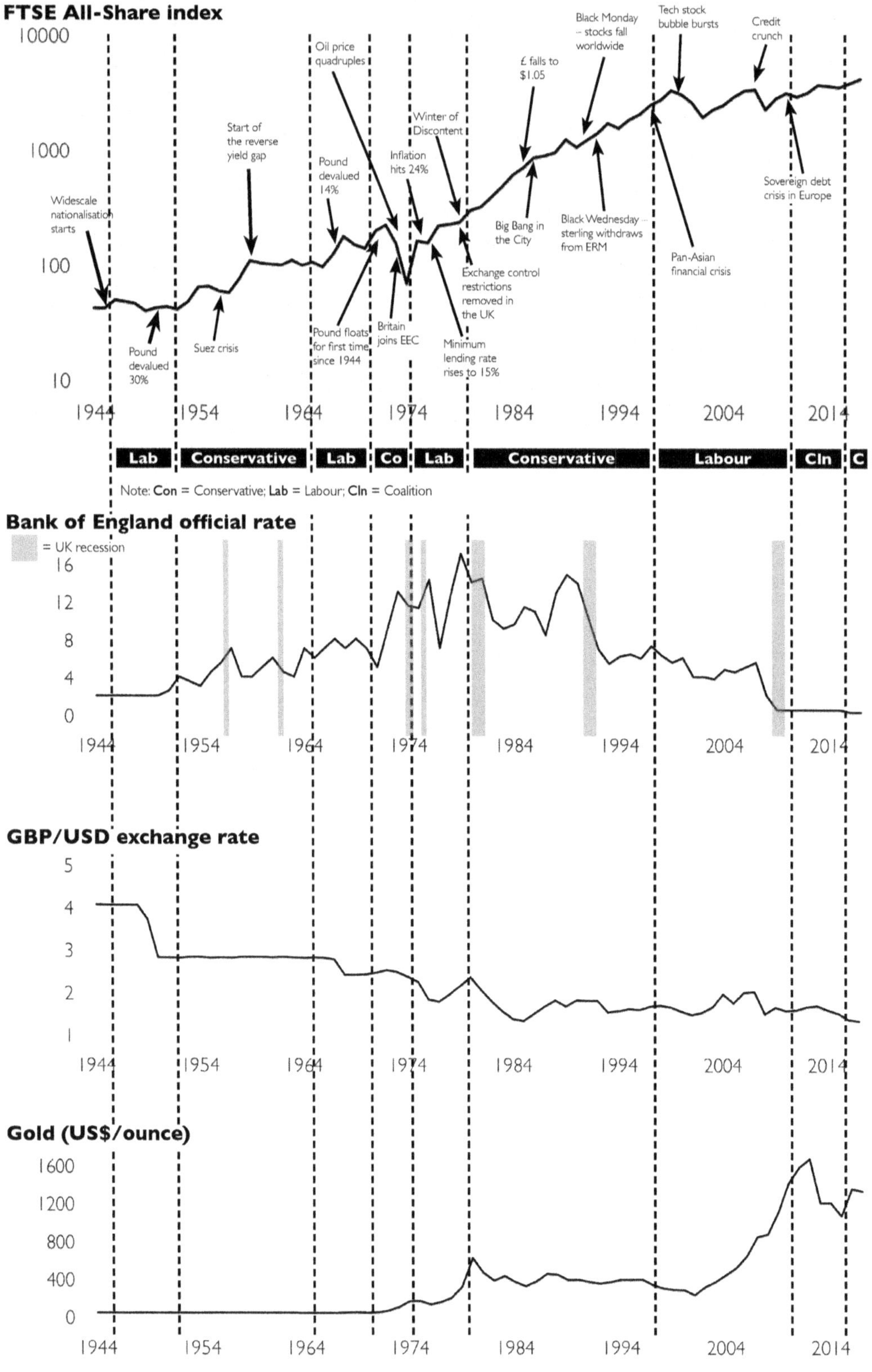

# GOLD

*Does the price of gold exhibit a monthly seasonality?*

On 17 March 1968 the system that fixed the price of gold at USD35.00 collapsed and the price of gold was allowed to fluctuate. Let's have a quick look at the chart to see how gold has performed since it floated in 1968.

Since 1968 when gold floated, its price has grown at a CAGR of 7.7%.

Let's look now at its monthly seasonality.

The following chart plots the average price returns for gold by month since 1968. For example, since 1968 the average return of the gold price in January has been 1.2%.

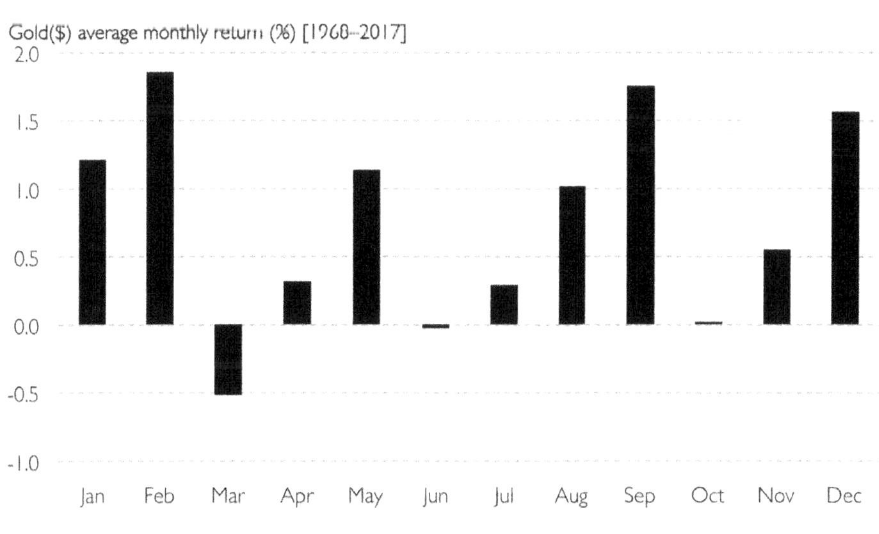

And the following chart plots the proportion of months that have seen positive returns. For example, in 60% of years since 1968 gold has had positive returns in February.

It can be seen that since 1968 gold has on average been strong in February, September and December. The weak months for gold have been March and October.

This profile of behaviour would seem to have some persistency as the same pattern can be seen for the more recent period 2000–17, for example the following chart plots the average monthly returns from 2000.

The main new features recently have been the strength of gold in the months January, August and November, and the weakness in December.

## Gold and equities

The following chart shows the ratio of the FTSE All-Share index to gold (priced in sterling) since 1968. One can regard the chart as the UK equity market priced in gold.

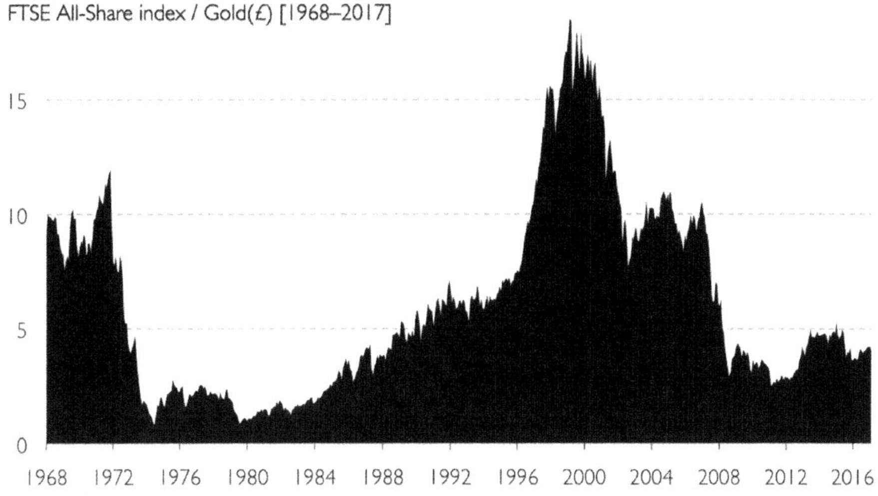


The ratio peaked at 18.8 in July 1999 and then fell to a low of 2.3 in September 2011. Since 1968 the ratio average is 6.1.

# INTEREST RATE

# UK BANK RATE CHANGES

*A brief analysis of the changes made to the bank rate since 1694.*

Since 1694 the Bank of England (BoE) has made 828 changes to the bank rate. Changes to the bank rate today are recommended by the Monetary Policy Committee (MPC), which meets once a month to consider changes to the bank rate.

The following chart plots all the changes to the bank rate from 1694. The size of each respective change is shown on the Y-axis. (NB. The Y-axis is truncated at +3 and −3 for legibility; in 1914 the rate did see changes of +4 and −4.)

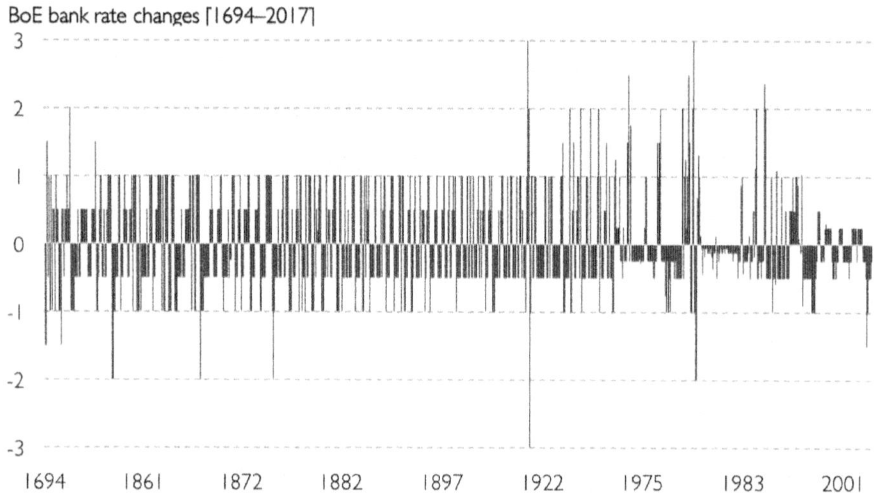


Until the beginning of the 20th century the great majority of rate changes were +/− 0.5 and +/− 1. And also the balance of the size of positive and negative rate changes was roughly equal.

Towards the end of the 20th century the Bank started experimenting with larger and smaller increments of change. And the balance of rate changes also changed; periods of small negative changes would be interrupted by larger positive rate adjustments.

In 1982 the Bank began a cautious period of frequent rate reductions of just 0.125 (the smallest rate reduction up to this time). The last time the bank rate was reduced by such a small amount was in 1989.

The frequency distribution of size of rate changes is shown in the following chart.

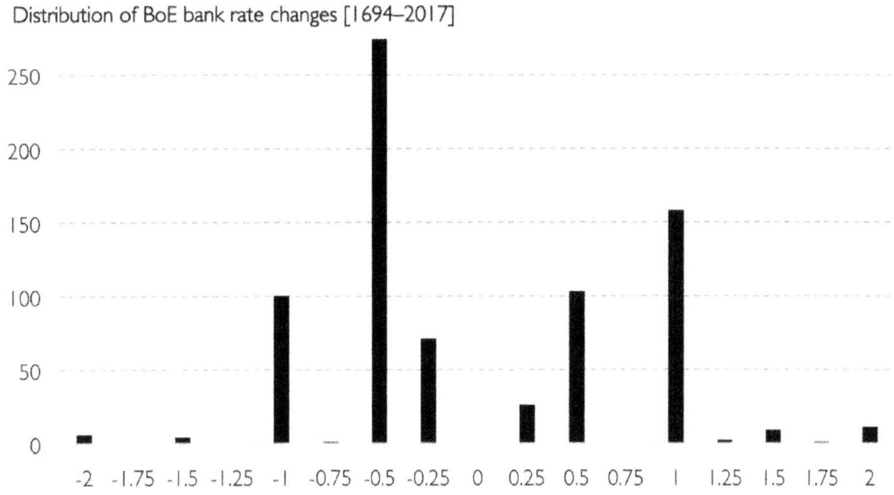


As can be seen, the most common rate change has been a reduction of half a percentage point. (Since 1694, 33% of all rate changes have been for −0.5.) After that the most frequent rate change was plus one percentage point.

The above chart supports the (well known) observation that rates are reduced cautiously with small increments and increased with more aggressive, larger increments.

The following chart breaks this frequency distribution down by century.

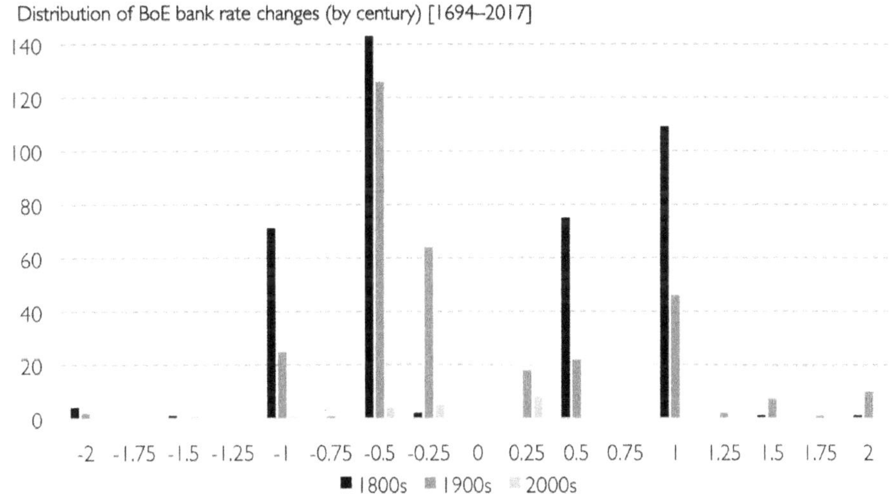


The above chart supports the previous observation that, whereas in the 19th century the Bank restricted its changes to a narrow band of increments, in the 20th century the size of the rate changes were more varied.

# UK INTEREST RATE CYCLE

*A brief analysis of the interest rate cycle in the UK.*

When growth in an economy is thought to be too low, interest rates may be reduced to increase consumption and investment. However, at a certain stage low interest rates may lead to inflation, with over-investment in property and other assets. At this point, to limit inflation, interest rates may be raised.

This cycle of interest rates increasing and decreasing is roughly related to the economic cycle: low growth leads to lower interest rates, and high growth leads to higher interest rates.

When central banks are lowering interest rates this is often referred to as the *easing phase* of the interest rate cycle; when rates are being raised this is the *tightening phase* of the cycle.

For the purposes of the study here, rates are said to be in an easing phase if the previous rate change was down. They stay in this phase until a positive rate change occurs, at which point rates move into a tightening phase.

We'll now look in some more detail at these alternating phases of easing and tightening.

Firstly, for a brief recap, the chart below plots the level of the bank rate since 1901.

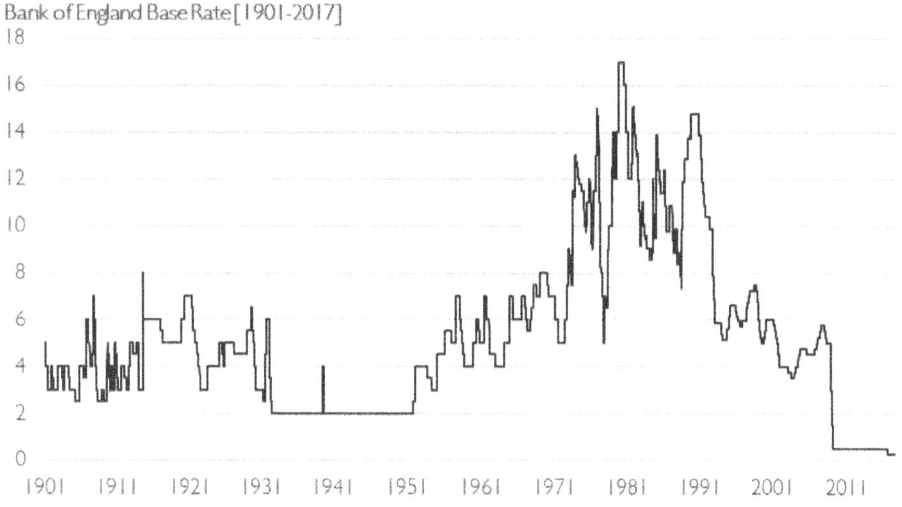


The following chart reproduces the above chart but overlays vertical bars to highlight the **tightening phase** of the interest rate cycle (i.e. periods when the bank rate is being increased). The periods without grey bars are therefore **easing phases**.

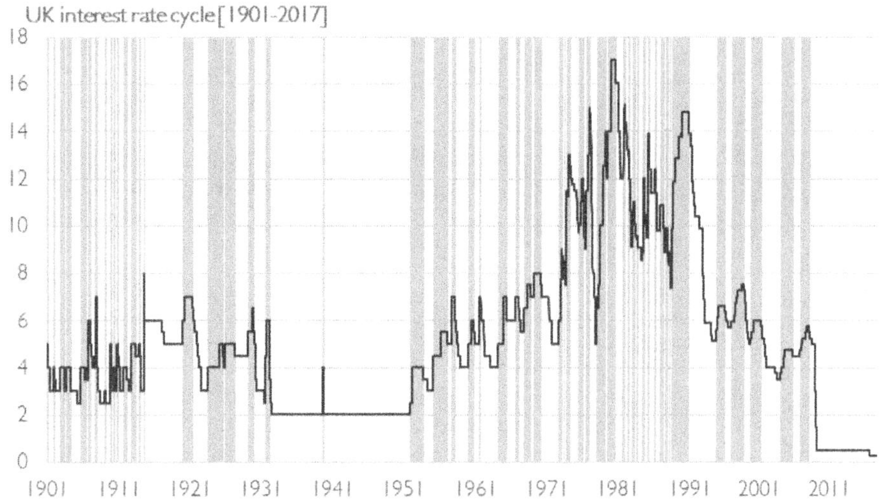


The following table gives a summary of the length of time the base rate stayed in the respective phases.

| Period | Market days | Easing | Tightening |
|---|---|---|---|
| 1901–1969 | 17,995 | 70% | 30% |
| 1970–1999 | 7,590 | 59% | 41% |
| 2000–2017 | 4,422 | 76% | 24% |
| 1901–2017 | 30,007 | 68% | 32% |

Over the whole period, rates stayed in an easing phase (68%) for twice as long as they did in a tightening phase (32%).

The following chart is similar to the above, but zooms in to the shorter time period: 1970–2017.

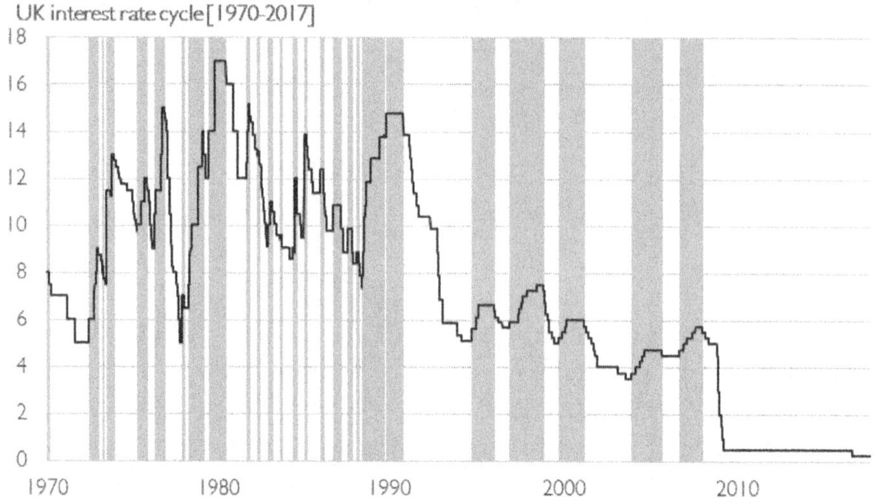


It can be seen that before 1988 monetary policy changed direction frequently (i.e. the average interest rate cycle was short). After 1988, monetary policy settled down and the interest rate cycle became much longer.

For example, in the five years, 1983–1988, there were seven full rate cycles (i.e. an easing phase followed by a tightening phase), the same number as occurred in the 28 years since 1988.

For reference, the following chart overlays the FTSE All-Share index on the Bank of England base rate.

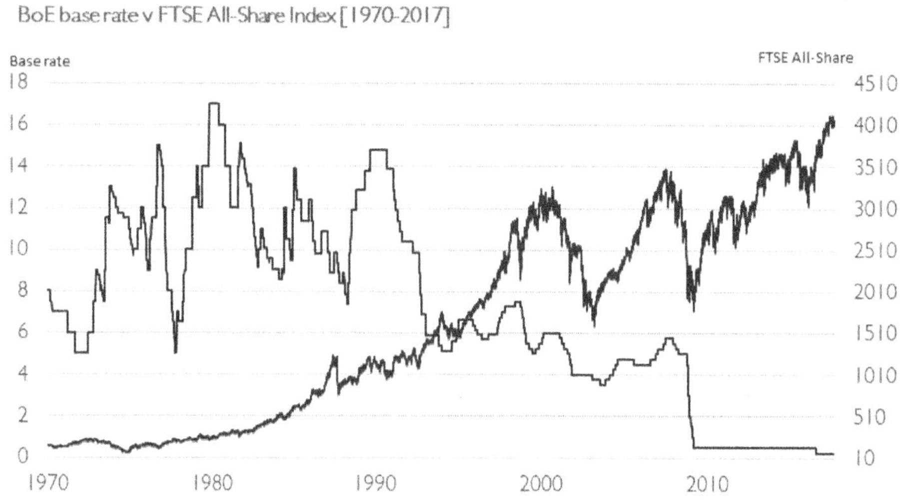


It can be seen that the period of great credit expansion that occurred from 1980–2000 was accompanied by an overall decline in interest rates from 17% to 5%.

The following chart (crudely) shows what happened to equities over this period during the discrete periods of interest rates being eased and tightened.

- **Portfolio EASE**: a portfolio that invested in the equity market only during the easing phase of interest rates.
- **Portfolio TIGHT**: a portfolio that invested in the equity market only during the tightening phase of interest rates.
- **Portfolio FTAS**: a buy-and-hold portfolio that invested continuously in the FTSE All-Share.

All portfolio values start at 100.

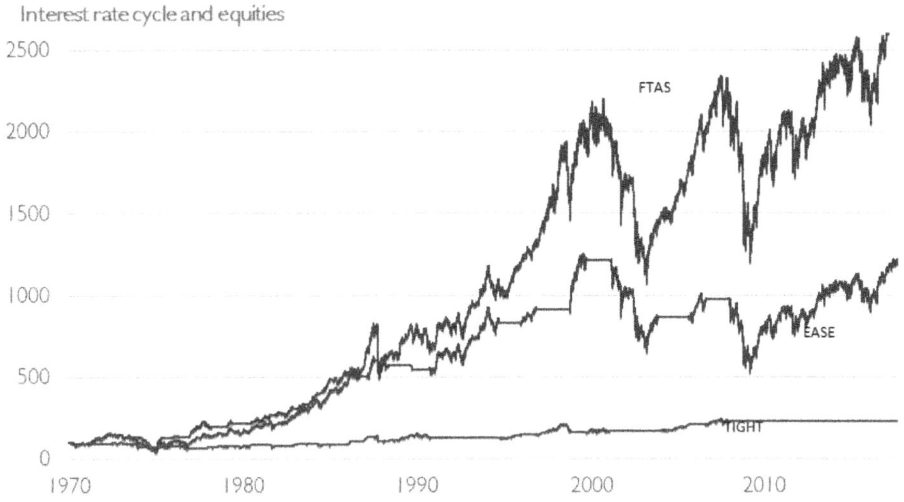


By 2017, the Easing Portfolio had a value of 1199, while the Tightening Portfolio a value of 228. Obviously some of this difference in performance is attributable to the fact that the Easing Portfolio was invested in the market for twice as long as the Tightening Portfolio.

# 4.
# REFERENCE

# CONTENTS

## STOCK INDICES – UK

### FT Ordinary Share Index (FT 30)

The FT 30 was first calculated in 1935 by the *Financial Times*. The index started at a base level of 100, and was calculated from a subjective collection of 30 major companies – which in the early years were concentrated in the industrial and retailing sectors.

For a long time the index was the best known performance measure of the UK stock market. But the index become less representative of the whole market. Also the index was price-weighted (like the DJIA), and not market-capitalisation-weighted. Although the index was calculated every hour, the increasing sophistication of the market needed an index calculated every minute and so the FT 30 has been usurped by the FTSE 100.

### FTSE 100

Today, the FTSE 100 (sometimes called the "footsie") is the best known index tracking the performance of the UK market. The index comprises 100 of the top capitalised stocks listed on the LSE, and represents approximately 80% of the total market (by capitalisation). It is market capitalisation weighted and the composition of the index is reviewed every three months. The FTSE 100 is commonly used as the basis for investment funds and derivatives. The index was first calculated on 3 January 1984 with a base value of 1000.

The FTSE 100, and all the FTSE indices, are calculated by FTSE International – which started life as a joint venture between the *Financial Times* and the London Stock Exchange, but is now wholly owned by the LSE.

### FTSE 250

Similar in construction to the FTSE 100, except this index comprises the next 250 highest capitalised stocks listed on the LSE after the top 100. It's sometimes referred to as the index of 'mid-cap' stocks, and comprises approximately 18% of the total market capitalisation.

### FTSE 350

The FTSE 350 is an index comprising all the stocks in the FTSE 100 and FTSE 250.

### FTSE Small Cap

Comprised of companies with a market capitalisation below the FTSE 250 but above a fixed limit. This lower limit is periodically reviewed. Consequently the FTSE Small Cap does not have a fixed number of constituents. By mid-2016, there were 275 companies in the index, which represented about 2% of the total market by capitalisation.

### FTSE All-Share

The FTSE All-Share is the aggregation of the FTSE 100, FTSE 250 and FTSE Small Cap indices. Effectively it is comprised of all those LSE listed companies with a market capitalisation above the lower limit for inclusion in the FTSE Small Cap. The FTSE All-Share is the standard benchmark for measuring the performance of the broad UK market and represents 98% to 99% of the total UK market capitalisation.

## FTSE Fledgling

This index comprises the companies that do not meet the minimum size requirement of the FTSE Small Cap and are therefore outside of the FTSE All-Share. There are fewer than 200 companies in the FTSE Fledgling.

## FTSE All-Small

This consists of all the companies in the FTSE Small Cap and FTSE Fledgling indices.

# STOCK INDICES – INTERNATIONAL

### Dow Jones Industrial Average (DJIA)

The DJIA is the oldest continuing stock index of the US market and probably the most famous in the world. Created in 1896, it originally comprised 12 stocks, but over the years has expanded to reach the point where today it includes 30 stocks. The index is weighted by price, which is unusual for a stock index. It is calculated by summing the prices of the 30 stocks and dividing by the divisor. Originally the divisor was 30, but this has been adjusted periodically to reflect capital changes such as stock splits, and is currently about 0.13. This means that companies with high stock prices have the greatest influence on the index – not those with large market values. The longest established company in the index is General Electric, which joined in 1907.

### Standard & Poor's 500 (S&P 500)

This is the main benchmark index for the performance of the US market. The index is weighted by market value and constituents are chosen based upon their market size, liquidity and sector. The index was created in 1957, although values for it have been back-calculated several decades.

### NASDAQ 100

This index tracks the performance of the 100 largest stocks listed on the NASDAQ exchange. The index is calculated using a modified capitalisation weighting method ("modified" so that large companies like Apple don't overwhelm it). NASDAQ companies tend to be smaller and younger than those listed on the NYSE and although there is no attempt to select technology stocks, it is regarded as the tech stock index. The index can be traded as there's an ETF associated with it (the most actively traded ETF in the US). The ETF has the symbol QQQ and is sometimes referred to as the "Qs" or "Qubes".

### Nikkei 225

The Nikkei 225 is owned by the Nihon Keizai Shimbun ("Nikkei") newspaper. It was first calculated in 1949 (when it was known as the Nikkei-Dow index ) and is the most widely watched stock index in Japan. It is a price-weighted index of 225 top-rated Japanese companies listed in the First Section of the Tokyo Stock Exchange. The calculation method is therefore similar to that of the Dow Jones Industrial Average (upon which it was modelled).

### TOPIX

The TOPIX is calculated by the Tokyo Stock Exchange. Unlike the Nikkei 255, TOPIX is a market capitalisation-weighted index. TOPIX is calculated from all members of the First Section of the Tokyo SE, which is about 1500 companies. For these reasons, TOPIX is preferred over the Nikkei 225 as a benchmark for Japanese equity portfolios.

## Hang Seng

The Hang Seng was first calculated in 1964. Today it has 48 constituents representing some 60% of the total Hong Kong market by capitalisation.

## CAC 40

The CAC 40 is the main benchmark for Euronext Paris (what used to be the Paris Bourse). The index contains 40 stocks selected among the top 100 by market capitalisation and the most active stocks listed on Euronext Paris. The base value was 1000 at 31 December 1987.

## DAX 30

The DAX 30 is published by the Frankfurt Stock Exchange and is the main real-time German share index. It contains 30 stocks from the leading German stock markets. The DAX is a total return index (which is uncommon), whereby it measures not only the price appreciation of its constituents but also the return provided by the dividends paid.

# EPIC, TIDM, SEDOL, CUSIP AND ISIN CODES

This page describes the common codes associated with securities.

## EPIC

Some time ago the London Stock Exchange devised a system of code names for listed companies. These provide a short and unambiguous way to reference stocks. For example, the code for Marks & Spencer is MKS. This is easier to use than wondering whether one should call the company Marks & Spencer, Marks and Spencer or Marks & Spencer plc. These codes were called EPIC codes, after the name of the Stock Exchange's central computer prior to 1996.

## TIDM

After the introduction of the Sequence trading platform, EPIC codes were renamed Tradable Instrument Display Mnemonics (TIDMs), or Mnemonics for short. So, strictly, we should now be calling them TIDMs or Mnemonics – but almost everyone still refers to them as EPIC codes.

## SEDOL

SEDOL stands for Stock Exchange Daily Official List. These are seven digit security identifiers assigned by the London Stock Exchange. They are only assigned to UK-listed securities.

## CUSIP

CUSIP (Committee on Uniform Securities Identification Procedures) codes are nine-character alphanumeric identifiers used for Canadian and US securities.

## ISIN

ISIN stands for International Securities Identification Number. These are 12-digit alphanumeric identifiers assigned by the International Standards Organisation (ISO) in order to provide standardisation of international securities. The first two letters represent the country code; the next nine characters usually use some other code, such as CUSIP in the United States or SEDOL in the UK, with leading spaces padded with 0. The final digit is a check digit.

# DAILY TIMETABLE OF THE UK TRADING DAY

This table displays the basic structure of the UK trading day, with some comments from a trader.

| | |
|---|---|
| 07.00 | **Regulatory News Services open**<br>The period before the market opens at 08.00 is the most important hour of the day. By the time the opening auction begins at 07.50 traders will have a clear idea at what price any particular major stock should be opening at.<br>Scheduled announcements are normally in the Regulatory News. Having a good idea of what companies are reporting for the forthcoming week is essential. Quite a few banks, brokers and websites provide comprehensive forward diaries.<br>As well as checking the movement of the major stock indices overnight, check the early show for the futures contracts on the main indices, as well as any US company results that were released after hours. Unlike the UK, in the US it is common for companies to release results after the markets close. |
| 07.50-08.00 | **Pre-market auction**<br>There are fewer opportunities in the opening auction than the closing auction, partly because there are lower volumes in the opening auction. It is safer to trade against an 'at-market' order than against several orders from several other participants that appear to be at the wrong price – almost certainly they have seen something that you haven't.<br>Despite representing only a small proportion of the total day's volume, the opening uncrossing trade will often be (or very close to) the high or low trade of the day for that stock. |
| 08.00 | **UK market and FTSE 100 Index Futures open**<br>By 08.00 as the UK market opens you should be fully prepared for the day's trading. |
| 08.00-16.30 | **Continuous trading**<br>Trading is continuous until 16.30. During the day there is a calendar of key economic figures to look out for, as well as both ad hoc and scheduled announcements. Some company-scheduled trading figures come out at midday, particularly companies that are dual-quoted.<br>US index futures should be monitored throughout the day as well as other influential continental indices such as Germany's DAX.<br>Traders will often concentrate on watching the high volatility shares as these provide the most trading opportunities, although many will add 'guest' stocks to their watch list and go to where the day's action is and join 'event' traders. Stocks to watch during the day include the biggest movers on the day (both risers and fallers), those experiencing high volume and constant gainers (popular with momentum players). |

| | |
|---|---|
| 14.30 | **US markets open**<br>The US markets usually open at 14.30 UK time, although at certain times of the year, due to daylight saving, it may be an hour earlier or later. As the futures contracts on the US markets trade throughout morning trading in the UK, traders will always have a good idea where the US markets are due to open, subject to the release of economic figures at 13.30 UK time. |
| 16.30-16.35 | **Post-market auction**<br>There can often be opportunities in the closing auction, particularly on the last business day of the month or when there are index constituent changes. The general strategy is to take the other side of a large 'at-market' order that is forcing the uncrossing price away from the day's trading range, in the anticipation that the stock will revert to the previous ('normal') level the following day. |
| 17.30 | **FTSE 100 Index Futures close** |
| 18.30 | **Regulatory News Services close**<br>A number of key announcements can come out after the market close and although most newspapers will pick up any significant stories, it is worth scanning through the day's late announcements before the start of trading the following day. |

*Source: The UK Trader's Bible* by Dominic Connolly.

# FTSE 100 – 1984

The FTSE 100 index was started on 3 January 1984 with a base level of 1000. The table below shows the original constituents. Of the initial 100 companies only 18 remain in the index today (indicated in bold, and with their new names in brackets) – a sign of the great changes in UK PLC in 32 years.

Allied – Lyons
Associated British Foods
Associated Dairies Group
**Barclays Bank [Barclays]**
Barratt Developments
Bass
BAT Industries
Beecham Group
Berisford (S. & W.)
BICC
Blue Circle Industries
BOC Group
Boots Co.
Bowater Corporation
BPB Industries
British & Commonwealth
British Aerospace
British Elect. Traction Co.
British Home Stores
**British Petroleum [BP]**
Britoil
BTR
Burton Group
Cable & Wireless
Cadbury Schweppes
**Commercial Union Assurance [Aviva]**
Consolidated Gold Fields
Courtaulds
Dalgety Distillers Co.
CJ Rothschild
Edinburgh Investment Trust
English China Clays
Exco International
Ferranti
Fisons
General Accident Fire & Life
General Electric
Glaxo Holdings
Globe Investment Trust
Grand Metropolitan
**Great Universal Stores [Experian]**
Guardian Royal Exchange
Guest Keen & Nettlefolds
Hambro Life Assurance
Hammerson Prop.Inv. & Dev. 'A'
Hanson Trust Harrisons & Crossfield
Hawker Siddeley Group
House of Fraser
Imperial Chemical Industries
Imperial Cont. Gas Association
Imperial Group
Johnson Matthey
Ladbroke Group
**Land Securities**
**Legal & General Group**
**Lloyds Bank [Lloyds Banking Group]**
Lonrho
MEPC
MFI Furniture Group
**Marks & Spencer**
Midland Bank
National Westminster Bank
Northern Foods
P & O Steam Navigation Co.
**Pearson (S.) & Son [Pearson]**
Pilkington Brothers
Plessey Co.
**Prudential Corporation [Prudential]**
RMC Group
Racal Electronics
Rank Organisation
**Reckitt & Colman [Reckitt Benckiser Group]**
Redland
**Reed International [Reed Elsevier]**
**Rio Tinto – Zinc Corporation [Rio Tinto]**
Rowntree Mackintosh
**Royal Bank of Scotland Group**
Royal Insurance
**Sainsbury (J.)**
Scottish & Newcastle Breweries
Sears Holdings
Sedgwick Group
**Shell Trans. & Trad. Co. [Royal Dutch Shell]**
Smith & Nephew Associated Co's.
Standard Chartered Bank
Standard Telephones & Cables
Sun Alliance & London Insurance
Sun Life Assurance Society
THORN EMI
Tarmac
**Tesco**
Trafalgar House
Trusthouse Forte
Ultramar
**Unilever**
United Biscuits
Whitbread & Co. 'A'
Wimpey (George)

The following table compares the market capitalisations of the top five largest companies in the index in 1984 and today.

| | Rank (1984) | Capital (£m) | Rank (2017) | Capital (£m) |
|---|---|---|---|---|
| 1 | British Petroleum Co. | 7,401 | Royal Dutch Shell | 176,337 |
| 2 | Shell Trans. & Trad. Co. | 6,365 | HSBC Holdings | 150,749 |
| 3 | General Electric Co. | 4,915 | British American Tobacco | 110,444 |
| 4 | Imperial Chemical Industries | 3,917 | BP | 87,873 |
| 5 | Marks & Spencer | 2,829 | GlaxoSmithKline | 75,360 |

Oil is still there today, but industrial, chemical and retail have been replaced by bank, consumer goods and pharmaceutical.

In 1984, the total market capitalisation of the index was £100bn; in 2017 the total market capitalisation is £2,058bn. It's interesting to note that Shell's market cap today is 76% larger than the whole FTSE 100 in 1984.

# FT 30 INDEX 1935 – WHERE ARE THEY NOW?

The FT 30 index was started by the *Financial Times* on 1 July 1935. Today the most widely followed index is the FTSE 100, but for many years the FT 30 (originally called the FT Ordinaries) was the measure everyone knew. The table below lists the original companies in the FT 30 index in 1935 – a time when brokers wore bowler hats and share certificates were printed on something called paper. It's interesting to see what became of the stalwarts of UK PLC from over 70 years ago.

| Company | Notes |
|---|---|
| Associated Portland Cement | The name was changed to Blue Circle Industries in 1978, and then left the index in 2001 when it was bought by Lafarge. |
| Austin Motor | Left the index in 1947. In 1952 Austin merged with rival Morris Motors Limited to form The British Motor Corporation Limited (BMC). In 1966 BMC bought Jaguar and two years later merged with Leyland Motors Limited to form British Leyland Motor Corporation. In 1973 British Leyland produced the Austin-badged Allegro... (the story is too painful to continue). |
| Bass | Left the index in 1947. In 1967 merged with Charrington United Breweries to form Bass Charrington. In 2000 its brewing operations were sold to Interbrew (which was then instructed by the Competition Commission to dispose parts to Coors), while the hotel and pub holdings were renamed Six Continents. In 2003 Six Continents was split into a pubs business (Mitchells & Butlers) and a hotels and soft drinks business (InterContinental Hotels Group). |
| Bolsover Colliery | Left the index in 1947. The mines were acquired by the National Coal Board on nationalisation in 1947. Bolsover Colliery closed in 1993. |
| Callender's Cables & Construction | Left the index in 1947. Merged with British Insulated Cables in 1945 to form British Insulated Callender's Cables, which was renamed BICC Ltd in 1975. In 2000, having sold its cable operations, it renamed its contruction business Balfour Beatty. |
| Coats (J & P) | Left the index in 1959. Traded as Coats Patons Ltd after the takeover of Patons & Baldwins, then as Coats Viyella, finally as Coats plc. Finally taken over by Guinness Peat Group in 2004. |
| Courtaulds | Demerged its chemical and textile interests in the 1980s, with the former eventually being bought by Akzo Nobel and the latter by Sara Lee. Left the index in 1998. |
| Distillers | Purchased by Guinness in the infamous bid battle of 1986 when it left the index. |
| Dorman Long | Left the index in 1947. Joined British Steel following nationalisation in 1967. |

| Company | Notes |
|---|---|
| Dunlop Rubber | Left the index in 1983 and was bought in 1985 by BTR (which became Invensys). |
| Electrical & Musical Industries | In 1971 changed its name to EMI and later that year merged with THORN Electrical Industries to form Thorn EMI but then de-merged in 1996. In 2007 EMI Group plc was taken over by Terra Firma Capital Partners but following financial difficulties ownership passed to Citigroup in 2011. |
| Fine Spinners and Doublers | Fell out of the index in 1938, and was later bought by Courtaulds in 1963. |
| General Electric | General Electric was re-named Marconi in 1999, suffered disastrous losses in the dot-com crash and was bought by Ericsson in 2006. |
| Guest, Keen & Nettlefolds | Guest, Keen is better known as GKN and is still in the FT 30 today. |
| Harrods | Left the index in 1959 when it was bought by House of Fraser, and then later by Mohamed Al Fayed. |
| Hawker Siddeley | Left the index in 1991, and was then bought in 1992 by BTR (which became Invensys). |
| Imperial Chemical Industries | Spun out of Zeneca in 1993, and the rump (called ICI) was sold to Akzo Nobel in 2007. |
| Imperial Tobacco | Still going strong. |
| International Tea Co Stores | Fell out of the index in 1947, was acquired by BAT Industries in 1972 and ended up as Somerfield in 1994. |
| London Brick | Replaced in the index by Hanson which bought it in 1984. |
| Murex | Left the index in 1967 due to "poor share performance". Acquired by BOC Group in 1967. |
| Patons & Baldwins | Left the index in 1960 when bought by J & P Coats. |
| Pinchin Johnson & Associates | Left the index in 1960 when bought by Courtaulds. |
| Rolls-Royce | In 1971 RR was taken into state ownership, the motor car business was floated separately in 1973, and RR returned to the private sector in 1987. |
| Tate & Lyle | Still going strong, although its sugar refining and golden syrup business was sold to American Sugar Refining in 2010. |
| Turner & Newall | Left the index in 1982. The company was heavily involved with asbestos production, so it is not surprising that things ended badly. In 1998 the business was acquired by Federal-Mogul, which soon after filed for Chapter 11 protection as a result of asbestos claims. |

| Company | Notes |
|---|---|
| United Steel | Left the index in 1951. The iron and steel works on nationalisation became part of British Steel Corporation (and now part of Tata Steel); while the mining interests passed to the National Coal Board (now closed). |
| Vickers | Left the index in 1986. Bought by Rolls-Royce in 1999. |
| Watney Combe & Reid | Left the index in 1972 when it was bought by Grand Metropolitan, which itself became part of Diageo. |
| Woolworth (FW) | Left the index in 1971. Bought by the forerunner of Kingfisher in 1982, and then de-merged and re-listed in 2001. But the remaining Woolworths stores all closed by January 2009. |

Of the 30 companies only four exist today as listed companies: GKN, Imperial Tobacco, Rolls-Royce and Tate & Lyle (all of which are in the FTSE 100). And only GKN and Tate & Lyle are in today's FT 30.

The star performer from the original line-up has been Imperial Tobacco.

It's interesting to note the complete lack of representation of the four sectors that dominate the UK market today – no banks, telecom, oil or drug companies.

## Index performance

From 1935 to mid-2017, the FT 30 has risen 2907%; by comparison the FTSE All-Share over the same period has risen 11,799%. The following chart plots the year-end values of the FT 30 against the FTSE All-Share (the latter has been rebased to start at the same value as the FT 30).

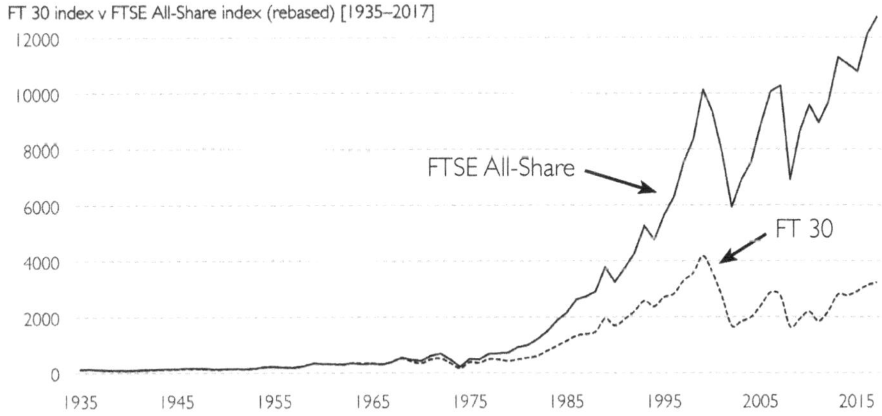


One of the reasons for the very large difference in performance is that the FT 30 is a price-weighted index (as are the Dow Jones Industrial Average and Nikkei 225); whereas most indices today (including the FTSE All-Share and FTSE 100) are weighted by market-capitalisation. When the FTSE 100 was introduced in 1984, if it had been price-weighted and performed in line with the FT 30, today it would have a value around 4144.

# COMPANY RESULTS ANNOUNCEMENT DATES

Note: Where table cells are blank, there are no results announcements in this week.

### January

| Week | Date | Interim | Preliminary |
|---|---|---|---|
| 1 | 1–7 Jan | Micro Focus International | Scottish Investment Trust |
| 2 | 8–14 Jan | SuperGroup | |
| 3 | 15–21 Jan | | Bankers Investment Trust |
| 4 | 22–28 Jan | Diageo, IG Group Holdings, PZ Cussons, Rank Group | Crest Nicholson Holdings |

### February

| Week | Date | Interim | Preliminary |
|---|---|---|---|
| 5 | 29 Jan–4 Feb | Renishaw | Aberforth Smaller Companies Trust, AstraZeneca, Centamin, Ocado Group, Royal Dutch Shell, Safestore Holdings, Unilever |
| 6 | 5–11 Feb | Ashmore Group, Dunelm Group, Hargreaves Lansdown, Redrow | Beazley, BP, GlaxoSmithKline, Randgold Resources Ltd, Rio Tinto, Smurfit Kappa Group, St Modwen Properties, Tullow Oil |
| 7 | 12–18 Feb | City of London Investment Trust | Acacia Mining, Coca-Cola, Drax Group, Lancashire Holdings, Reckitt Benckiser Group, Rolls-Royce, Shire, Spectris |
| 8 | 19–25 Feb | Barratt Developments, BHP Billiton, Galliford Try, Genesis Emerging Markets Fund Ltd, Genus, Hays, JPMorgan Emerging Markets Inv Trust Petra Diamonds | Anglo American, BAE Systems, Barclays, BGEO Group, British American Tobacco, Capital & Counties Properties, Centrica, Essentra, Glencore, Greencoat UK Wind, Hammerson, Howden Joinery Group, HSBC, Indivior, InterContinental Hotels Group, Intu Properties, KAZ Minerals, Lloyds Banking Group, Metro Bank, Millennium & Copthorne Hotels, Mondi, Petrofac Ltd, Playtech, Rathbone Brothers, RELX, Royal Bank of Scotland Group, RSA Insurance Group, Segro, Serco Group, Standard Life Aberdeen, Temple Bar Investment Trust, The Renewables Infrastructure Group Ltd, UBM, UNITE Group, Weir Group, Wood Group |

## March

| Week | Date | Interim | Preliminary |
|---|---|---|---|
| 9 | 26 Feb–4 Mar | Dechra Pharmaceuticals, Go-Ahead Group, WH Smith | Aldermore Group, Ascential, BBA Aviation, Bodycote, Bovis Homes Group, Bunzl, Capita, Carillion, Coats Group, Cobham, ConvaTec Group, CRH, Croda International, Derwent London, Elementis, Evraz, Fidessa Group, Fisher (James) & Sons, Fresnillo, GKN, Greggs, Hastings Group Holdings, Hiscox, Hunting, IMI, Inchcape, Informa, International Consolidated Airlines, ITV, IWG, Jardine Lloyd Thompson Group, Jimmy Choo, Jupiter Fund Management, Kennedy Wilson Europe Real Estate, Man Group, Meggitt, Melrose Industries, Merlin Entertainments, Moneysupermarket.com Group, Morgan Advanced Materials, National Express Group, Pearson, Pershing Square Holdings, Persimmon, Provident Financial, Rentokil Initial, Rightmove, RIT Capital Partners, Riverstone Energy, Rotork, Schroders, Senior, Spire Healthcare Group, St James's Place, Standard Chartered, Taylor Wimpey, TBC Bank Group, Travis Perkins, Vesuvius, Virgin Money Holdings UK, William Hill |
| 10 | 5–11 Mar | | Admiral Group, Aggreko, Aviva, Berendsen, Cineworld Group, CLS Holdings, Dignity, Direct Line Insurance Group, Domino's Pizza UK & IRL, FDM Group Holdings, G4S, Grafton Group, Hill & Smith Holdings, Hochschild Mining, Ibstock, Inmarsat, Intertek Group, IP Group, John Laing Group, Just Eat, Legal & General Group, London Stock Exchange Group, Morrison (Wm) Supermarkets, NMC Health, Old Mutual, Paddy Power Betfair, PageGroup, Paysafe Group, Restaurant Group, Spirax-Sarco Engineering, Synthomer, Tritax Big Box REIT, Ultra Electronics Holdings, Worldpay Group, WPP Group |
| 11 | 12–18 Mar | Close Brothers Group, Wetherspoon (J D) | Antofagasta, Balfour Beatty, Cairn Energy, Clarkson, Computacenter, esure Group, Fidelity European Values, Just Group, Marshalls, Murray International Trust, OneSavings Bank, Polymetal International, Prudential, SIG, TP ICAP, Witan Investment Trust |

| Week | Date | Interim | Preliminary |
|---|---|---|---|
| 12 | 19–25 Mar | Bellway, Kier Group, Softcat | Ferrexpo, GVC Holdings, Hansteen Holdings, John Laing Infrastructure Fund, Kingfisher, Next, Phoenix Group Holdings, Savills, Ted Baker, Vectura Group |

## April

| Week | Date | Interim | Preliminary |
|---|---|---|---|
| 13 | 26 Mar–1 Apr | Ferguson, Smiths Group | AA, Alliance Trust, Barr (A G), Card Factory, Foreign & Colonial Investment Trust, International Public Partnership, JPMorgan American Investment Trust, Ladbrokes Coral Group, Nostrum Oil & Gas, Polypipe Group, Saga, Sanne Group, Sirius Minerals |
| 14 | 2–8 Apr | McCarthy & Stone | F&C Commercial Property Trust, Mercantile Investment Trust, NB Global Floating Rate Income Fund |
| 15 | 9–15 Apr | | Hikma Pharmaceuticals, JD Sports Fashion, Tesco |
| 16 | 16–22 Apr | Associated British Foods | UK Commercial Property Trust, Vietnam Enterprise Investments |
| 17 | 23–29 Apr | Jupiter Fund Management, Redefine International | Amec Foster Wheeler, Brown (N) Group, Whitbread, Woodford Patient Capital Trust |

## May

| Week | Date | Interim | Preliminary |
|---|---|---|---|
| 18 | 30 Apr–6 May | Imperial Brands, Safestore Holdings, Sage Group | P2P Global Investments, Sainsbury (J) |
| 19 | 7–13 May | Compass Group, Finsbury Growth & Income Trust | 3i Infrastructure, BT Group, Burberry Group, Stobart Group, TalkTalk Telecom Group |
| 20 | 14–20 May | Brewin Dolphin Holdings, Countryside Properties, CYBG, Diploma, easyJet, Euromoney Institutional Investor, Marston's, Mitchells & Butlers, SSP Group, Thomas Cook Group, TUI, Victrex | 3i Group, Booker Group, British Land Co, BTG, Dairy Crest Group, DCC, Experian, Harbourvest Global Private Equity, Investec, Land Securities Group, National Grid, NewRiver REIT, Royal Mail Group, Scottish Mortgage Investment Trust, Sophos Group, SSE, Vodafone Group |

| Week | Date | Interim | Preliminary |
|---|---|---|---|
| 21 | 21–27 May | Britvic, GCP Infrastructure Investments, Grainger, Greencore Group, Paragon Group of Companies, Shaftesbury, UDG Healthcare, ZPG | Assura, Aveva Group, B&M European Value Retail, Babcock International Group, Big Yellow Group, Caledonia Investments, Cranswick, Electrocomponents, Entertainment One, Great Portland Estates, Halfords Group, HICL Infrastructure Company, Homeserve, Intermediate Capital Group, Marks & Spencer, Mediclinic International, PayPoint, Pennon Group, Pets at Home Group, QinetiQ Group, Severn Trent, Tate & Lyle, TR Property Investment Trust, United Utilities Group, Vedanta Resources, Wizz Air Holding |

## June

| Week | Date | Interim | Preliminary |
|---|---|---|---|
| 22 | 28 May–3 Jun | British Empire Trust, Electra Private Equity, JPMorgan Indian Investment Trust | Edinburgh Investment Trust, FirstGroup, Johnson Matthey, Londonmetric Property, NEX Group, Perpetual Income & Growth Investment Trust |
| 23 | 4–10 Jun | | Auto Trader Group, Personal Assets Trust, RPC Group, Templeton Emerging Markets Investment Trust, Workspace Group |
| 24 | 11–17 Jun | Crest Nicholson Holdings | Fidelity China Special Situation, Halma, Mitie Group, Telecom plus, Worldwide Healthcare Trust |
| 25 | 18–24 Jun | Carnival, Scottish Investment Trust | Ashtead Group, Berkeley Group Holdings |

## July

| Week | Date | Interim | Preliminary |
|---|---|---|---|
| 26 | 25 Jun–1 Jul | | Dixons Carphone, DS Smith, Greene King, Monks Investment Trust, Northgate, Stagecoach Group |
| 27 | 2–8 Jul | Ocado Group, St Modwen Properties | SuperGroup, Syncona |
| 28 | 9–15 Jul | Bankers Investment Trust | Daejan Holdings, Micro Focus International, Polar Capital Technology Trust |
| 29 | 16–22 Jul | Drax Group, Howden Joinery, IP Group, Moneysupermarket.com Group, Unilever | IG Group Holdings, Sports Direct International |

| Week | Date | Interim | Preliminary |
|---|---|---|---|
| 30 | 23–29 Jul | Aberforth Smaller Companies Trust, Acacia Mining, Alliance Trust, Anglo American, Ascential, AstraZeneca, Beazley, Berendsen, Bodycote, British American Tobacco, Capital & Counties Properties, Croda International, Domino's Pizza UK & IRL, Foreign & Colonial Investment Trust, GKN, GlaxoSmithKline, Greencoat UK Wind, Hammerson, Inchcape, Indivior, Informa, Intu Properties, ITV, Jardine Lloyd Thompson Group, Just Eat, Lancashire Holdings, Metro Bank, National Express Group, Provident Financial, Rathbone Brothers, Reckitt Benckiser, RELX, Rentokil Initial, Royal Dutch Shell, Schroders, Segro, Smith & Nephew, Spectris, St James's Place, Temple Bar Investment Trust, Tullow Oil, UNITE Group, Vesuvius, Virgin Money Holdings UK, Weir Group | Diageo, PZ Cussons, Renishaw, Sky |

## August

| Week | Date | Interim | Preliminary |
|---|---|---|---|
| 31 | 30 Jul–5 Aug | Aggreko, Aviva, BAE Systems, Barclays, BBA Aviation, BP, Centamin, Centrica, Coats Group, Cobham, ConvaTec Group, Dignity, Direct Line Insurance Group, Elementis, Essentra, esure Group, FDM Group Holdings, Ferrexpo, Fidelity European Values, Fidessa Group, Fresnillo, Greggs, Hiscox, HSBC, IMI, Inmarsat, International Consolidated Airlines, Intertek Group, Lloyds Banking, London Stock Exchange Group, Man Group, Meggitt, Mondi, Morgan Advanced Materials, Old Mutual, Randgold Resources, Rightmove, Rio Tinto, Rolls-Royce, Royal Bank of Scotland Group, RSA Insurance Group, Senior, Serco Group, Smurfit Kappa Group, Standard Chartered, Taylor Wimpey, Travis Perkins, UBM, William Hill | |

| Week | Date | Interim | Preliminary |
|---|---|---|---|
| 32 | 6–12 Aug | Aldermore Group, Amec Foster Wheeler, Cineworld Group, Coca-Cola HBC AG, Derwent London, Evraz, G4S, Glencore, Hastings Group Holdings, Hill & Smith Holdings, Ibstock, InterContinental Hotels, IWG, JPMorgan American Investment Trust, Kennedy Wilson Europe Real Estate, Legal & General Group, Merlin Entertainments, Millennium & Copthorne Hotels, Paddy Power Betfair, PageGroup, Paysafe Group, Pearson, Polypipe Group, Prudential, Riverstone Energy, Rotork, Savills, Shire, SIG, Spirax-Sarco Engineering, Standard Life Aberdeen, Synthomer, TP ICAP, Tritax Big Box REIT, Ultra Electronics Holdings, Witan Investment Trust, Woodford Patient Capital Trust, Worldpay Group | |
| 33 | 13–19 Aug | Admiral Group, Balfour Beatty, BGEO Group, Clarkson, CLS Holdings, Hikma Pharmaceuticals, Hochschild Mining, KAZ Minerals, Marshalls, Murray International Trust, NB Global Floating Rate Income Fund, RIT Capital Partners, Sirius Minerals | Hargreaves Lansdown, Rank Group |
| 34 | 20–26 Aug | Antofagasta, Cairn Energy, CRH, Hansteen Holdings, Hunting, John Laing Group, NMC Health, OneSavings Bank, Pershing Square Holdings, Persimmon, Phoenix Group Holdings, Playtech, TBC Bank Group, The Renewables Infrastructure Group, Wood Group (John), WPP Group | BHP Billiton |

## September

| Week | Date | Interim | Preliminary |
|---|---|---|---|
| 35 | 27 Aug–2 Sep | Bunzl, Computacenter, F&C Commercial Property Trust, Fisher (James) & Sons, Grafton Group, Jimmy Choo, Ladbrokes Coral Group, Melrose Industries, Nostrum Oil & Gas, P2P Global Investments, Petrofac, Polymetal International, Restaurant Group, UK Commercial Property Trust, Vietnam Enterprise Investments | Hays |

| Week | Date | Interim | Preliminary |
|---|---|---|---|
| 36 | 3–9 Sep | Bovis Homes Group, International Public Partnership, Sanne Group, Vectura Group | Ashmore Group, Barratt Developments, Dechra Pharmaceuticals, Genus, Go-Ahead Group, Redrow |
| 37 | 10–16 Sep | GVC Holdings, JD Sports Fashion, John Laing Infrastructure Fund, Just Group, Morrison (Wm) Supermarkets, Next, Spire Healthcare Group | Dunelm Group, Galliford Try, Wetherspoon (J D) |
| 38 | 17–23 Sep | Capita, Kingfisher, Saga | City of London Investment Trust, Kier Group, Petra Diamonds, Smith & Nephew, Smiths Group |
| 39 | 24–30 Sep | AA, Barr (A G), Card Factory, Carillion, Harbourvest Global Private Equity, Mercantile Investment Trust | Close Brothers Group |

## October

| Week | Date | Interim | Preliminary |
|---|---|---|---|
| 40 | 1 Oct–7 Oct | Tesco | Ferguson, JPMorgan Emerging Markets Inv Trust |
| 41 | 8–14 Oct | Booker Group, Brown (N) Group, Ted Baker | Genesis Emerging Markets Fund, WH Smith |
| 42 | 15–21 Oct | Stobart Group | Bellway, Softcat |
| 43 | 22–28 Oct | BT Group, Whitbread | Redefine International |

## November

| Week | Date | Interim | Preliminary |
|---|---|---|---|
| 44 | 29 Oct–4 Nov | 3i Infrastructure, Tate & Lyle | |
| 45 | 5–11 Nov | 3i Group, Auto Trader Group, Aveva Group, Burberry Group, Dairy Crest Group, Edinburgh Investment Trust, Halfords Group, Marks & Spencer, National Grid, Sainsbury (J), Scottish Mortgage Investment Trust, Sophos Group, SSE, Vedanta Resources, Wizz Air Holding, Workspace Group, Worldwide Healthcare Trust | Associated British Foods, Imperial Brands |

| Week | Date | Interim | Preliminary |
|---|---|---|---|
| 46 | 12 –18 Nov | B&M European Value Retail, British Land Co, BTG, DCC, Experian, FirstGroup, Great Portland Estates, HICL Infrastructure Company, Intermediate Capital Group, Investec, Land Securities Group, Mediclinic International, QinetiQ Group, Royal Mail Group, TalkTalk Telecom Group, Vodafone Group | British Empire Trust, McCarthy & Stone |
| 47 | 19 –25 Nov | Assura, Babcock International Group, Caledonia Investments, Daejan Holdings, Electrocomponents, Entertainment One, Fidelity China Special Situation, Halma, Homeserve, Johnson Matthey, Mitie Group, NewRiver REIT, NEX Group, PayPoint, Perpetual Income & Growth Investment Trust, Personal Assets Trust, Severn Trent, Syncona, Telecom plus, Templeton Emerging Markets Investment Trust, TR Property Investment Trust, United Utilities Group | Compass Group, Countryside Properties, CYBG, Diploma, easyJet, Euromoney Institutional Investor, Paragon Group of Companies, Sage Group, SSP Group, Thomas Cook Group |

## December

| Week | Date | Interim | Preliminary |
|---|---|---|---|
| 48 | 26 Nov–2 Dec | Big Yellow Group, Cranswick, Greene King, Londonmetric Property, Pennon Group, Pets at Home Group, RPC Group | Brewin Dolphin Holdings, Britvic, Grainger, Greencore Group, Marston's, Mitchells & Butlers, Shaftesbury, UDG Healthcare, ZPG |
| 49 | 3–9 Dec | DS Smith, Monks Investment Trust, Northgate, Stagecoach Group | Victrex |
| 50 | 10–16 Dec | Ashtead Group, Dixons Carphone, Sports Direct International | GCP Infrastructure Investments, JPMorgan Indian Investment Trust, TUI |
| 51 | 17–23 Dec | | Carnival |
| 52 | 24–30 Dec | Berkeley Group Holdings, Polar Capital Technology Trust | Electra Private Equity, Finsbury Growth & Income Trust |

Lightning Source UK Ltd.
Milton Keynes UK
UKOW05n0334191117
312929UK00005B/56/P

9 780857 196057